GRINGO
NIGHTMARE

GRINGO NIGHTMARE

A Young American

Framed for Murder in Nicaragua

ERIC VOLZ

ST. MARTIN'S PRESS

NEW YORK

The fact that the author's Web site is mentioned in this book as a source of information does not mean that the publisher endorses the information it may provide. The publisher has not sponsored, prepared, or approved—and is not connected with—the author's Web site, www.gringonightmare .com.

GRINGO NIGHTMARE. Copyright © 2010 by Eric Volz. All rights reserved. Printed in the United States of America. For information, address St. Martin's Press, 175 Fifth Avenue, New York, N.Y. 10010.

www.stmartins.com

Library of Congress Cataloging-in-Publication Data

Volz, Eric (Eric Stanley), 1979–
    Gringo nightmare : a young American framed for murder in Nicaragua / Eric Volz. — 1st ed.
        p.   cm.
    ISBN 978-0-312-55727-0
    1. Volz, Eric (Eric Stanley), 1979—Imprisonment.   2. Murder—Nicaragua—Case studies.   3. Criminal justice, Administration of —Nicaragua—Case studies.   4. Prisoners, Foreign—Nicaragua—Biography.   5. Americans—Nicaragua—Biography.   I. Title.
    HV6535.N5V65 2010
    364.152'3092—dc22

                                                                                    2009045699

First Edition: May 2010

10 9 8 7 6 5 4 3 2 1

I dedicate this book to Doris Jiménez

& my grandparents,

Enrique "Kiki" and Amalia Gordín.

Contents

Author's Note

This book chronicles my arrest, trial, conviction, and subsequent imprisonment in the Republic of Nicaragua for a horrific crime—the rape and murder of a dear friend—I did not commit.

I have tried to shape the story as an engrossing narrative, but I also intend that it will serve as a piece of evidence, as an insider's investigative report of an unsolved murder and the ongoing legal case surrounding it. I've incorporated a significant amount of detail, covering a two-year period. I began writing, clandestinely, what would become the foundation for this book in 2006, during my imprisonment. By the time of my release, I had filled forty-eight journals with notes and observations, which have been essential to the completion of this work.

The truth about Doris Jiménez's murder has been the subject of heated debate in many circles since the moment the crime was made public. In the most general terms, the consensus opinion in the United States is that I am an innocent man who was framed, while most Nicaraguans believe I am guilty of the crime and should be behind bars. Naïve and ill-informed perspectives have resulted in several twisted misunderstandings, and for many there are numerous questions left unanswered. In this book, I hope not only to clarify the facts but also to take the reader beyond the specific events of the case and to offer a new understanding of certain international realities. I also share specifics on the unique political coalition that was built by my defense team and on the behind-the-scenes strategies implemented to bring about my release.

At the same time, the book will perhaps serve as a cautionary tale, demonstrating some of the very real dangers faced by North Americans and other foreigners living, investing, and traveling in Nicaragua today.

On a more personal level, I pray that the story shared in these pages will help bring some sense of closure to Doris's many family members and friends, if such closure is possible.

A few notes on language: I have translated conversations that took place in Spanish as faithfully and accurately as possible. In addition, dialogue offered in scenes at which I was not present have been carefully reconstructed from interviews with individuals who were present at that scene. I also tend to use the pronoun *we* instead of *I* when describing discoveries, decisions, or actions made regarding my defense. I am a free man because of the collective work of many, many committed individuals and wish to avoid any implication that my defense was anything other than a group effort.

Acknowledgments

This manuscript would never have materialized without the assistance of a number of individuals who contributed to its development by the furnishing of clues to sources, data, research, knowledge sharing, legal counsel, intelligence, and editorial guidance.

I am deeply grateful to David Sobel, who collaborated with me in the creation of this project, providing invaluable assistance in writing, editing, and revision. I have fond memories of our first meetings and brainstorms in various Manhattan parks, diners, and university cafeterias.

I especially want to thank my literary agent, Faith Hamlin, from Sanford J. Greenburger Associates, along with her gracious colleagues Courtney Miller-Callihan and Stefanie Diaz. I am grateful to my editor, Charles Spicer of St. Martin's Press, for his expertise and generous support and the contagious enthusiasm of his colleagues, Yaniv Soha and John Murphy.

I owe a special tribute to Melissa Campbell, whose expertise in media relations not only played a crucial role in generating the appropriate attention around my story but also managed the difficult but necessary task of protecting our family's privacy. Melissa's work kept me alive, and this book would not exist without her.

Words cannot describe the deep admiration and affection I have for my Nicaraguan attorney, Fabbrith Gomez, for his factual research and legal counsel and, even more important, for his unfailing trust. Thank you, Jackie Becerra, for your continued friendship. Likewise, I thank Jim Zumwalt, who has spent many late afternoons dealing with logistics and whose legal counsel helped formulate a successful venture.

To Drew Tulumello, Claudia Barrett, and Lissa Percopo from the Washington, D.C., office of Gibson, Dunn & Crutcher for their generous pro bono work and assistance navigating the Inter-American Commission on Human Rights and for enriching my perspective of justice and the rule of law as it applies to my experience.

I would also like to thank my mother, Maggie Anthony; her husband, Dane Anthony; and my uncle, Roberto Lady, for their factual review of the manuscript. I also need to acknowledge the amazing compassion displayed by my mother, Dane, and my father, Jan Volz, in the countless hours comforting me as I wrestled with the emotional challenge of this writing process.

In Nicaragua, an affectionate salute goes to Adolfo Calero, Xavier Reyes Alba, and Maria Alicia Reyes for helping me understand the various forms and threats to judicial independence and democracy as these served to impact my case and this project. In addition, I thank those individuals requesting anonymity, who contributed important clues to sources, information of social allegiances, and intelligence.

My understanding of what happened in my case on a diplomatic level benefited greatly from several frank discussions with members of the U.S. Embassy in Nicaragua, U.S. Department of State in Washington, and U.S. Senate and with officers at the U.S. Agency for International Development. Thank you to Cesar Zamora, Ricardo Castillo, Marc Meznar, Mike Poehlitz, Kerry Sanders, and Tania Lindsey, who provided crucial information on specific topics.

To my friend Holly Benyousky, for her incredible support and encouragement of this endeavor, I am grateful beyond words.

I am deeply indebted to Susan Houston for her relentless efficiency and endless patience. To Charlie Peacock and Andi Ashworth of the Art House and to Christopher Cook, Nick Purdy, Shawn Harstad, Richard McKinney, and Jim Thomas, who were each kind enough to review sections of the manuscript and offer helpful suggestions. To Ben Pearson and Chris Wellhausen for donating photographs and to Adam Paredes of Zion Media Group for creative direction and photo editing. The entire staff at St. Martin's Press has been a pleasure to work with, offering helpful comments and graciously accepting last-minute changes.

Finally, I would not have been able to complete this work without the patience and support of my family and friends and the contributions of others whose names may not appear here. I am eternally grateful to each one of them and am blessed to have them in my corner.

Easy-to-Use Online Exhibit Hall

Throughout this book the reader will find the superscript "EX.xx", indicating that there is an exhibit in an online archive that corresponds to that point in the text. Readers will have access to in-depth material such as photographs and video from inside the prisons, headshots of characters, audiotapes from the trial, autopsy reports, government documents, witness statements, crime-scene photos, the original police case file, defense motions, court rulings, and newspaper articles. Much of this material has never been publicly available until now.

To access this archive, visit www.gringonightmare.com and enter the number of the exhibit in the box on the home page. For example, exhibit 14 will be represented in the text by the superscript note EX.14.

You will need the log-in information below to access
the Exhibit Hall archive:

access code: hG495px1

www.gringonightmare.com

List of Persons

SILVIO **AGUIRRE**—crime scene investigator, Rivas Police Department

ARNOLDO **ALEMÁN** LACAYO—former president of Nicaragua, 1997–2002

DANE **ANTHONY**—Eric's stepfather

MAGGIE **ANTHONY**—Eric's mother

MERCEDES **ALVARADO** LANZAS—Doris's mother

DAN **BAZAN**—U.S. consular official in Nicaragua

JACKIE **BECERRA**—Washington attorney

OMAR **CABEZAS**—Solicitor-General of Human Rights

ADOLFO **CALERO** PORTOCARRERO—former Contra army general

MELISSA **CAMPBELL**—public relations specialist

RICARDO **CASTILLO**—defense witness

CAMILO DE **CASTRO**—Nicaraguan journalist, *Esta Semana*

JULIO **CENTENO** GOMEZ—attorney general of Nicaragua

LENIN **CERNA**—director of Nicaragua's internal intelligence agency

NOEL MARTIN **COREA**—crime-lab expert

ARTURO JOSÉ **CRUZ** SEQUEIRO—Nicaraguan ambassador in Washington

NELSON ANTONIO LOPEZ **DANGLAS** AKA KRUSTY—Nicaraguan citizen

ALEJANDRO **ESTRADA** SEQUEIRO—Granada appeals court magistrate

DR. OSCAR **FLORES**—prosecution witness, medical examiner, Managua

FREDDY—police officer, Rivas Police Department

FABBRITH **GOMEZ**—attorney

LARA **HARRIS**—U.S. consular official in Nicaragua

JOSE JUARQUIN **HERRERA**—prosecution witness

JONATHAN **HUBERT** ZAPATA—prison inmate

ISOLDA **IBARRA** AGUELLO—head prosecutor, Rivas District

DORIS IVANIA **JIMÉNEZ** ALVARADO—victim

VANESA ARCIA **JUAREZ**—prosecution witness, medical examiner, Rivas

ROBERTO (TIO BOB) **LADY**—fixer / Latin American specialist

ARMANDO AGUSTÍN **LLANES** NAVARRO—U.S. citizen

ALFONSO AGUSTÍN **LLANES** WHITESELL—Armando Llanes's father, prominent Nicaraguan and U.S. citizen

JOHANNA HOLLMANN DE **LLANES**—Armando Llanes's aunt by marriage, cousin of San Juan del Sur mayor, Eduardo Hollmann

RICARDO **LLANES** WHITESELL—Armando Llanes's uncle

ROSY **LOPEZ**—defense witness

ALLAN VELASQUEZ **MARTINEZ**—trial prosecutor

MANUEL **MARTINEZ** SEVILLA—president of Supreme Court of Nicaragua

MARC **MEZNAR**—U.S. cónsul general, Nicaragua

NORMAN **MIRANDA**—Granada appeals court magistrate

OSCAR **MOLINA** CAVARÍA—warden at La Modelo

JULIO CESAR **MONTES**—former guerilla commander, Guatemalan human rights activist

ANA ISABEL **MORALES**—minister of government

MUSTACHE COP—detective, Auxilio Judicial, Managua Division

CARLOS JOSE **NAJAR**—vice minister of Government

EDGAR NAVAS **NAVAS**—Supreme Court justice

OTTO **NAVAS**—former district-level judge in Granada, son of Edgar Navas

DANIEL **ORTEGA** SAVEDA—President of Republic of Nicaragua

PETER **PALMA**—Rivas judge

MARIA ESPERANZA **PEÑA** NUÑEZ—prosecutor at initial hearings

MIKE **POEHLITZ**—regional security officer for U.S. Embassy in Nicaragua

NICK **PURDY**—defense witness

CHEVEZ **POZO**—prison inmate

LESBER **QUINTERO**—journalist, *El nuevo diario*

ALBA LUZ **RAMOS**—Supreme Court justice

JOE **REEDER**—Washington attorney, Greenburg Traurig

EMIGDIO **REYES** PÉREZ GONZÁLEZ—Commissioner of Detectives, Auxilio Judicial, Rivas Division

XAVIER **REYES** ALBA—editor, *La trinchera*

FRANCISCO ROBERTO **RODRIGUEZ** BALTODANO—Granada appeals
  court magistrate

RAMON **ROJAS**—attorney

JULIO MARTÍN CHAMORRO LOPEZ AKA **ROSITA**—Nicaraguan citizen

LEONARDO **SANDOLVAL** GIRÓN—second cell mate in La Modelo

THOMAS **SHANNON**—Assistant Secretary of State, Western Hemisphere

EL PREFECTO CARLOS **SOBALVARRO**—director of Federal Penitentiary System
  in Nicaragua

GABI VANESA **SOBALVARRO**—prosecution witness

RAFAEL **SOLÍS** CERDA—Supreme Court justice

SIMON **STRONG**—private investigator

ROSEMARY **THORNTON**—journalist and police operator

DENIS **TINOCO**—Commissioner of Detectives, Auxilio Judicial, Managua
  Division

IVETTE **TORUÑO** BLANCO—Rivas trial judge

PAUL **TRIVELLI**—U.S. ambassador in Nicaragua

JORGE **URIARTE**—detective, Auxilio Judicial, Managua Division

CAPTAIN **VALERIO**—Captain, Rivas Police Department

AGNIELLY **VEGA**—operations manager, *EP* magazine

JAN **VOLZ**—Eric's father

Nicaraguan Government Acronyms

FSLN- Frente Sandinista Liberacion Nacional (Sandinista political
  party)
MIG- Ministry of Government
PLC- Liberal Constitution Party (opposition to FSLN)
SPN- National Penitentiary System

Foreword

by BILL KURTIS

San Juan del Sur, Nicaragua, evokes the same reaction in every visitor: "Let's stay an extra day." Tiny by Acapulco standards, it has the same wide, half-moon beach framed by short, green-jungle hills. The streets are dusty, lined with just enough open-air bars to keep tourists happy but not enough to disturb the feeling that this town is the real thing—an authentic, undiscovered, unspoiled Central American beach town.

But in the fall of 2006, this small community was rocked by a brutal murder. Doris Jiménez, a beautiful young woman who owned a local clothing boutique, was found dead in her shop. Within days, Eric Volz, a young American magazine publisher and real estate investor who had dated Doris, found himself accused of her murder. Thus began a chain of events that would change Eric's life forever, expose a judicial system dominated by corruption and special interests, and lead to a diplomatic meltdown between the Nicaraguan and United States governments.

Eric's first impression of San Juan del Sur had been sweet, but it wasn't accurate. It missed the red-tiled rooftops of half-a-million-dollar homes, occupied by wealthy Nicaraguan families and American expatriates who had also discovered this little pirate cove and decided to stay more than "an extra day."

After Volz arrived and put it all together, he smelled *boomtown* and launched a successful bilingual magazine called *El Puente*—the Bridge. The Pacific waves seemed to be breaking his way. And it wasn't hard for him to stand out in the sleepy little village, especially when he started dating the local beauty, Doris Jiménez.

But a plotline too good to be true usually is. For Eric Volz, the end to paradise came with a phone call to his office in Managua, several hours away. Doris was dead, murdered in the back of her small gift shop on one of San Juan del Sur's dusty streets, where the sun beat its fury the hardest.

Eric's story could've ended there. Instead, it was just the beginning.

Even though he was hours away at the time of the murder, police found it easy to believe some local toughs who fingered the "gringo." Eric was soon slipping down the rabbit hole of Nicaraguan justice, wrongfully accused, and then, wrongfully convicted of murder.

Everything worked against him. While North Americans brought money to the shops of San Juan del Sur, they also represented an enemy of the Sandinista revolution. Doris's mother was a political activist who kept the newspapers filled with reminders that Eric was from the United States. The switch of prejudice was an easy one to turn on. Finally, being an American inside a Nicaraguan prison completed his journey down the River Styx.

Eric Volz is a graphic reminder that one's rights as an American citizen end at our borders. His story should be issued with every passport.

GRINGO
NIGHTMARE

Prologue

"¡A donde me llevas, cabrones?!" "¡A donde me llevas?!"

No answer. I kept asking, kept demanding to know. *Where are you taking me?!*

It was the middle of February, 2007—Valentine's week—and only a few moments before, Judge Ivette Toruño had brought down her gavel on my trial, declaring me guilty of the cold-blooded first-degree murder of Doris Jiménez. *Asesinato atroz.* Armed police guards loaded me and the codefendant, Rosita, into a pickup truck. Rosita sat exposed in the rear bed, surrounded by four guards who packed sidearms and AK-47s. They pushed me onto the backseat of the truck's cab, with guards on either side of me and two more in the front seat. The truck, part of a three-car convoy, sped away from the courthouse in the small Nicaraguan city of Rivas and pulled onto the Pan-American Highway, the main north-south road through Central America.

We had only been on the road for a few minutes when the truck we were in separated from the other two cars and took off down a tiny dirt road. We headed into the endless sea of sugarcane crops, and suddenly we were alone.

The deeper we got into the cane, the more it began to feel like a one-way trip for me. Before the trial had ended, my team and I had tried to anticipate the outcome and to calculate what each particular scenario might reveal. A conviction would tell us without a doubt that there were larger forces at work, forces that reached high up into the Nicaraguan government and that wanted me captive. And that meant that the normal rules no longer applied, or, as one Nicaraguan put it to my mother, that

I

getting me out would be like "resurrecting a dead body." Now, as the truck sped farther and farther into what felt to me like oblivion, every mile raised the tension and anxiety.

I heard only the rattling of the truck as it bounced along the rough dirt road and tried to will the fear away. There was something in me that refused to accept this fate. I took a couple of deep, centering breaths and tried to imagine breaking free. I scanned the cab, checking and rechecking the number of police, locating their weapons, formulating plans. Maybe I could kick this one with my right foot, maybe I could get that one's sidearm before he could react. I went over it and over it, but it never added up. There was no way I wouldn't end up dead.

I could hear Rosita shouting in the back of the truck. "¡No me pueden hacer esto!" *You can't do this to me.* Rosita was Nicaraguan, or Nica. He, like every Central American, knows what happens in the sugarcane.

After twenty minutes, the truck came into a tiny village and pulled up to a shabby little jailhouse. Several carloads worth of police officers stood outside the jail with guns drawn, blocking the road. The fear I felt while driving through the cane must have distracted me from the events of the day, and, as they walked me to a cell, it all came rushing back. I was going back to jail, back into hell, and maybe I'd never come out again. With that realization came a horrible rush of adrenaline, a gut-twisting surge of pain unlike anything I had ever felt. My head started to swim, but the police captain's voice snapped me back to attention.

The captain was telling me to take off my bulletproof vest, and this simple request made a lot of things clear to me. I understood that the police were frightened, too. The number of guards, the heavy weapons, and the sudden evasive detour off the highway were to protect them from an armed ambush. They must have figured that my security team would use this transfer, this brief moment of vulnerability, to come after me, attack the police convoy, and break me out. And the captain further figured that if my team saw me without a vest, they'd never start shooting. The captain wanted me unprotected, to protect himself.

They kept us in the little jail for half an hour or so. For thirty minutes I sat alone with my mind racing, my imagination running wild, my belly churning with hunger and stress, my heart pounding, adrenaline pulsing through me. As dusk fell, the police must have decided that no rescue team was coming, and they rushed Rosita and me back into the truck and, with the siren wailing the entire time, sped back through the sugarcane to the highway.

Even after we left the cane fields, we seemed to have the road to ourselves, which spooked me even more. Then, in the last sliver of sunlight before nightfall, another car approached from the opposite direction. As they passed, I could see into the car and was stunned to look into the faces of my former business partner, JT, and his wife, Arelis. Our eyes met for an instant as they shot past us.

If I hadn't been so strung out and terrified, I might have laughed. Here was JT, the guy who got me down to Nicaragua in the first place, and Arelis, the woman whose open, vicious hatred of Doris Jiménez, the murder victim, hung like a shadow over everything that had happened to me in the last three months. For all I knew, they could be the last familiar faces I'd see, the last people to see me before the hidden forces of Nicaragua took me wherever the hell they were taking me.

When the Pan-American Highway forked into northwest and northeast, the truck took the eastern road, to the colonial city of Granada. About forty-five minutes later, the police were pulling me out of the truck at the penitentiary on the outskirts of the city, and the entire prison erupted, like someone had set off an explosion. It seemed like all six hundred prisoners were shouting at once. I will never forget the horrible noise; it haunts me to this day. I could hear hysterical, shrieking laughter, and the raw, chilling sound of men howling and literally barking like wild dogs. They banged against the bars of their cells and windows with plates or chairs, and underneath it all was the blare of dozens of television sets, all turned to the news. The news about me.

The sound that rang in my ears as the prison guards hustled me off was the sound of my own name being shouted through the prison. Just like the guards, the inmates knew who they had on their hands.

"¡Volz! ¡Volz!"

"¡Ya llegó el gringo!"

I.

Road to República

The path I followed to Nicaragua may not have been direct, but it was never random. Although the first time I set foot in Nicaragua I hadn't been looking for much more than some good, uncrowded surf, I didn't end up living there by accident. My interest in, and later my affection for, Nica grew out of a unique combination of circumstances, from my family's heritage and my own academic background, growing involvement with social development, and natural sense of adventure to what I would later come to understand as God's will.

By the time I got to Nicaragua I, like a lot of people of my generation, had had the luxury of trying on a few different personas. Some part of each of those had stuck with me, combining to form my character. Over the long months of my trial and imprisonment, I had to tap into the many varied experiences of my life for the skills and wisdom I would need to survive.

I grew up in Northern California, where I was born in 1979, and my life had centered more on sports and the outdoors than on books and school. It turns out that I wasn't such a bad athlete either. I had the fortune of not just being quick and strong but of having a knack for balancing focus and instinct on the playing field. I loved it, and it became a central component of my identity. I played a lot of sports, but for a long time my passion was soccer.

My dad started out as a professional musician. When I was young, he had been part of the 77s, one of the country's first and most successful alternative "Christian rock" bands. Later, my dad left the band and started an artist-management company based in Nashville, Tennessee. Growing up, I picked up many little things just from watching him at work, from coping with life on the road to managing your own or someone else's public image to financing and promoting projects.

My mom grew up as Maria Margarita on the southern border of Arizona. Now everyone calls her Maggie. Her parents were Mexican, and, although she grew up dominant in the English language, Spanish was commonly spoken around the house. Her parents were very traditional, conservative Mexicans, but, like many children of immigrants, my mom identified more with American culture than she did with that of her parents. Mom had trained as an interior decorator but devoted herself to taking care of my sister and me, which was challenging enough when my father was out touring and got harder when their relationship grew rocky.

By the time I was thirteen, we had left California. We were living in Tennessee, and my parents had split up. My dad needed to be in Nashville for his work, but, for my sister and me, the country-music capital represented a huge culture shock. Everybody sounded different, acted different, and sometimes even looked different from what we were used to. I think adolescence is tough under any circumstances, but getting uprooted and dropped into a strange environment made it an extraconfusing time for me.

As I got older, my attention turned away from organized team sports. Eventually, I discovered rock climbing, which consumed me to the point where it was all I did. Climbing opened up new worlds for me. As physically challenging as anything I had ever done, it was also a deeply meditative activity, an opportunity to train my mind as well as my body. People who do yoga or other activities that involve hyperawareness of one's own body, precise muscle control, and total concentration will talk about the same kind of mystical qualities that I found in climbing. But climbing has another element, something that fundamentally changes the nature of the experience: the constant presence of danger, the possibility of life-changing injury or death. A good climber learns to compartmentalize his or her thoughts. You still get scared, but you learn how to stay cool. Climbing is about problem solving, and if your brain is overwhelmed by the fear of falling, it can't process or solve the practical problems like, Will my foot fit on that edge? or, Is the rope secure?

Eventually, I came under the wing of the late Lars Holbeck, a well-known pioneer kayaker and Yosemite climber who became the first of a handful of influential mentors in my life. When my climbing skills got good enough, I took it to another level, and started free soloing—climbing without ropes or other protective equipment. I had always found climbing to be both exhilarating and soothing at the same time, and I felt those qualities even more strongly when soloing. On the one hand, there are no distractions. You have fewer questions and fewer decisions if you don't have to think about hammering pitons into the wall or clipping your rope into carabineers. It's just you and the rock, and every time you go up, you can't help facing the possibility of death. You actually become accustomed to situations in which you could die. You learn to manage the fear and channel adrenaline into focus and concentration, which results in peak performance.

Climbing also helped get me through an adolescence complicated not only by our move to Tennessee but also by my parents' divorce. It gave me some escape, a place where I could be part of a community of people and yet still be alone, on the rock face. It was not, however, the only escape I found. When I was in high school, friends introduced me to a place not too far away called The Farm. In the simplest terms, The Farm is a hippie commune straight out of another era. While most of the communes established in the 1960s were short-lived, The Farm thrived and is now probably one of the best known of these experimental communities. I never lived there, but weekends and camping trips at The Farm exposed me to some different ways of understanding the world. It was a safe place for me at a time when I needed it. At The Farm, I made many lifelong friends. I also fell in love with a girl who opened up another huge door for me. Audrey had lived and traveled in Central America and could speak Spanish, and knowing her triggered my desire to connect with my own heritage, to understand the experience of my mother and her parents. I started asking questions and hearing stories I had never heard before. Although I had grown up understanding the Spanish spoken to me by my mother's family, I had never actually taken an interest in speaking Spanish. I always responded in English for some reason. But now, with a new desire to know my roots, I began to learn to speak the Spanish language for the first time.

The next several years of my life were devoted, in one way or another, to building this bridge between the "America" in which I had grown up and the culture of my grandparents that I felt calling to me. It was as if I missed something that I never even knew. I studied briefly in Mexico and then went back to California to spend time with my grandmother, Amalia, before she passed. My grandfather's nickname was Kiki. He had come from a very poor family and, together with my grandmother, had fulfilled the common Mexican-American dream of starting a business that grew and prospered. I think that when she was growing up, my mom was as eager to reject her *fronteriza* roots—her experience growing up near the border immersed in Mexican culture—as I was to embrace them at the same age. It seemed to me, in those years, that in order to know myself, I needed to know about this culture of the border. I think that I needed to find a way to cross it.

After three years in community college, I finally had the credits to get accepted to the University of California, San Diego, where the political science department emphasized not just Latin American studies but what many scholars refer to as border studies; there, I had the good fortune to meet a number of politically engaged teachers who strongly influenced developing perspectives in their fields. First, I met Ignacio Ochoa— "Nacho"—a young Guatemalan dissident. Nacho and I became close enough that, years later, when he needed a safe place to lay low after his activism in Guatemala put his life in danger, I arranged for his protection in Nicaragua. After he left the university, I ran into him again when we both enrolled in a San Diego State course taught by the Mexican human-rights activist Victor Clark Alfaro. Victor's class actually met in Tijuana, and, although it was officially sanctioned, he kept the class under low profile and always had one or two armed men standing guard over our meetings. Victor was constantly receiving death threats and had had some close calls. I bonded with Victor in much the same way I had with Nacho, and I remember riding in his car through the backstreets of TJ with all my senses on fire, alert to the danger. This was the first of many times I would be in a group that would use car swapping as a safety precaution.

Through Nacho, I met Julio Cesar Montes, the notorious Guatemalan revolutionary and activist with whom I developed an equally close relationship. Known as El Comandante, Montes had founded the Rebel Armed Forces (FAR) in the early 1960s, later commanded the Guerrilla Army of the Poor (EGP) during Guatemala's thirty-six-year civil war, and served the Farabundo Martí National Liberation Front (FMLN) in El Salvador and even fought alongside my future captors—the Sandinistas of Nicaragua.

Montes knew that I had also become interested in filmmaking, and about a half a year after our meeting, I found myself in Guatemala with him, shooting video for a documentary. Cesar Montes was the real deal, a modern revolutionary, grassroots activist, and soldier, a man who lived in shadows, except when he would give a speech at an event. In Cesar's world, you had to stay sharp and alert. Everybody had a gun, and everybody had a secret. It was an intense existence, and while the possibility of violence constantly hung in the air, you learned that letting the fear get the better of you endangered the lives of everyone around you, not to mention the cause for which they were making so many sacrifices. As in climbing, I had to learn to channel fear into focus, and also as in climbing, we all had to be light and fast and sure of every step.

Seeing the world through Cesar Montes's eyes changed my understanding on many levels. I saw the painful past and present of Central America up close, in the kind of detail that most North Americans never see. I saw people risking everything, including their own lives, for something larger. Following Montes around the mountains and jungles of Guatemala was at times a little sketchy, but it was always inspirational.

Together, people like Nacho and Victor and Montes woke me up to a different kind of life. Now, spending time hanging by ropes off the side of a mountain seemed trivial and self-indulgent. Through these men and others my consciousness began to shift. It wasn't just that I saw that I *could* contribute, it's that I realized I wanted to. I wasn't interested in joining a guerrilla army somewhere, but I knew that I could help with message and communication, through words and images. As a middle-class American, I had access to education and financial resources, and I felt a responsibility to put these things to use in some socially meaningful way. I still feel that way.

I made a special arrangement with UCSD to finish my undergraduate degree and senior thesis abroad, in the Dominican Republic. The United States and Mexico aren't the only countries with border issues. The dynamics between the peoples of Haiti and the Dominican Republic, two tiny countries sharing a small Caribbean island, were as fragile and volatile and relevant as anything I could study in the United States. My experience there allowed me to see how easily and quickly random trouble can flare up around innocent people.

When I returned to California my life had come to be more about the world south of the border. Most gringo boys like me were busy chasing big waves and surfer chicks, but I guess I had become a little nerdy, obsessed with politics and ethnic studies. I spoke as much Spanish as I did English. I found myself immersed in all these underworlds of the immigrant experience, such as that of my Mexican friends who would paddle their boards up from south of the border and surf into the United States on the morning tide.

Maybe I was driven by sadness or even guilt about missing the chance to get to know my Mexican grandparents better. It just felt like I would never understand myself or really be comfortable in my own skin until I understood the world of the border. Over the next few years, I continued to practice various forms of journalism. I went to Puerto Rico to do a photo-essay about the thousands of Dominicans who came there crammed into tiny little *yolas*—fishing boats braving the dangerous currents of the Caribbean Sea. I made one of my first 16mm films, a fictional narrative about a pair of lovers who can only see each other through the border fence, called "Smuggling Roses." I even traveled to Iraq to document the war in pictures.

Iraq opened my eyes in ways that my travels in Central America never had. I saw up close the kind of focus and attention the soldiers put into the daily business of staying alive. I was lucky—if that's what you want to call it—to go out on patrol, or at least to travel in some small groups of soldiers, and I watched how they developed procedures and protocols for anything they might encounter. They take every possible precaution to get home safely, and I never forgot what I learned from these courageous young men and women.

In the year 2000, after a long semester at school, I took off on a backpacking-surfing trip to Central America, starting in northern Panama, where a friend had bought some land on an island. That North American surfers and other tourists had discovered remote places like Bocas del Toro, on Panama's Caribbean coast, and were eager to relocate and retire there showed just how much things had changed in that part of the world. And still there was so much left to explore. For the past twenty-five years, Costa Rica has been the hot Central American vacation destination for Americans and Europeans. It's gorgeous, to be sure, and comparatively prosperous. Between the rain forests, beaches, volcanoes, eco-lodges, and countless adventure-travel-guide outfits, it's ideal for American families looking for a somewhat exotic, yet still relatively safe, vacation. In recent years, you may have heard tourists talking about Belize or Bay Islands of Honduras in the same way, but nobody was talking much about vacationing in Nicaragua. Though Nica has much of the natural appeal of its neighbors, most gringos still think of it as too sketchy, if they think of it at all. The word *Nicaragua* has long been associated with images like Cuban cigars, jungles, AK-47s, Che Guevara, the Iran-Contra scandal, poverty—not to mention the constant political turmoil—and definitely not with the culture of tourism you find in places like Costa Rica.

But every now and then I'd come across some long-time traveler or crusty old surfer who had been to Nica and who described it as an enchanting and undiscovered place, if you knew how to take care of yourself. Being someone who couldn't resist the chance to explore new places, I eventually gathered up my board and my backpack and got on a bus to Nicaragua.

I know this will be hard to believe, but the moment the bus crossed the northern border of Costa Rica into Nicaragua, I sensed a different vibe. The first thing you come across is an old abandoned government building that was used as the border inspection station during the civil war that ensued after the 1979 revolution. Physically, everything seemed more rustic and raw, old and patched up, but also not yet fully formed. You only had to look out the window of the bus to see the legacies of civil war and of isolation from the international community. The political history of Nicaragua over the last forty or fifty years is as painful as it is complex. It also happens to be directly relevant to almost everything that happened to me there.

People my age sometimes find it hard to imagine that thirty years ago this impoverished nation—what some of our parents would refer to as the "third world"—played such a major part on the world stage. Historians largely credit Christopher Columbus with being the first European to arrive in what is now Nicaragua, in 1502. A little more than twenty years later, the first Spanish settlement was established, and within a generation various *conquistadores* fought for control of the land, leaving a trail of devastation. Whatever portion of the indigenous population that survived lived under Spanish colonial rule for the next three hundred years, until the nation gained independence in 1838. The first trouble between the United States and Nicaragua appeared in 1909, when the United States sent in an occupying force of marines, ostensibly to protect American business interests during political unrest but really to prop up a friendly regime. A rebellion led by Augusto Sandino—whose politics and activism inspired the Sandinista party, which adopted his name, in the latter half of the twentieth century—convinced the United States to withdraw its troops. But before they retreated, the United States made sure that a leader friendly to its interests, Anastasio Somoza, took control of the government and that he was supported by a strong national guard that was trained and equipped by the United States.

Power rested in the hands of the Somoza family dynasty, first under the dictatorship of Anastasio Somoza and later under his two sons, for the next forty years. The history and nature of the Somoza regime is a delicate and controversial subject among Nicaraguans. Some claim that Somoza ruled by terror while others revere him as a brilliant leader who was ironfisted but who could be credited with major achievements for his country. More important, those who stand by Somoza's legacy feel that it is only fair to point out that his form of governing was nowhere near as ruthless or savage as the regime run by the Sandinistas in the eighties. The Somozas, indeed, controlled the government and the military, and had a stranglehold over the national economy, but their policies resulted in Nicaragua's status as the wealthiest country in Central America at the time. There were even elections. However, many claimed that there was no real democracy. The populace began to organize in the early 1960s, but dissension didn't come out into the open completely for another ten years. After a massive earthquake leveled most of the capital city of Managua in 1972, the wholesale corruption of the Somoza regime came into clear focus for the Nicaraguan people. The recovery effort never really got off the ground, as most of the foreign-aid money was mishandled and misdirected—much of it into private pockets. In some ways, the city and the country are still feeling the devastation of that earthquake. The growing resentment within the population finally boiled over into open rebellion, and in 1979 the Somoza regime fell, to be replaced by the Sandinista party, led by Daniel Ortega.

The Sandinista revolution and the period of Sandinista Communist rule over Nicaragua changed the political landscape in Central America and thrust Nicaragua into the global spotlight. It also triggered events that rocked the Reagan administration in Washington. With the cold war still going strong, Latin America was, as far as Washington was concerned, a fertile breeding ground for Communist revolution, such as had happened in Cuba. Ronald Reagan, focused as he was on bringing the cold war to an end and protecting U.S. economic interests, distrusted any left-leaning individual or movement that was close to his borders and that might come under the influence of the Soviet Union.

The Sandinistas had their hands full getting the country moving again in the aftermath of their bloody revolt, but with Ortega wanting the spirit of revolution to spread throughout the region, the United States decided to take action, and Central America once again would become the backyard where the cold war would turn hot. The U.S. government began to fund a counterrevolutionary army—*contrarrevolucionarios*, or more familiarly *Contras*—made up of former Somoza loyalists as well as other opposition groups who had vied for control with the Sandinistas. When the U.S. Congress cut off funding for the Contras in 1983, officials in the Reagan administration set up a complicated scheme in which the money from the sale of arms to Iran (at that time involved in a long war with Iraq) were secretly channeled to the Nicaraguan Contras. When the operation was exposed, Washington erupted. Congressional hearings riveted the American people for months and dealt a severe blow to Reagan's credibility. In the course of the investigations, further allegations came out connecting the operation to drug trafficking, although those allegations were never proved. I would later learn the real story in prison from one of the pilots involved.

Additionally, the United States put economic pressure on the Nicaraguan government by imposing a complete trade embargo, which had immediate repercussions for the population in Nicaragua. Goods and services became even more scarce, meaning that living conditions, which had already been grim for the average Nicaraguan, grew worse. It's no wonder that Ortega's strategy for assistance was directed to the only reasonable ally in the area—Cuba. And, in those years before the fall of the Berlin wall, a relationship with Cuba almost certainly meant some kind of relationship with the Soviet Union, even if it was hazy and loosely defined. Ironically, Reagan's own fears made the United States turn its back on the Sandinistas and on Nicaragua. Daniel Ortega would never have accepted assistance from the United States anyway, which he claimed was the great and evil "Yankee imperialist," responsible for the very conditions that had brought about the revolution. But the antagonism he felt from Washington likely helped drive the Sandinistas right into the arms of the United States's enemy.

Ten years after the Nicaraguan revolution, much had changed in the world. The Soviet empire had collapsed, leaving Cuba—and by extension, Nicaragua—out in the cold. With the U.S. embargo in place and the pipeline from Russia and Cuba gone, living conditions got worse and worse. Things hadn't been perfect under Somoza, but now under Ortega many Nicaraguans had trouble meeting even their most basic needs. With no trading partners or outside sources of supply, industry and agriculture were drying up. Although Ortega could point to some real accomplishments, such as dramatically increased literacy rates throughout the country, the constant food shortages and crumbling infrastructure made most Nicaraguans less and less sympathetic to the ideals of the revolution. The mandatory draft that Ortega instituted may have been the final straw in the Nicaraguan people's disillusionment. Too many young men were dying, too many sons were lost by too many mothers, and too little, if anything at all, was gained by their sacrifice. Ortega's refusal to abolish the draft is what most Nicas will tell you ultimately brought down his regime.

Something else had seeped into the lives of the people as well. Along with all the economic assistance from Cuba and the Soviet Union had come some of the darker realities of Soviet cold-war culture. The state security forces that had held the population under its thumb during the long years of dictatorship might have changed uniforms but were still strong and created a thick fog of fear and suspicion. There were eyes and ears on every corner. Neighbors and coworkers were encouraged to inform on each other, and even a slight slip of the tongue could land a person in prison or worse. Nobody ever quite knew who they could trust. Political affiliation and allegiance became the unofficial currency. If you ever needed help from a local official, for example, you knew you needed to find one with quality ties to the Sandinistas. Even later, after the Sandinistas were voted out, this "Russian shadow" remained, part of the legacy of the revolution.

In 1990, Ortega and the Sandinistas lost control of the executive branch in a closely watched election. People both inside and outside the country worried that Ortega would try to hold on to control of the government despite the vote, but he stepped aside to let Violetta Chamorro serve as president. Chamorro, the widow of the assassinated editor of Nicaragua's leading newspaper, *La prensa*, led a coalition of political parties that opposed the Sandinista rule. Ortega's graceful departure may not have been as noble as it appeared; at the time it was known that he intended to go on governing "from below," confident that a network of Sandinista loyalists remained in place throughout all levels of government and in the streets that he could call to action. Nowhere was this more true than in the judiciary. Ortega was able to use the legal system to squeeze his enemies and to manipulate various situations for his own benefit. This network was still in place more than fifteen years after Ortega stepped down from the presidency. Through the courts, Ortega would attempt to neutralize opposition leaders, from former president Arnoldo Alemán, who was jailed for corruption, to Ortega's newest political rival, Eduardo Montealegre.

Nicaragua started to open up during the 1990s. The tourism that had propelled neighbors like Belize and especially Costa Rica into a higher level of prosperity had started making inroads into Nicaragua. The gringos were coming. And, as might be expected, many Nicas had conflicting feelings about outsiders, especially North Americans. They didn't forget the painful history of U.S. support for the Contras or the devastating embargo imposed or the way they were used as pawns in the global power struggle between the United States and the Soviets. There wasn't much that could soften their animosity toward U.S. citizens—except, of course, for U.S. dollars. Although some Nicas resented Americans, they were forced to brush it off because foreign investment could help change the economic situation. Of course nothing is ever black and white. Not all

Nicas hated the United States, and some even saw Washington as a savior. Many distrusted Ortega and the revolution and got out of the country, emigrating to other Central American countries and to Miami. However, Ortega found widespread support in the millions who bought into his promises and who believed that anything would be better than Somoza.

So, this was the Nicaragua I found when I first stepped off that bus in San Juan del Sur. When I got there in 2000 it was still a dusty village by the sea but was already on the way to becoming a hot surfer destination. Back then, it was anybody's guess what direction the country would take, but it certainly seemed possible that in a few years San Juan could end up lined with souvenir shops and American-style hotels and pizzerias, like Tamarindo in Costa Rica. Maybe in another generation it would be a spring-break zoo for American college kids, like Cabo San Lucas or Puerto Vallarta in Mexico.

The signs were already there when I arrived. In fact, I could have seen all the signs of what was to come in one of the very first people I met in San Juan, a local street kid who acted tough and who called himself Rosita. You find guys like this in any tourist town—savvy survivors who attach themselves to tourists by offering themselves as "guides" but who are just as down to hook you up with drugs or local women or whatever you're looking for—but in the face of the kind of generational poverty you find in Nicaragua, they seem a little hungrier. I had traveled enough that I could spot the Rositas of the world a mile away, but I let him show me around anyway. I didn't mind buying him a couple meals—after all, he was providing a service and I was focused on finding the surf breaks I had heard about. It was Rosita who took me by bus to the best surfing beach in the area and who tried to attach himself to me in any way he could. I think maybe he thought he had scored a real sucker when he found me and was pissed when he discovered that wasn't the case. I didn't see him again for a while after that trip to the beach, but when I did finally run into him at a bar a few days later, he nearly started a fight with me when I declined to buy him a beer.

The first person who I actually met in San Juan was another young American, JT, with whom I would later start a magazine. JT and I became fast friends, bonding easily and almost immediately over our interest in community development and in socially conscious media. You couldn't call JT a tourist in San Juan, nor was he a simple do-gooder. Up to that point in my travels, I had seen nothing like him. This guy was more Nicaraguan than American; he spoke with a perfect local accent and peppered his speech with street slang. What JT cared about most was the people in the town, and the work he had done there had earned him the deep respect from the elders and the affection of most everyone.

After I returned home to California, in 2000, at the end of my backpacking adventure and JT had gone back to his home in Atlanta, we kept in touch. Over the next four years, whenever we would talk or get together, the conversation would always get around to the kinds of projects we'd like to launch someday and to JT's desire to return to Nicaragua. When he finally called with a specific project in mind and asked me to come back to San Juan with him, I didn't waste any time saying yes.

JT had a vision. He wanted to go back to Nica to start a publication—which he referred to at the time as a newsletter—called *El Puente* ("The Bridge"), which he intended would be an effort to fill the gap between local folks from San Juan and visitors from North America and Europe, whether travelers or real-estate investors. It would be the first bilingual publication of its kind in the region. JT's wife, Arelis Castro, never wanted to return to Nicaragua but was willing to for her husband's project. Knowing my interest in photojournalism, JT invited me down to Nicaragua for a week to take photographs and build up a small library of stock images he could use in the newsletter.

I made the trip, took the pictures, and came back to California, which is actually where the first issue was put together. In that short time, my involvement with the project deepened. I had been counseling JT about ways to strengthen the brand of the publication by expanding its scope beyond social issues and economic development and creating a more distinctive look and editorial voice. Before the week was out, JT invited me to become his partner, and we agreed to move forward together, splitting everything right down the middle.

We returned to Nicaragua for the printing and the launch, which turned out to be a great success. We only printed 2,500 copies of the first issue of *El Puente*, but the excitement it seemed to create made it feel like something bigger. I remember the cover of that first issue, with a photograph of an old hand laying a brick, a simple image that conveyed the idea of development, which gave *El Puente* both a reason and a purpose, and the everyday labor of the *pueblo*. I saw something deeper in that photo as well. It spoke to me of the beginning that I was making and that JT and I were making together. This was the foundation we were laying down for our future.

I relocated to San Juan right away and got immediately wrapped up in our project—planning; recruiting writers, photographers, designers, advertisers; securing financing; doing marketing; and so on. It was a wonderfully exciting time, not only because we were creating something of our own but also because the nature of the project quickly linked me up with movers and shakers throughout Nicaragua. I got to know journalists and politicians, business owners and local representatives of foreign companies with offices there. I remember being amazed at how easily one connection would lead to another and how quickly the network would take us to people of real influence. I also got a very fast lesson on how things really work in Nicaragua. In the absence of the kind of oversight and regulation businesses in the United States are used to, success depended, in a very direct way, on knowing the right people and staying on their good side.

I built this social and professional network more quickly than I ever dreamed possible, but strangely, JT hadn't thrown himself into it in the same way. It was easy for me, I suppose. I was single and didn't really have a career or even a steady job when JT had first proposed his idea. JT was on a different trip, though. After he returned home to Atlanta after the launch of *El Puente* in San Juan, he had done well in his job and didn't find it so easy to give up. And he had a new wife and a new house. He said he needed to save a nest egg before he could move down permanently, but it dawned on me after a while that JT was dragging his feet, and I began pressuring him to make a commitment and get down to Nicaragua. Eventually, he and Arelis made the move, but I sensed it hadn't been easy for them. I didn't realize it at the time, but things had changed in our relationship and would never quite feel right again.

Early on in the process, I had gone to try to sell advertising space to the San Juan office of the American real-estate company Century 21, who had established an early foothold on the Nicaraguan coast. Century 21 was busy connecting individuals and corporate developers from the United States and elsewhere to local residents and wealthy landowners who saw the chance to make a quick score selling in the property boom. Not surprisingly, the company needed people who could relate to both the buyers and the sellers, people who knew their way around the local culture and language but who could also relate to the gringos with money to spend and their rigid and "by the book" way of doing business. The local office manager must have sized me up as someone who had those skills, and he offered me a job.

Selling real estate had never been part of my plan. That wasn't why I had moved so far away from home, and it wasn't how I planned to make my mark. Nonetheless, I immediately saw the advantages of taking the job, and after much discussion JT and I decided I should go for it. First, and most obviously, it meant an income, and actually a pretty good one after not too long. Second, I could put some of that money toward fueling the magazine until it got on its feet. Third, I thought it would be a position that would give me a unique understanding of the inner workings of the rapidly changing socioeconomics of the region. Finally, I told myself that by being directly involved with new real-estate and tourism development and with the influx of foreigners and their venture funds, I could perhaps see that the principles of responsible development, which meant so much to our magazine, could be put directly into action. I could guide the development. As for that last part, it didn't always work out the way I would have wanted. Every now and then, we'd be able to get a buyer to rebuild a classroom, dig a well for a community, or invest in some green technology for their neighborhood. I knew at the time that often their true motivation was not to "lend a hand" as much as it was to buy a form of "local insurance" on their new beachfront property or investment holding. Plenty of people talked a good game and nodded enthusiastically whenever we suggested something green, progressive, or community minded, but only a select few of them followed through. We met with plenty of disappointment. I watched a lot of people get rich, really rich. Millions got moved around with a couple of strokes of the keyboard. I brought in big revenue for the office, although some of the compromises along the way left me feeling a little uncomfortable. I was generating capital, rising up in the company, and making connections.

Six months after the first edition of *El Puente*, the whole idea of the project had grown. We had started by focusing our attention on San Juan del Sur and its immediate neighborhood, but right away we had caught the attention of people all over the country, including those in metropolitan Managua. We started hearing from writers and journalists, politicos, the white-collar business sector, and advertisers. It was clear to me that we could expand this into something much bigger. By the time we were ready to bring out the second edition, *El Puente* had evolved into a magazine with a print run of ten thousand. It was a success, and we decided to not look back and to go for it all the way. The third issue, now retitled *EP*, had a print run of twenty thousand copies and a readership that reached beyond Nicaragua's borders. We heard from readers in Costa Rica and had made copies available in Panama, and we started selling subscriptions to Central Americans in the United States. Delta Air Lines wanted it as one of their in-flight magazines, and within Nicaragua and Costa Rica we could already see imitators starting to appear. Clearly, we were on to something, something with potential to grow quickly and grow big.

2.

Doris Ivania Jiménez

As a man, I never thought about it much before, but I see now that being a beautiful girl in a small town can't be easy. You can't escape the jealous eyes and the sharp tongues of other women, and the men are either too intimidated by your looks or bitter over some past rejection. If you are outgoing and friendly, you run the risk of people thinking of you as a gold digger, or worse. If you're shy, they take you for stuck up and aloof. They look at you and see only great looks—your ticket out of town or to a better future—but nobody understands how easily that blessing can become a curse. You withdraw, becoming an outsider in your own little world.

Doris Jiménez was not just another pretty girl, although that's how the press usually referred to her, if the press even referred to her at all. There was something exotic in her looks, a touch of Caribbean, that set her far apart from even the many young and attractive Latina women on the dusty streets and beaches of the Pacific coast of Nicaragua. Slender and small boned but not delicate, Doris was what Latinos call *morena* because she had brown skin and thick black hair and huge brown eyes. When she smiled, her full lips seemed to spread across her face and her neat white teeth would shine. But there was more, a quiet intensity that let you know that something deeper was going on behind her beauty. Something subtle in her lively and friendly face, maybe wariness or fear or some hidden hurt, spoke of experience.

In her hometown of San Juan del Sur, the unique pressures of small-town life were magnified. For as long as most people can remember, the sleepy seaside village had escaped the notice of the outside world, despite the charms of its pristine beaches or the stunning views from the thickly forested hills rising up above the sea. The embattled Communist history of Daniel Ortega and his Sandinista government had kept Nicaragua effectively off the radar of North American or European tourists and entrepreneurs since coming into power in the revolution of 1979, first as leader of the ruling junta, and then as president from 1985 until 1990. Before Ortega, the few foreigners who found their way to this strip of coastline were most likely the more adventurous travelers and employees of big fruit companies from the north. Now, at the beginning of the new century, Nicaragua had suddenly opened up, and San Juan del Sur was seeing the first wave of a new influx of tourists and surfers, real-estate developers and business people with an eye on an untapped market, and even retirees looking for a quiet place to kick back and escape the cold winters of home.

Naturally, a gorgeous girl like Doris was one of the first things that caught the eyes of some of these opportunists and pleasure seekers. How exciting it must have been to have so many strange new people in town, including men with mobility and confidence, singling her out. It would take a special kind of worldly smarts to negotiate the tricky interaction between the culture she knew—a culture of poverty, little interpersonal trust, of old-world Catholic values—and the faster, looser, and more extravagant attitudes of the foreigners. According to Doris herself, she had found herself on the wrong side of that equation more than once.

When I first met Doris, she was living with her aunt Elena in a house up a winding dirt road in the hills overlooking town. Before that, Doris had been living with a serious boyfriend, something that girls only did in that part of the world on the understanding that marriage would soon follow. When the relationship fell apart, Doris returned in shame to her family, many of whom turned their backs on her, as did so many others in town. After that failure—that *fracaso*—Doris was branded what they call in Nicaragua *una chica fácil*, or "damaged goods."

Not that her own family was a model of traditional values. Her parents had split up some years before, her father now living in the nearby town of Rivas with a new wife and children, and her mother in the capital city of Managua, living with a semi-influential businessman there, with whom she, too, had had more children.

Despite all the turmoil in her own home life, Doris was devoted to the idea of family. She had been raised mostly by her aunt and lavished the same kind of love on her beloved little cousin, Valentina, the sweetest four-year-old I had ever met. I recall coming home one night after a day's work so exhausted I couldn't even make it to the bedroom. I flopped down on the couch, but no sooner had I closed my eyes when I felt a weight thump down on my chest. I opened my eyes to see Valentina sitting on me, with Doris standing right behind her, the two of them clapping and giggling happily.

"¡Sorpresa!" they shouted between peals of laughter. Guess what! "We're going out for pizza and ice cream! And you're taking us!"

There was so much joy and love in their faces that my fatigue and crankiness just vanished. I put my shoes back on and we climbed in my Jeep, where Doris and I each kept a hand on Valentina as she stood on the gearbox and helped me shift. So focused was she on her copilot duties that the beautiful little girl didn't see me wink at Doris, nor did she see Doris flash her brilliant smile at me in return. It's a moment I will cherish always.

In some ways, Doris surrendered to her new lowered status in the community. Although she knew everyone in San Juan del Sur and everyone knew her, she kept mostly to herself, with only a couple of true friends she felt she could count on. At the same time, however, Doris was making a new life for herself, studying business at a local university and earning money waiting tables at a seafood restaurant on the beach, just down from the real-estate office where I worked.

The first time Doris and I laid eyes on each other, as she walked past my beachfront office on her way to work one morning, there was instant chemistry between us. I couldn't imagine—and still can't—how anyone could have borne her any ill will. Doris didn't have a mean bone in her body. In fact, she was deeply empathetic, always thinking about other people. I remember one night, for instance, when Doris quietly went through an enormous amount of trouble to cook up a great feast for me and some of my buddies. She loved to cook all the classic Nica dishes, several of which she served up that night. After the meal, my buddies and I sprawled out to watch a movie, and without saying a word, Doris gathered up the leftovers, of which there were a lot, and brought them to a poor family who lived a couple of doors down. Doris spent the rest of the evening chatting with the neighbors while they enjoyed their gift of food in their candlelit shanty. It's the kind of thing she did all the time.

Still, it took some time before Doris was able to give herself up to another romantic relationship. She couldn't bear the possibility of another *fracaso*, and, though she never quite said so, I knew that she didn't want to get involved in anything temporary. The next thing needed to be the real thing. Her experience had made her intensely self-conscious, like she knew that the local gossip queens and busybodies were just waiting for her to give them something to talk about. At the same time, I sensed that whether she realized it or not, Doris really wanted to be with a man who would provide for her and protect her, a man she could build her life around.

For my part, I guess I was charmed by her vulnerability. Without doubt, I could identify with her outsider status in the community. I had only arrived six months before and was still getting my bearings. There was something else, though, something that complicated our relationship before it even got started. When I first told JT, whose Nicaraguan wife, Arelis, had grown up in San Juan del Sur, about Doris, something strange happened between us.

"My wife is not gonna be stoked to hear about that," he said, taking me totally by surprise. It turns out that Arelis had known Doris for nearly her entire life, and for reasons that never became totally clear to me, simply could not stand her. To this day, I can't say if Arelis's animosity had to do with Doris's standing as a "fallen" woman or was because of something specific that happened between them years before or was a case of simple jealousy. Whatever the cause, Arelis's hatred of Doris poisoned my relationship with JT and would eventually force me to make a choice about my loyalties. Either I would abandon Doris, showing a commitment to JT and the magazine by placating his wife, or I would stick by Doris, who, as far as I knew, had done nothing to trigger such ill will. Of course I stayed with Doris, a decision that not only infuriated Arelis and put JT in an untenable position but also put me in a different light in the eyes of a lot of people in San Juan. Arelis wasn't the only person there carrying some kind of grudge.

There's a Spanish saying: *Pueblo pequeño, infierno grande* ("Small town, big hell"). The smaller a place is, the more socially tangled and claustro-phobic it becomes. Grudges and resentments mean more than they would in other places. The gossip is nastier and spreads faster, and it feels like no one has the slightest bit of privacy. Doris had been living in that kind of hell for years. Now I was learning how true that old saying really was. In those days, it was only annoying. Of course, I had no idea how hot that inferno was going to get.

Doris and I held out against the inevitable for a while but eventually came together as a couple. We made our own little community of two, each of us helping the other in our own way. In small ways I could bring pieces of the larger world into San Juan for her and help her see possibilities that might not have occurred to her, whether about her place in the world or more practical matters like making a living. And Doris could introduce me into her fascinating world and help me understand the local dynamics that were critical to my own ambitions.

The ironies in Doris's life still amaze me. A beautiful, driven woman in a town just starting to boom with development and excitement should have been able to break the glass ceiling that most local women ran into. And yet things always seemed to work against her. The charming sea-food restaurant where she worked had been owned and run by a loving group of women, all from the same local family. Then, in a sign of the bigger changes going on in San Juan, the restaurant had been bought by a Canadian man who wanted to turn it into some kind of nightclub where the girls on staff wore more sexy, revealing outfits. Doris just wasn't comfortable with the new atmosphere, and we decided she should leave, which was a blow to the new owner's ego. He, of course, had developed a crush on her and now became another enemy for both of us. Her studies, too, turned out to be less useful than they should have been. She never seemed to bring schoolwork home, and eventually she told me that she spent most of her time at school fending off advances from her male professors.

No wonder that Doris eventually became closed off to most people. She had learned to build a protective shell around herself, and, as we talked through her options, I saw quickly that this was a woman who might never feel comfortable in working relationships with men and that her best bet might be to go into business for herself.

Of course, the first thing you need when starting up any business is money, and this is where one of the other major cracks in Doris's life became apparent. Her mother, Mercedes, having gone off to Managua, was cold and distant, and I can recall finding Doris off by herself crying on birthdays and holidays because her mother hadn't bothered to pick up a phone. Mercedes still played the matriarch from time to time, controlling access to whatever money the family might have, and there turned out to be more there than anyone expected. For generations, the family had lived on a piece of land on a scenic hillside overlooking the bay, land that was now prime real estate to the gringo developers. Mercedes had arranged to sell the property for over $110,000 and had promised $30,000 of that to Doris.

The impending windfall comforted Doris but also worried her. It was nice to know she'd have a stake for her own business, but, at the same time, she knew that the money represented her entire inheritance. It never occurred to her, however, that there was a possibility she might never see it. In Nicaragua, even broken, estranged families passed assets along from generation to generation, according to tradition, knowing that to deny a child an inheritance would invite public scorn.

According to Doris, Mercedes had no such qualms. I remember Doris, sobbing with shock and disappointment. Her mother had decided to give her daughter only $2,000 she said. Mercedes kept most of the money for herself, using it to leave her boyfriend in Managua and relocate to Rivas. Any illusions Doris may have still had about her mother were shattered. The thought that Mercedes would choose money and her own creature comfort over the welfare of her own daughter left Doris devastated. Unfortunately, this wasn't the first time, nor would it be the last.

Now Doris faced a much more uncertain future, and we set about revising her short-term plan. Although she eventually got a couple of thousand dollars more out of her mother, with the help of her aunt Elena, Doris knew her dream of a restaurant was now out of reach. With so little capital, she didn't have many options, but one that did come to mind was a small clothing boutique. Maybe Doris sensed that the qualities that made her a natural for the restaurant business would transfer to a retail shop. The simple truth is that she had a way of drawing the public in, even when she wasn't trying to.

Sol Fashion opened in March 2006, in a small space close to the center of town, and was an immediate success, financially and otherwise. Doris recouped her investment threefold in just a few months, and the venture seemed to help bring her back out of her shell. The store quickly developed a reputation as a cool place to shop or just hang out. With the local hipsters going in and out of the shop all day, Doris began to feel more a part of the town's social life, reconnecting with people. The gringos and other foreigners also made a habit of stopping by, exposing Doris to even more of the outside world. She made regular trips to Managua to shop for new inventory. She liked being self-sufficient, and for the first time began to envision a future for herself in which she would have some control over her own fate. Her wisdom was deepening, and she was happier than she had been in a long time.

Early in 2006, it looked like everything was falling into place, at least on the surface. After only a year in Nicaragua, *EP* was about to take off, Doris and I had found each other, and I had landed a job that could keep

it all going. I could envision a real future in the region. But as the old saying goes, "If you want to make God chuckle, just tell him your plans."

I could sense JT pulling back. At first the signs were subtle. He would
be distracted or make some choice that seemed to indicate that EP was no
longer his priority. Soon it became obvious that he was distancing himself, either from the magazine or from me personally or both. He started
missing meetings and then stopped coming to the office altogether. The
original concept of a humble newsletter had been JT's brainchild, but after six months or so and two issues under our belt, it had evolved into
something pretty far removed from his original idea. JT was more of an
idealist than I and had always been less comfortable with the edgy elements we had added to the magazine—the documentary, lifestyle and
fashion, and travel material that had helped bring in advertisers and that
had made it possible to publish the more serious material about sustainable development and cross-cultural relations. On top of this, or maybe
because of this, I had quickly become the more public face of EP, cement-
ing business relationships, closing deals, finding investors, and lining up
the lion's share of the creative work as well.

JT began to spend more time doing what he loved most—outreach
and community organizing. JT remained true to his vision of working in-
timately with a small group on local projects. Now that the communications project he had cofounded was moving into a wider arena and taking
on more commercial characteristics, it became less interesting to him.
Clearly we weren't on the same page anymore.

JT's situation was complicated. His wife was tugging in another direction. For Arelis, getting out of San Juan and Nicaragua had been a real
achievement, and she had been in no hurry to return from the United
States. In truth, JT had dragged his feet about moving back to Nica and
committing to EP and had never been able to kick in any capital. What had
started as a fifty-fifty arrangement between him and me was mostly in my
hands.

As stated before, my relationship with JT was also complicated by his
wife Arelis's unexplained hatred for Doris. When Doris and I began

dating, it was like someone had flipped a switch inside Arelis, revealing a side of her personality I had never seen. I know sometimes your friends act weird about your new romantic partners, and maybe even gently hint that you're making a bad choice or something, but Arelis's reaction was way out of proportion. She didn't just give me a gentle warning; she started spitting venom. Arelis immediately told me that I was making a terrible mistake, that Doris was nothing but trouble. She called Doris the most horrible of names, painting her as not only a lowlife slut but as completely evil, like something terrible would happen if I kept dating her. Even today, I have no idea where all this hatred and doom came from, but Arelis never let up. At first it freaked me out, not because I would ever believe the nasty things Arelis said but because I couldn't really understand how the Doris I knew could have caused someone to hate her so much. After a while, it just made me angry, not just at Arelis but at JT, too. I thought Arelis was out of line to take such a strong position about my personal life to begin with, but I really resented that she was turning it into a wedge between me and JT. He was in a terrible spot. I was his friend, but Arelis was his wife, and on this particular subject, he either couldn't or wouldn't stand up to her.

I was in a spot myself. Without ever coming out and saying so, it was clear that Arelis wasn't going to back off as long as Doris was in the picture. Arelis wanted me to make a choice also: a relationship with Doris or a smooth and successful venture with her husband. I went on seeing Doris, although that relationship would play itself out on its own in less than a year. During that time, JT and I parted company. I bought out his shares of the company and was determined to see the magazine move forward and grow. The release of the third issue was a big deal, attracting lots of press hoopla, including television coverage, and heralded by a huge launch party. JT was there for the party, even though his relationship to *EP* had formally ended by then.

EP's sudden and exciting growth became one of the contributing factors to the end of my romance with Doris. After her murder, and especially during my trial, the stories about what went on between Doris and me took on exaggerated and dramatic qualities, but the truth is that there wasn't much of a story to tell about our breakup. It really wasn't high drama of any kind. We were two people in our twenties who had met and dated and then had broken up. There wasn't anything unusual about it.

As *EP* got bigger and bigger, with readers from a growing area, I started to feel that it made more sense for us to be headquartered in the capital city of Managua. Doris, however, had her own growing business to look after, and that meant staying put in San Juan. Sol Fashion wasn't just a successful shop. In many ways, it had been Doris's ticket back into the mainstream of her hometown, and so it meant more to her than anybody can truly understand. Our brief romance was passionate, but all my spare time and energy went into the magazine or into earning money to support it.

I became more and more focused on work, and I think Doris began to sense my lack of commitment to her. The more distracted I got, the more effort Doris put into maintaining our relationship, making me pull away even more. Once this cycle took hold of us, the breakup was inevitable. It's a sad and painful memory of mine, and I spent many lonely nights in jail beating myself up over how I had been so foolish to single-mindedly put my magazine first.

There is one strange twist though. About a month after I started dating Doris, but before my partnership with JT fell apart, I received an anonymous e-mail message blasting Doris. It was pure, vicious hate mail, spewing vulgar insults and accusations. Over the next eleven months, the e-mails kept coming, calling Doris a *puta*, talking about all kinds of relationships with sleazy men that she had kept secret, making references to homemade porn tapes she allegedly had appeared in, and so on. The notes went into all kinds of obscene detail, painting a picture of Doris as a filthy and greedy prostitute.

I told Doris about the e-mails, and it broke her heart. Together, we tried to figure out who could have written them or even could have had any reason to hurt her that way. We tried to track the IP address, to see if we could find out where they were coming from, but our search led us to a random street address in Atlanta, Georgia. The fact that we couldn't understand or explain the e-mails made them seem even more bizarre and evil. They came sporadically. Just as we'd forget about them, another would appear, triggering the cycle of anxiety all over again.

After a little less than a year, Doris and I finally broke it off. It was a mutual decision and came about in conjunction with my packing up and moving to Managua. Things didn't end as cleanly as I planned, but I don't think they ever do. Even after I moved away, we stayed in touch. Doris would call for advice for her business and even visit me in Managua on buying trips for the shop, but I sensed that she was having trouble moving past our relationship. We even fell back into our physical relationship on a couple of occasions, even though I had begun seeing other women. A clean break would have made it easier for Doris to move on, but that just wasn't the way it played out.

In Managua, I threw myself into the magazine, which, although still small by U.S. standards, was a busy operation. I got a house that also doubled as the magazine's office. The life of the magazine and my own life merged into one. My home was my office, and my coworkers were my friends. Among these were Agnielly Vega, *EP*'s operations manager; Shawn Harstad, the graphic designer; Adam Paredes, art director; Noah Goodman, editorial manager; and Sandra Torres, an attorney from Century 21 who did some legal work for *EP* on the side.

I had come to Nicaragua intending to take pictures for a week or two. I had hoped to go back home and see if I could make a living as a photojournalist, maybe even a filmmaker. But so much had happened. Not quite a year and a half had passed. A friend and I had started a new business, which had taken off in unexpected directions. We were no longer partners or even friends. A real estate company, of all things, had noticed me and offered me a job at which I quickly became successful. I had become immersed in the life and culture of Central America, something that happened so quickly and so naturally. This was my life as the Christmas season of 2006 approached.

In early November, there were signs that life was changing for Doris, too. We got used to being apart and even started to talk to each other, in that cagey, incomplete way that former lovers do, about the new people we were seeing. From what Doris would tell me, I knew that a variety of men seemed to be chasing her, as they always had. There was another American in the picture, apparently, a young guy from Nicaragua who had grown up in Miami. She didn't tell me all the details, but it didn't surprise me when Doris called me one night and told me in a quiet, hesitant voice that she wouldn't be able to see me anymore.

I can't forget that phone call. I heard a tiny catch in Doris's voice, like she was saying something she didn't want to say. Maybe even like she was afraid of something. I've replayed that conversation over and over in my head. Sometimes I remember her sounding as if she were being forced to say certain things, as if someone had a gun to her head. Other times I think she just sounded wistful, as if finally acknowledging that our relationship was really and truly over. I do remember that we never really said good-bye that night, that our conversation sort of faded out until we both hung up, in a moment of sadness. The next day, Doris was dead.

3.

Doris Dead

On Tuesday, November 21, 2006, we had a lot going on in the *EP* office—in fact, we were about to make some pretty big changes—yet the day started out like most others.

Agnielly Vega had left that morning for Costa Rica to sign a lease on an office space in San Jose. The time had come to move the magazine out of Nicaragua, first because the more metropolitan Costa Rica was a better place to be headquartered, and second because the political climate in Nicaragua was changing quickly. Daniel Ortega had spent sixteen years campaigning and rebuilding his base of support, and, just about two weeks before, he had finally won back the presidency. Control of the Nica government was once again in the hands of the Sandinistas, or the FSLN, as most people referred to the party. We could only assume that meant crackdowns of some kind in the near future—tighter controls over the media and probably over everything else—as well as a resurgence of the institutionalized anti-Americanism he promoted. People in the know had started telling me that the magazine would need some kind of political protection and thought that the best way to get that would be to bring in a prominent Nica investor, preferably someone aligned with the Sandinistas. For me that wasn't an option. I had a responsibility to the company and knew we needed to move if we wanted to keep thriving and growing.

Actually, there was already a small ownership group in place. A few individuals had provided an infusion of cash in exchange for a very small stake in EP. On that Tuesday I was in the process of making plans to travel to the United States for a kind of promotional tour, both to talk to advertisers and potential contributors and to pitch to a new round of investors.

In the late morning, a very-well-known Nica journalist named Ricardo Castillo came to the offices for a meeting. Ricardo had taken notice of *EP* and had become intrigued. We met that morning to get to know each other and discuss ways in which he might become directly involved in the magazine. I didn't tell him at the time, but I was hoping he would turn out to be a good fit for editor in chief. I needed to transition myself out of the creative area to focus on running the company as publisher. We set up a telephone conference call with Nick Purdy, a consultant in Atlanta I had retained, and the three of us spoke for just under an hour. Ricardo and I spoke from separate rooms in the office, so we were both able to have our own phone. During the phone conference, I carried on a separate dialogue with Nick by instant messaging. We had started our instant-message conversation earlier that morning regarding other *EP* issues. Once we were on the phone with Ricardo, we picked up where we had left off, sharing our reactions to Ricardo as well as prompting each other with interview questions. The electronic records of this event would later become a critical piece of my defense. When the call ended, Ricardo hung around and had lunch with us, after which I followed up on the morning's activities with my colleagues, including Shawn Harstad, Adam Paredes, and Noah Goodman.

My cell phone rang at 2:42 in the afternoon, and when I answered I heard the voice of JT's wife, Arelis, and what she was saying was so random, so jolting, that I couldn't process it at first. She said that there was something she had to tell me.

"¡Doris está muerta! Ella se ahorcó en su tienda." *Doris is dead! She hung herself in her store.*

Arelis let that hang in the air. After a moment of silence, she said, "I'm sorry," and then she hung up.

There was something wrong with Arelis's tone. There was no pain, no shared loss, no sympathy or warmth. She sounded flat and disconnected. I can't say if it was really there or if I imagined this, but it almost seemed like she was happy to rub this horrible news in my face. And why was Arelis the one making this call, anyway? She hated Doris and resented me. We hadn't talked in over six months, and she wouldn't even say hi if we passed each other walking on the beach with no other people around. I thought to myself, what a cruel sick joke. I felt anger rising up in me, but I didn't have time to deal with that. The flip phone rang again just as I was closing it from Arelis's call. This time it was Gabi, Doris's closest friend in San Juan, and she was hysterical.

"¡Doris está muerta, Eric! ¡Se ahorcó! ¡Está muerta! ¡Está muerta!"

Gabi was barely coherent and just kept repeating the same words over and over. I tried to calm her down and get what little information I could. Leaving the office and walking outside to the sidewalk, I sat down, unsure what to do or even what to think. Waves of conflicting emotions came over me, but really I think I was in some kind of state of shock. One of my closest friends was dead, and as I sat there trying to make some sense out of what I had just heard, the initial anger from Arelis's call gave way to sadness—and guilt, as I recalled that final phone call from Doris the night before. Had that call been her last cry for help? Had she been so down she could really have thought of killing herself? And had I just blown her off? Carlitos, our security guard, stood quietly off to the side and watched me but didn't interfere. (Later, when he offered to testify at my trial about the genuine emotion he witnessed in me, his request was denied by the judge.)

Over the coming months, I tried to piece together part of what happened that day—an effort that is still ongoing. San Juan is a very small town in a culture driven by gossip, so word of Doris's death had spread in what must have been a few short minutes. Doris's cousin Oscar had discovered Doris's body, but beyond that nobody had any real facts to pass along. People only knew that she had died, and in those early moments they talked about the death as a suicide. I know that Arelis had reached JT by phone while he was out on a fishing boat with one of his closest friends, an American named Austin. Doris had talked to me about Austin—they had dated years back and might have still had feelings for each other. I didn't know for sure.

I also learned that as the news of Doris's death spread through San

Juan del Sur, most people had the same first reaction: *We better call Eric.* I
know a lot of people in San Juan had mixed feelings about me, especially
after I left and moved to Managua. I wasn't a local anymore. Even when I
lived there, many people interpreted my quietness and the fact I didn't
hang out in bars and make small talk as aloofness or arrogance. I always
focused on work, and my social status in the local community suffered as
a result. Surely some people saw me as too slick or ambitious. The kind of
work ethic that many Americans tend to admire is seen as extreme in
other cultures. But the qualities that maybe made them think of me as a
hustler were the same qualities that made them seek me out now. They
saw me as someone who knew how the system worked and who got things
done. I think I got that much respect, at least, even from people who didn't
like me.

Back in the office, I collected myself and sat down with the staff, all of
whom had known Doris, to tell them what had happened. I remember
thinking about the best way to break the news to the team. Some of them
had known Doris well, and it was going to hurt. The whole thing was just
impossible to explain. It's true that I didn't have any facts, but I'm not
sure that even if I had information to share anything would have made
sense at that point. The art director of *EP*, Adam, was from the Dominican Republic, and we actually had a short discussion about whether or
not I should go to San Juan. He told me it was a bad idea and could be
dangerous. That advice may sound strange or even incriminating. Many
people describe Nicaragua as *el pais de maravillas*—"the country of marvels."
The expression refers not, say, to its wondrous beauty but to the audacity
of the institutional corruption. Authorities pull off stunts that leave
people stunned and speechless and yet are just part of the normal course of
business for them. In the Dominican Republic, where people talk about
their own country this way, Adam knew all too well how *maravillas* can
unfold. If you've grown used to the culture of paranoia and suspicion and
corruption found in many developing countries, you are aware that anything can happen and innocent people get dragged into trouble all the
time. In San Juan, many people had been jealous of my relationship with

Doris, like guys who wished they could have her—and this in a country where gringos seemed to always be winning. The chances of somebody blaming me for something in San Juan were high.

Nonetheless, I was so shaken and distraught about the news that I couldn't imagine not going. A small part of me refused to believe that anything bad could really happen. After all, everybody knew I was in Managua and had been miles away from Doris and San Juan at the time of the crime. So without reluctance, I started making arrangements to get myself there.

Two things happened in the next hour and a half before I could leave for San Juan that would come back to haunt me later. The first is that I had my hair cut. In retrospect, of course, it seems like an utterly foolish and insensitive thing to do. After all, someone I cared deeply about had just been found dead. Why would I be concerned about such a trivial chore? I wish I had some other explanation for my actions. All I can say is that at the time, in my shocked, disoriented state, it made sense to me. The appointment had been made days in advance, and the haircutter showed up at the house (as is custom in Nicaragua), ready to go to work. It never crossed my mind to send her home. Rosy, the woman who cut my hair, had known Doris, too, and she blended into the scene of grief and confusion in the house. I must also have been aware that I looked scruffy and scraggly, and I knew I would be going to a funeral in the next day or two. Cleaning myself up was to my disoriented mind an act of respect, the same way a person might (as I later did) pack dress clothes for a funeral. Everyone reacts to a crisis differently, and I have learned that I deal with the stress by focusing my attention on practical demands, what needs to be done. It's a coping mechanism, and we had an enormous amount to cope with that day. Flights and reservations for the upcoming promotional tour had to be canceled or rescheduled, not to mention the daily business of running a magazine office. Part of me might have considered jumping into the nearest available car and leaving with all these details hanging; but, for whatever reasons, that just wasn't the way I responded.

The second thing is that I arranged to rent a car, even though I owned one at the time. My car was a beat-up Land Cruiser, nearly fifteen years old. It was fine for beaches and dirt roads or short trips around town but wasn't reliable enough for longer highway trips. But the main reason that I decided not to drive my Jeep was that the insurance had just expired. (I would later offer proof of this to the police and the D.A. several times, but they ignored the document.) I had also rented cars so often for photo shoots or other magazine business that I had established a relationship with the Hertz office in Managua. The *EP* administrative assistant (Adam's girlfriend who came with him from the Dominican Republic), Leidy de los Santos, took care of ordering a car, which an employee from Hertz named Victor delivered to the house. Again, this simple act would be used against me. Later, when the prosecution and the salacious Nica press went after me, they fabricated all kinds of ways to make my renting a car seem like the suspicious action of a guilty man.

I packed a bag with a black suit and made sure some key business matters would be dealt with while I was gone, and just after 4:30 Shawn and I got into the rented car and headed to San Juan del Sur. As we drove, my cell phone was blowing up, ringing every time I hung up on a call. After a while, I just handed my cell to Shawn and asked him to deal with the calls. At several points in the few times I took a call, the conversation turned to how everyone knew what the medical facilities in Rivas were like and suggested that an autopsy performed there would probably be worthless. Several people suggested that if anyone was on the scene and saw the cops starting to remove Doris's body, they should insist it be sent to Managua.

On the way, we stopped in Rivas to pick up Doris's father. There was already a mob scene at his house. I pushed through the mass of people until I ran into Doris's sister, who threw herself into my arms, sobbing. In the house, I found her father, just hanging up the phone, his body shaking as he cried. As we embraced, I offered to drive him to San Juan, and he gratefully accepted. Neither of us knew quite what to say on the short drive. For a little while, we simply held hands. The poor man simply stared straight ahead, asking only, "How could this have happened to my daughter?"

Even with the stop off at Doris's father's house, we made the trip in amazingly little time, another fact that the prosecution would later use against me. It was dark by the time we got to San Juan. I pulled the car right up to the crowd of people at the crime scene and got out with Doris's father, both of us terrified of what we might see but at the same time determined to find out what had happened and what was being done now. My stomach was churning as we approached the store because I knew Doris's dead body was somewhere near.

We made our way through the huge crowd gathered outside on the street, and I remember hearing someone say, "Es el novio." *He's the boyfriend.* With that, the crowd sort of fell back, parting to let us through. We walked past Doris's mother and her aunt Elena, who had thrown themselves on the ground, surrounded by other woman, and were wailing. "¡Doris! ¡No, no! ¡Mamita! ¡Aayy no!" I don't mean to sound cold or disrespectful, but I remember thinking that the whole scene felt staged, as if there was an unwritten script or protocol that everybody knew to follow, having witnessed so many deaths over so many years. Even Doris's mother's wailing had that quality, like it was something she knew she had to do, whether or not it came naturally from her heart.

The cops had left the door to the store open, exposing the scene in a way that immediately got my sugar up. Before I even got close enough to talk to them, I was angry, and when her father went up to the cop at the door and demanded to know what was going on, I had already adopted an assertive tone. When the cop blew us off, I got furious, not because I had any right to know anything, but there was Doris's father standing right next to me, and they acted like they couldn't care less about him. We got no information, and when I asked why the cops couldn't show some common decency and shut the door to the death scene ^{EX.01} or at least block off the entrance, they simply ignored me.

Taking charge of the scene and of the investigation was a man named Emigdio Reyes, the Rivas head of Auxilio Judicial, the special detective unit. Reyes began asking me questions right there at the scene, as I stood there with Doris's father. He let us know that Doris had not hung herself or even committed suicide. The police were investigating a murder and believed that the killer or killers were on the loose. The thought crossed my mind that Reyes and his team looked at me not just as an important source of information but also as a potential suspect. I had no reason to be afraid, though. That was the right way to question a former boyfriend, and I knew I had nothing to hide. There was nothing to hint at the world of trouble that Reyes would cause for me over the coming weeks and months.

I had met Mercedes, Doris's mother, only one time before that evening. When she approached me on the street outside Sol Fashion that night we were essentially strangers, but of course we had heard about each other from Doris or other members of the family. Mercedes was open and respectful that night, as if acknowledging that the pain of Doris's death was something that we shared. She referred to me as *amor* and asked for my help, suggesting that I come to the house and go through Doris's belongings with her. I remember thinking that was a good idea and suggesting that we begin as soon as possible, on the chance that we could find a letter or something, anything, that would offer a clue about her murder. Mercedes also asked me when I thought they should have the funeral. I felt they should lay her to rest quickly and not have that hanging over everyone any longer than necessary. Mercedes decided to wait, so that Doris's oldest friend had a chance to make the trip from Costa Rica, but I remember politely telling her I didn't think that was fair to all the others there who loved Doris and were suffering. Mercedes would later tell people about how eager I was to get the body in the ground, probably because I needed evidence gone. In that conversation with Doris's mother, I also repeated what I had said earlier on the phone—that we should try to get Doris's body to Managua, where a proper autopsy with better forensic work could be done. I remember, too, that at some point that first night, the subject of money came up. Various family members were grumbling about the expenses—the mortician, the coffin, the funeral, and so on—and Mercedes simply turned to me with a look of expectation in her eyes. I offered to pay, which she very quickly accepted.

When the police finished their study of the crime scene, they let Doris's mother and aunt in to see the body and were going to let her father and me in next. When our turn came they stopped me at the door and let him pass. The cops directed me over to a senior detective from Auxilio Judicial in Managua who had just arrived on the scene, and we went by car to the San Juan police station, where we talked for about an hour. I remember sitting outside the station with this detective, named Arcenio. He seemed to be more experienced with this kind of thing than the local police, and he was laid-back, treating me with courtesy and professionalism. He asked the kind of intelligent questions I would have expected, about Doris's life and background, her friends and associates, her current financial situation, and about my whereabouts during the day. I told him everything I knew, never thinking for a second that I had any reason to be worried about anything. In Nicaragua they say, "el que no debe, no teme." *He who owes no explanation has nothing to fear.* About halfway through the conversation with Arcenio, the lights went out. One of Nicaragua's all-too-common power failures. I know now that this blackout occurred precisely at the moment the police were removing Doris's body from the store, outside of which hundreds of people still stood hoping to catch a glimpse. It was as if God had decided that she was entitled to that last little bit of privacy.

At the police station, Arcenio asked me if they could take samples— hair, skin, and saliva—for forensics, to which I agreed without any hesitation. I mentioned to Arcenio, as I had to Doris's mother, that I was concerned about the autopsy being done correctly and even offered to pay for the procedure in Managua, if necessary. Arcenio took the offer in good faith and simply answered, "Okay. I'll let you know. . . ." Arcenio actually gave me his cell number and said to call him if I had any questions or new information. The only other people at the station that night were the medical examiner who collected my bio-samples and another vaguely mysterious policeman. This tall, handsome cop with a heavy, dark mustache wore a uniform and remained virtually silent, although somehow I came to understand that he, too, had come from Auxilio Judicial in Managua. I would see this man again, although to this day his identity is a mystery.

By the time I left the police station and went directly to Doris's house, her body was already there. It had been put into a coffin at the store and taken up to her aunt's house, where the family would hold *la vela*, the traditional wake. I learned later that by the time the body was brought up to the house that night, it had already been examined at the crime scene by a medical forensic "specialist" and had been analyzed and photographed by a crime-scene investigator. Both individuals would testify later in court, and the CSI eventually got fired as higher-ranking officers tried to wash their hands of the misconduct connected to my case that would later be revealed. A policeman also leaked out later (although it has never been known publicly) that the police carefully hid the fact that the first person with medical experience on the scene—a nurse from the local clinic—had tampered with the body. This would have been enough to call any physical evidence into question.

When we got to the house that first evening, knowing the police had made it clear that Doris had been murdered, some of my friends started chatting about how San Juan wasn't safe for me or others close to Doris. In my head, I suppose I knew they were right, given the corruption we all knew existed. In the coming days, people would remind me that I was "the ex," which automatically made me a suspect. And still I never entertained the possibility of leaving. Besides, I was there for Doris and her family, not for anything or anyone else.

Even that night, with Doris laying close by and her grieving family all around me, I couldn't keep from asking the millions of questions flying through my head. I made a point of taking her cousin Oscar aside, the young man who had actually discovered Doris's body at her store, and asking if he knew anything. I specifically asked if he could tell me if there was anyone new in Doris's life. He was pretty vague about it, but he did mention "a kid from Miami" who had recently moved to Nicaragua and been spending time in San Juan. I knew this had to be the same guy Doris had mentioned. All the cousin really knew was that Doris had gone out with the guy once, maybe twice. He had picked her up out front of the shop on a four-wheeler, but Oscar didn't know the details of their relationship.

I'm struck by one memory in particular of that cold night. I was sitting outside the house, looking out over a common scene of Nicaraguan poverty. A muddy, unpaved road led up to the house, a simple wood structure with a zinc roof just a few steps up from a tin shanty. A few broken-down old cars sat with tall weeds growing up around them, and the patches of bare dirt around the house were strewn with garbage. What made the scene particularly bitter was the barbed wire. Doris's mother had recently sold her piece of the family property to the developer of a big resort called Pelican Eyes, which occupied the adjacent parcel of land. The owner, Chris Berry, appraised the property at $26 million; he financed the land it was built on from Doris's grandfather for $80,000 according to Doris. The resort had lined the entrance road with barbed-wire fencing, cutting off easy access to the house. In my mind, the wire was like the final irony of that painful scene, symbolizing the new forces in town, or maybe even the deal with the devil that I was later convinced Mercedes had made. As I sat there surveying it all, Doris's beautiful little cousin Valentina tiptoed up to me. We looked at each other wordlessly for one moment, and then she threw her arms around my neck and gave me a big kiss on the side of my face, bringing on one more flood of tears.

The next morning, Wednesday, the situation began to change quickly and in strange ways. The first thing I learned was that the police had searched JT and Arelis's house at 6 A.M. I took that to mean that somehow they had learned about Arelis's inexplicable bad blood with Doris, which meant, more important, that the police were in the process of a legitimate investigation of the crime. They were seeking information and acting on leads.

Also early that morning, I had a conversation, by phone, with a criminal lawyer in Managua. I connected with this lawyer through the family of Agnielly, from the EP office, and the advice I was seeking was for Doris's family. It seemed to me and to the friends I was talking to that the family needed someone who understood how the legal system functioned to help ensure that the police did what they were supposed to, that the investigation would proceed and not get swept under the rug as is all too common. That lawyer also had some very clear and specific advice for me: Get out of San Juan, he told me. He told me to come immediately back to Managua, where he could protect me. Protect me from what? I wondered, and he explained that if the police didn't find the real killers quickly they would inevitably start looking at me. I was the former boyfriend, a gringo. No doubt I would be a handy scapegoat. He wasn't the first one to tell me this, but still I didn't act on his advice. Part of me thought that this lawyer was just trying to get his hooks into a gringo client with money. Another part of me thought that even if he was right, I wasn't going to abandon Doris.

I spent part of the morning visiting Doris's aunt at the house. The body had been removed for embalming and would be back for that night's *vela*. I was surprised to find Austin, JT's friend, at the house when I got there. Austin had done well in real estate back home in Atlanta and had moved to Nicaragua hoping to participate in the tourism boom. That day he was cleaned up nice and was in a private conversation with Doris's aunt. I knew that he and Doris had been friends, but I couldn't understand how he had come to feel close enough to the family to be hanging around at such a time.

I ran into Austin again after lunch. I had driven over to Rivas to buy flowers for the funeral, and there was Austin in the flower shop, apparently doing the same thing. Again it struck me that this wasn't something that a casual acquaintance would be doing, and I started to consider the possibility that Austin's relationship with Doris might have gone deeper than anyone knew. He didn't mention anything about that then but just hugged me and cried and told me how sorry he was, as if the loss had been more mine than his. The shop said they'd need about an hour to get the flowers ready, so I took advantage of the time and went to a local cybercafé and printed off copies of the hate mail that I had received about Doris.

The day seemed to grow stranger each minute. My cell phone rang while I was standing in the shop trying to understand what was up with Austin. I heard the panicked voice of Tyson, one on my Century 21 co-workers, a young American whose Nicaraguan girlfriend had received two sinister but anonymous text messages on her phone just a couple of minutes before.

"Vos sos la que sigue," the first message read. *You're next.*

The second message was even more frightening. "Fallamos la primera vez, pero no fallaremos la segunda." *We failed the first time, but we won't fail the second.* It turned out that this woman had narrowly escaped being hit by a car about a week before, and she felt certain it had been a deliberate attack. The two of them were completely freaked out, asking what I thought they should do. It seemed the only sensible thing for them to do was to come immediately to Rivas, and we'd go together to the police. I told him not to delete the text messages and to bring the phone with them.

About fifteen minutes later, I met Tyson and his girlfriend Migdalia and we went to the Rivas police station, where I had my first formal sit-down with Emigdio Reyes, the cop who had been in charge at the crime scene the night before. I'll never forget the sight of Reyes's office, a shabby, nearly empty little room in a raggedy old building. Panes of glass were missing from the rusted window frames. Paint flaked and peeled from the walls, and the lighting was dim at best. Reyes's office had an old desk, a scattering of folding chairs, a phone in the room, and not much else. The only sign of his status as commissioner of the Rivas division of the Auxilio Judicial was a stack of used phone cards on the desk with the seal scratched off exposing the PIN. Phone cards. Even the top cop in the district couldn't be trusted with open access to a long-distance phone line. In Nicaragua, *minutos*, or "phone minutes," are the stuff of barter and bribe, a negotiable commodity.

Reyes listened to Tyson and Migdalia with what seemed like total disinterest. When they finished telling their story, he was deadpan. "Muy bien." He said he'd look into it, but he let them take the phone with them when they left, and he didn't even make a record of her number. It seemed obvious that he had no intention of following up. I protested, asking if he planned to trace the calls or something. He shrugged and thanked me again.

My cell phone rang again while I was in Reyes's office. The thing hadn't stopped ringing since I'd left Managua. This time, the caller identified himself as Mike Poehlitz, the RSO—regional security officer—of the American embassy in Nicaragua. The RSO is responsible not only for the safety and security of the diplomatic personnel but also serves as official liaison between the United States and the host country's law-enforcement or other agencies. Doris's murder in San Juan del Sur was already making news. Poehlitz needed some eyes and ears "on the ground," someone who could tell him exactly what was happening in San Juan so he could anticipate if there would be fallout for Americans there. It's not a big country, so you can imagine how small the community of Americans there is. If Poehlitz asked around, as I'm sure he did, any number of sources would have given him my name. In fact, the American embassy already knew me; I had been meeting regularly with the economic officer there with updates on the progress of EP. Poehlitz mostly just listened to what I knew of the murder and the current situation in San Juan. He said little, except to tell me, "Be careful and keep me updated."

I asked Reyes if we could continue on privately and then hit him up with questions. Did they have any leads? Had they found any evidence or any clues? Could he tell me any details about what happened to Doris? Reyes clearly had no interest in sharing any information with me or in pursuing our conversation at all. I turned the topic to Doris's missing cell phone. I had gathered from the questions the police asked me on the night of the murder that her phone was gone and that they assumed that the killer or killers had stolen it along with her purse. I wanted to know what the police were doing to try and track it down. Had they at least requested a subpoena for the phone records? I knew enough to know that police often feel obligated to follow up on something simply because it's been suggested to them, because they can't afford to let it come back and bite them in the ass later as a legitimate lead that they failed to explore. I told Reyes that we had been trying to call Doris's phone for the last day and a half and that someone actually would answer but just laugh and then hang up. He wouldn't even tell me if they were triangulating the signal to find out where the phone might be, and I was persistent on this point.

We spoke respectfully to each other, but there was no doubt that we were pissing each other off. In retrospect, I'm pretty sure my assertiveness contributed to Reyes's desire to want to teach me a lesson. Maybe he saw that my movements could be presented as suspicious. He could say that I was trying to find out what they knew as part of a plan to cover my tracks. I told him about the e-mails and handed over the set of copies I had printed for him, which he basically ignored. Reyes told me straight out that he wanted to hear about my relationship with Doris and proceeded to ask me exactly the same questions that other cops had asked me the night before, and I went through it all over again. Then, his vibe suddenly changed.

"How many times have you hit Doris?" he asked. "You get violent when you drink, don't you, Eric?" Then, "You're a pretty jealous guy, aren't you, Eric?" His last question was the most bizarre, "Why is it that gringos don't take showers regularly?"

Now I was mad. "Look, *comisionado*, I know my rights," I said, "and with all due respect, you have an accusatory tone. If you have an accusation to make, go ahead and make it, and I'll go ahead and get an attorney. Why don't you research my alibi? I'm here trying to help and cooperate. The clock is ticking, and you're wasting time."

Reyes seemed not to like that. He couldn't have been used to people standing up to him or even understanding the law, much less their civil rights. And he certainly didn't appreciate this coming from a young American. There was an edge to his interactions with the foreigners that night at the crime scene, with Tyson when he went to report the threatening text messages, and now with me that gave me the impression that he wasn't too fond of gringos. My refusal to be pushed around seemed to make Reyes dislike me even more. I sensed his mood get icy. He pushed a piece of paper in front of me and asked me to sign it, but I refused without even reading it. He said, "Well, it doesn't matter anyway, because anything you say in the presence of a police officer can be submitted in court." The paper was a declaration, supposedly based on the notes of our conversation taken by a chubby cop, who had been sitting scribbling in the room. Reyes got up from his desk and literally showed me the door. We were done.

In the early evening, I stopped into the police station back in San Juan, again, just to see if there was any new information. I sensed the cops all sit up and pay attention when I walked in. They took me to meet the new man in charge, who had come to San Juan to oversee this investigation. He was introduced as a homicide detective, Jorge Uriarte, who outranked Reyes. The two of them worked for the Direccion Auxilio Judicial in Managua. I had no way of knowing it at the time, but the highest-ranking officers at this deeply corrupt investigative division were calling the shots on how Uriarte was to handle evidence and deliver a culprit. The short and fat Uriarte, who never wore a policeman's uniform, looked particularly unpleasant when I met him, maybe because he was sitting next to the tall, mysterious cop with the dark mustache who had been hanging around the day before.

Even though I had gone to the police to ask my own questions, Uriarte immediately turned the tables and started probing me. I gave them tons of information, absolutely everything I knew about Doris's business and finances, her relationships, anything I could think of. When they started asking questions about my own personal financial situation, my instincts told me to proceed with caution, and in fact I gave them some numbers that were completely untrue. I sensed that they wanted to know if I had the means to hire killers or maybe they were sizing me up to see if I would be worth extorting, so I made it sound like I earned far less than I actually did. I knew they were grilling me for a reason, that I was on their radar as a possible suspect, but I continued to cooperate in every way. I went directly from the police to Doris's aunt's house, for the more formal *vela* planned for that night. By now, the body had been embalmed and prepared for viewing. I saw Doris then but did not linger. Next to her casket I placed a photograph of her that I had taken. The photo showed her standing on a hillside overlooking the town, vibrant and beautiful, and ironically became the most widely circulated image of her in the months to come. Many times it would be printed in slanderous articles against me.

That second night at the house had a different feel than the night before. The previous night had been very cool, but this night was frigid, by far the coldest night anyone could remember in San Juan. To me it felt like a wave of unexplainable evil energy somehow connected to this tragedy. One vivid memory from the *vela* is of a moment with Doris's uncle, a man who had been close with her and protective of her and who embraced me with great warmth that night, like a friend or even a family member with whom he shared the bond of love for Doris. Soon enough this man would become part of a group who vowed to sacrifice their own lives to kill me in order to avenge Doris's death.

My most powerful memory of that night is of my last moment with Doris. Before I left, I went to say my personal good-bye. People kept back what distance they could as I pulled up a chair and sat by the coffin, but the house was so small, and there was no chance of real privacy. I sat there anyway and reached out a hand and laid it on the coffin, unleashing the first overwhelming wave of uncontrollable grief. It was like a huge release of pent-up anger and concern and tension and confusion, and I cried like I hadn't cried since childhood. I pulled the hood of the sweatshirt up over my head to create a sense of privacy alone with Doris. I remember that I told her I was sorry. Sorry for marginalizing her for my magazine and for being a selfish boy-man instead of the man that she deserved. I realized that everyone around me started crying, too, as if my losing it in that way was a signal or a trigger of some kind. Still, nobody came near. They knew it was my time and they respected that. Even outside the house, people were huddled together against the cold and the sadness, all of them sobbing. I walked away through this crowd, feeling totally isolated and alone.

At around midnight, the police showed up and announced that they needed Doris's body. They were taking it to Managua for an autopsy. Doris's mother reacted by throwing a fit, refusing to let them take her daughter away. She said something about letting her daughter's body be at peace and not slicing her up. She fought loudly with the police, but they prevailed and left with the body. Nobody mentioned the obvious problem—that more than a day had passed since Doris had been found dead, during which time her body had been handled, moved, cleaned, and even embalmed. Could a forensic examination under those circumstances be useful?

I woke up Thursday morning, the day of Doris's funeral, feeling wasted, but the day had a few more twists in store. Austin approached me with something serious on his mind. He reminded me that I had told him earlier that year about the venomous e-mails that Doris and I had received, and he told me that morning that he knew who wrote them. The news was shocking in a way, but at the same time not at all surprising. I asked Austin if he would go with me to the police about this, and he quickly agreed. I then called Uriarte on the spot to let him know we'd be coming by to see him after the funeral.

I remember the funeral mass as being much more raw emotionally and even in a way more unorganized than I expected. At times, the scene reminded me of the *vela* at the house the night before, with people wailing and weeping loudly and openly. The service itself was mostly subdued. Only one of the two people who took the priest up on his offer to share something personal on the mic made a statement that I found memorable or significant. The man who spoke had been a professor of Doris's, one who some of the students looked up to as cooler or hipper than other teachers. He stood up in the church and spoke harshly about the wave of development that was washing away the peaceful and sleepy old San Juan del Sur that people still remembered. He wasn't talking about me specifically, and I didn't even disagree with everything he was saying, but there was something chilling about his talk, something that left everyone feeling like a terrible thing like this would never, could never, have happened in their quiet old village before the gringos came down and changed the place.

It took me a long time to get up the nerve to stand up and speak. I had just gotten up and was making my way toward the front of the church when the priest concluded the ceremony. I found myself somewhat awkwardly standing up near the coffin, when one of Doris's cousins grabbed my arm and asked me to help carry it out of the church, an honor reserved for those known to be very close with the deceased. This was an open gesture of respect from Doris's cousin, and he intentionally put me at the front. Three other men served as pallbearers. I was on the left side, with Doris's casket resting on my right shoulder. Behind me was a shorter man who kept having to readjust the weight by pushing the casket in such a way that it dug painfully into my skin. We walked her down the center aisle of the church, and I remember meeting eyes with nearly everyone seated there as we passed. Outside, we waited with the coffin on our shoulders for the arrival of a flatbed truck. My shoulder was aching when we finally lifted Doris onto the truck bed. The truck drove off very slowly through the town, with all of us walking slowly behind it, our procession accompanied by music from a mariachi band.

The funeral passed through the center of San Juan. People came out of their houses or closed their shops to join in and pay their final respects. Many fell in with the procession as we went by. I have a vivid image in my mind of one man who seemed to materialize out of the shadows and join in, almost right beside me: It was the tall detective with the mustache. There he was, walking down the town's main street, as if he were my shadow. We made eye contact, and he winked at me. I interpreted the gesture as his telling me that he was still investigating, checking things out to see if he noticed anything strange or telling. I didn't know that he was there to keep tabs on me, to make sure I never got out of his sight. I didn't know that the police had by then decided to arrest me and that it was this man's job to make sure I never left San Juan. They had a plan. I looked around and saw that the detective with the mustache wasn't alone.

Another policeman was floating around recording everything with a video camera, and more than once I looked up to see the camera pointing directly at me.

Nicaraguan funerals don't end with what we would call a burial. Instead, the family builds a little cement crypt above ground, like a heavy rectangular box, into which they slide the coffin. There is no grave to fill in with dirt. Rather, the open end of the crypt is then closed with cinder blocks and sealed with wet cement by a mason as the mourners watch. At this part of the ceremony, I began to sense even more coldness toward me in the eyes of some of the people who had known Doris, which I didn't fully understand. I remember being next to Gabi, Doris's good friend who had called me with the news of the murder; she was a mess, and I put my arm around her.

She immediately stiffened, and when she pulled away, she looked at me squarely and said, "Maybe if you had taken Doris to Managua with you, this wouldn't have happened."

The funeral broke up slowly. As long as everyone was together, focusing on Doris, it was almost as if she were still somehow a part of things, but turning your back meant moving on, and some people couldn't bring themselves to leave the graveside. I stayed there for a while, with a handful of her oldest friends, mostly young women she had known since childhood. I went and sat in the grass alone off to the side of the scene, and I looked over to see three of Doris's friends huddled up talking very softly so that I couldn't hear, but from the way they all kept looking up at me, I suspected they were talking about me. It felt oddly disorienting, like something was going on that everybody but me knew about. When I finally got into a friend's car to leave with Austin, one of them, a young girl named Helen, who had worked for Doris in the store, broke away and ran up to the window of the car.

"Eric!" she said. "Take care of yourself, okay?"

We went directly from the cemetery to where I had my rental car parked. Austin and I then drove to the police station, where I introduced Austin as someone who had information about the e-mails. The cops interrupted me and announced that Detective Uriarte wanted to speak with me. They showed me to the entrance of the station, where nine policemen were waiting. They surrounded me and told me to empty my pockets. "Huh?... My pockets?" I repeated. One of them announced that I was being "detained," on the grounds that I had "refused to finish an interview with Commissioner Reyes yesterday in Rivas." They examined the items as I pulled them out of my pockets. They hung on to all the business cards and documents and the keys to the rental car I had brought from Managua. They told me to hang on to my cell phone and tried to take my cash, but I refused and gave it to Austin. All of this was happening literally as the police hustled me toward the street. I was told I was being taken to be interviewed again by Reyes, so it didn't make any sense at all when the police grabbed my arms and snapped handcuffs on my wrists. Never in my life had I worn handcuffs, even in play, and I angrily demanded an explanation. I never got one.

"¡Llevate lo!" *Hurry! Get him outta here*, Uriarte yelled.

They put me in the back of a police pickup, which they then drove through town very slowly, as if parading me, displaying me to the people of San Juan del Sur. When I tried to duck down low and get out of the line of sight, they would forcefully sit me back up so people could see. They even took an unnecessarily roundabout route down the town's main street, to make sure everyone knew. Once we left the town the driver gunned it at top speed, despite the broken pavement of the street. He was actually driving dangerously as he dodged in and out around the sea of potholes. The truck headed toward Rivas, passing cars filled with people who had spent the day at Doris's funeral, and I can still see the confused looks on their faces as they looked up and saw me in custody. The truck sped along the Pan American Highway through the fields along the shoreline of Lake Nicaragua, and the thought crossed my mind that it was all over for me. I had just been arbitrarily detained. They never showed me an arrest warrant or read me any rights. If I was going to an "interview with Reyes," why couldn't I have just driven my own car? I had committed no crime, but my liberty had

just been taken away. It didn't add up. The cops in the truck had been handling me very roughly, as if they no longer felt any need for courtesy or fair
play. There was something very dangerous about their skittish and impulsive energy. Yet I could sense that my detention had been planned. Forced
disappearance was not unheard of in Nicaragua, and I actually had a notion that the cops might try to kill me. I was scared and my world was spinning.

One of the people in the cars we passed on the road was Sandra, who
did legal work for Century 21, and when she saw me she must have immediately sprung into action, because by the time I got to the jail in Rivas,
another lawyer I knew was already waiting outside, arguing with the police, trying to get some control of the situation. I was not allowed to speak
with him.

Inside the jail, they took my belt, watch, cell phone, and a gold chain
that Doris had given me, whatever hadn't been taken in San Juan. I kept
demanding to know what was going on, since I was supposed to be there
to speak again with Reyes. The guard in charge just looked at me as if he
had no idea what I was talking about and told me I had been arrested and
to "sign here" as he slid a document across the counter. It was some sort of
jail form, and for the first time I saw the words.

"Violación y asesinato de Doris Jiménez." *Rape and murder of Doris
Jiménez.*

In that instant the focus of this case changed completely. Even though
the charge contained her name, the story was no longer about Doris Jiménez. It had just become *El Caso Volz*—"the Eric Volz case."

4 ·

Suddenly the Enemy

I'll never forget the barking.

I would hear it again in other Nicaraguan prisons, but hearing it now for the first time as the truck pulled through the gates of the Rivas jail, I began to tremble. I could handle the hooting and the shouting, the clanging and banging against the rusted bars of the windows, but what I heard now went beyond anything I could have imagined. And through all that crazy noise, the sound of barking stood out, and I knew instantly that there were no dogs, that these were men I was hearing, men reduced to their lowest, most animal level, barking at me like wild, hungry, rabid dogs. The sound was the most evil thing I had ever heard.

Although it is the capital of the *departmento*, or "state," Rivas is a small town. The sight of a nicely dressed Anglo man (I was still wearing the suit from the funeral) being pulled out of a pickup truck in handcuffs must have been shocking to a jail that is full of thugs and borderline psychos. At the very least, I'm sure I looked like a fresh and easy target to them. Occasional shouts of "gringo" would reach my ears. I could see through to one cell, where a young man had leapt up onto the bars and was hanging on and shaking them, as if he were some kind of sick monkey in a zoo.

Even then, I hadn't been read my rights or told on what grounds I had been arrested. Inside the Rivas station, the anger and fear were boiling over inside me, but I forced myself to keep calm. The guard walked me to a cell—a big holding tank, really—in which about twenty men shuffled around. Some kept to themselves in the dark corners or stood quietly, staring me down and sizing me up. Others were in different states of agitation, pacing or fidgeting around like men who were going mad. Even through my panic, I could tell that I wouldn't last long in there, but somehow I knew enough to hide my fear. I was innocent, absolutely and completely, but that didn't matter at that moment. In a place like this innocence is one thing, vulnerability is another.

I'm not sure what made me think to get in that guard's face just then. Something in me I didn't completely recognize took over, as if all the tight situations I'd been in had become a part of me without my realizing it. Standing in front of the door to the holding cell, I put my face an inch away from his and as coldly as I could, I said, "If you want to sleep tonight, don't put me in that cell. I'm not in the mood to be fucked with."

It may have been an act, but it had the benefit of being absolutely true. Something told me that there would be trouble, and I wanted him to be thinking the same thing. For a moment, he didn't move. We watched each other, and I could see the wheels turning in his head. Did he really want to get up in the middle of the night, to break up a fight, or worse? Did he really want to have to report some kind of trouble to his bosses? The tension eased just a fraction. His body and his expression relaxed almost imperceptibly, but enough to let me know he was giving in.

He led me away to another cell, the only empty one. He couldn't budge the heavy metal door that was bent crooked, which I suppose explains why the cell looked like it hadn't been used in a while. The guard strained against the door, putting all his weight into it, but could not get it to open. I still can't believe that I did this, but I took a step forward and helped him. I gripped the bars and tugged with everything I had. It may have been my jail cell, but right then it felt like my only chance of getting through the night. Together we pulled and heaved and grunted until the cell door opened.

All of sudden, I was alone in the dark and the cold. The tiny cell was bare except for a concrete slab to sleep on and a hole in the floor for a toilet. No sheets or blankets so prisoners couldn't hang themselves. Nothing that could be broken or held as a weapon. As the air on this frigid night moved through the decrepit jail built for tropical heat and hit my thin dress shirt, I began to shiver uncontrollably. I took off my shoes and fashioned a little pillow out of them, just something to put under my neck, and lay down. Curled up in a fetal ball, trying to wrap my arms around myself to fight off the chill, I listened to the sounds of the jail that night, the murmurs and conversations, the drug-fueled laughter and screams.

As I lay there shivering, the noise of the other inmates seemed to grow louder in my ears. I tried to focus my mind on something other than the cold and the dark and the solitude and the menace on the other side of the walls. I found it almost comforting to think about some other people I had glimpsed in the cells who seemed as out of place or at least as confused or as frightened as I felt. I remembered some young teenagers, boys really, who must have gotten way over their heads into some kind of mischief. You couldn't miss them, mostly because they were trying so hard to make themselves invisible. Also sitting off by herself was a grandmotherly looking woman with silver hair, who seemed to be concentrating on keeping her dignity.

At about 7:00 that first evening, I was taken out of the jail and walked a couple of blocks to another location in Rivas for a physical examination. The woman who checked me over was the same woman who had taken samples of my hair and cotton swabbed under my fingernails for the police in San Juan del Sur. Turns out she had also been at the crime scene, performing that first cursory forensic examination of Doris's body. She was never introduced to me in any way, and here in Rivas, it was hard to tell if she was actually a doctor or medical professional. She worked out of a simple storefront "office" with a plain wooden desk and chair and no sign of medical equipment. The office seemed to double as a makeshift pharmacy, with a few items—toothpaste, combs and brushes, soap and shampoo, and such—in a small display case. She never took any blood from me, either in San Juan or that night in Rivas, but she did examine all over visually, looking, I suppose, for fresh wounds or other signs of struggle that might connect me directly to the murder. This examiner clearly saw the bruises left on my shoulder from carrying Doris's coffin but never asked me about it. In fact, I didn't even know they were there. It wasn't until later I learned that she wrote down in her report that "the injuries were similar to those produced by fingernails, with two or three days of evolution."

Before I knew it, I was sitting in my cell again but still couldn't fully grasp what was happening to me. At that moment, it was inconceivable to me that the terrible mistake of my arrest wouldn't get cleared up in a matter of days, if not hours. I expected that at any minute, someone would walk in and tell me to gather my things and get ready to go. It actually occurred to me that if the real killers were found, the cops would probably bring them to the same jail, and I'd have a chance to see them face-to-face.

At one point in the middle of that first night, the guard who had promised he wouldn't put anyone in the cell with me brought in a frightened kid who had gotten into a fight in town, and later two more street thugs were thrown in as well. Even as I kept myself half hidden in the corner shadows of the cell and adopted the body language of someone hard and dangerous, I stared at those guys, steaming with the thought that one or all of them might have killed Doris. I remember looking across into the crowded common cells on that next morning, trying to see if anyone gave me a sense that they might be the one. There was one guy about my age, dressed and groomed nicely enough that he seemed out of place with all the hoods in the common cells, who caught my attention. He kept looking at me like he knew something I didn't. In my mind, hyper with exhaustion, he started to look like the type of dude that Doris might have gotten mixed up with. Of course, I had no clue who or what she might have been mixed up with, and that guy in cell across from me turned out to have nothing whatsoever to do with the case.

Frigid, dark, and covered in filth, the Rivas jail felt like the underworld. You'd be amazed at the kinds of things you can get used to. The first night sleeping on a slab of cold concrete, I would either feel shooting pain through my hips and shoulders and limbs or complete numbness in these parts from the pressure on a particular nerve. Quickly, though, I started to figure out the little tricks—the right way to wrap my shirt or jacket into a pillow and place under one of my joints or how to position my shoes just so under my neck to make the long nights somehow bearable. I even started to get used to the disgusting stench from the vomit and feces smeared around the holes in the cement floor we were expected to use as toilets. Many came in drunk and spent their first couple of hours detoxing over the toilet hole. The men themselves all stank, especially if they had been there a while, with the stale, rank odor of sweat and dirt and suffering.

The guards would bring around a pot of rice and beans twice a day, but you were on your own as far as a plate was concerned. From the first day, I had to figure out how to scramble just to get a few bites of food. Like every prison, there's a pecking order among the inmates, and there's always someone who seems to have access to something the others need. The Rivas police jail only houses transients—people awaiting processing or trial for petty crimes or convicted murderers and rapists on their way into the penitentiary system—but even there, you needed to know which guys could get you a plate or something else you needed in exchange for some other favor. Right from the beginning, a prisoner has to negotiate for the most basic things. I felt immediately like that put me at a disadvantage, but strangely that kind of survival mentality forces the inmates to depend on, even while abusing, one another. I was getting just a tiny glimpse of what it was going to mean to be part of *el sistema*, "the prison system."

The little world of the Rivas jailhouse revealed itself to me in the short time I was kept there. The small, decaying building housed about sixty prisoners. The shape of the building—a giant letter *U* surrounding a central holding cell—allowed you to see into all the other cells except for those immediately on either side of your own cell and made the place feel like an insane amphitheater. With nothing else to do, inmates would find a way to grab center stage, keeping themselves and one another entertained. Some of the men would just rave madly, but a few made me sit up and pay attention. One fat dude kept up a constant stream of patter, like a stand-up comic with the foulest, most demented material I ever heard. I don't know how I would have reacted to him in a different setting, but in the jailhouse, he was hilarious.

Another young kid would sing the same mournful song over and over again. Every night, when things got quiet after lockdown, he would stand at the door of his cell, and, with his hands wrapped tightly around the bars, he would sing from somewhere deep down in his heart a song by a young Panamanian reggaeton artist called El Rookie. It was an eerie kind of ritual; as soon as he would start to sing, all of the other inmates, even the baddest of the bad, would stop whatever they were doing and come listen at the doors of their cells. I had heard the song [EX.02]—"Buay del barrio" ("Kid from the Ghetto")—more times than I could count. It opens with the line, "In there, sitting, you think about how to escape, because in a trial you lost your freedom, kid from the ghetto [buay del barrio]. I'm singing to you . . ." and speaks of the mothers and loved ones suffering on the outside. The song, which concludes that God is the only light worth walking toward, took on a whole different meaning in jail than the simple dance tune that I remembered from discotecas all over Latin America. This kid sang loudly enough for all of us to hear, but really he was singing to himself, like a mother sings a lullaby to a baby. The last thing I heard most nights as the prison settled down to sleep was this boy's sad and beautiful song.

But it isn't like there was silence and solitude when nobody was performing. The noise *never* let up in the jailhouse, and it's the most traumatizing thing about prison life. I could retreat into the corner of my cell, make myself nearly invisible, but I couldn't shut out the banging and clanging and shouting and maniacal laughter that filled every moment. The noise alone kept my nerves on edge, the stress and tension in my body high.

Just as I was watching everything and everyone in the jail, they were watching me, too. The loss of privacy in prison is total. If you're new, the others watch your every move, studying you, sizing you up, trying to figure what kind of man you are. Are you a victim or are you hard? gullible or street smart? They watched me with even more intensity than usual, I'm sure, since probably none of them had ever encountered someone like me in jail—a white man in good clothes, but a gringo who spoke Spanish like they did. Even before the case became a national sensation and a strange sort of cause célèbre grew around me, I knew I was something unique in the world of Nicaraguan prisons.

I could feel their eyes on me all the time. That first morning, a guard came and got me out of my cell and brought me to be fingerprinted. The procedure was rustic and low tech, with an old-fashioned ink roller and a piece of paper on which I pressed my fingertips. Knowing how my interaction with the guards would be analyzed by the inmates watching, I made some trouble right away, deliberately dragging my fingers a little to smudge the print. I guess I wasn't the first to pull this little trick, and the guard was unimpressed, but it seemed important to show some kind of attitude, to show I wasn't a coward.

The guards felt my alien status even more acutely than the inmates. They would have been cautious if I had just been a rich or highly placed Nicaraguan, but an American was something more mysterious. It's easy to forget how little exposure to the rest of the world people in developing countries get. Even though the shrinking world has brought more than a few foreigners into Rivas, most of the people who live there probably haven't seen much beyond their immediate community. If they've had a chance to leave the country, it would most likely have been to go to one of the neighboring Central American countries. Nicas were becoming used to seeing gringos on the streets and beaches and in the shops but not in their prisons. To have an American—well traveled, educated, and rich as far they were concerned—in their jail must have felt like they had been handed some exotic specimen. None of the normal rules applied, which most likely made the guards nearly as nervous and unsure of themselves as I was.

After the guard had fingerprinted me, he took me off into another small room and had me take my shirt off so he could take some photos of my back and shoulders. I hadn't been complaining about any injuries, and no damage showed on my clothing in those areas, so there was no obvious reason for anyone to be interested in photographs of my bare skin. I could only assume that someone had handed these instructions down, perhaps to verify that indeed I did not have any tattoos as they had asked the night before. In any event, those photos[EX.03] were to become a critical part of the prosecution's case and were later exploited by the press to inflame public opinion against me.

Less than an hour later, I received my first friendly visit in jail, from Sandra, who did legal work for Century 21. Sandra herself was from Rivas and personally knew some of the police and other local officials, relationships that helped her get in to see me. I also know that another more senior attorney had been counseling her on what to do. Sandra had me tell her everything that had happened since the day before, and when I told her about the police taking photos of my body, she immediately pulled a small digital camera out of her purse, and right there in the visiting room made me take off my shirt so she could take her own set of pictures. It turns out one of the frames is from precisely the same angle as the police photo. Sandra's photos[EX.04] later made it clear how much the photos that appeared in the Nica press had been digitally altered and doctored to look even more incriminating.

Sandra proved to be indispensable in those early days. Through her contacts in Rivas, that first evening after my arrest she heard rumors that arrest warrants had been issued for Shawn, the art director from *EP* who had driven with me to San Juan del Sur, and the other members of the *EP* editorial team in Managua. She got through to all of them and made sure that they got out of the office and even avoided their own homes so they wouldn't get picked up by the cops. She even brought Shawn to her own house in Rivas and hid him there.

I hadn't gotten myself an attorney yet, still confident that everything would be cleared up and I'd be freed in no time. I simply figured that once my alibi was confirmed, they would see that there was no way I could have been in San Juan at the time of the murder and that I had no motive. At the same time, I knew about the rampant corruption in law enforcement. Maybe getting out of jail would involve knowing the right people, or more likely if I was extorted, it might mean having to pay. Before Sandra left, I told her she was free to get some cash through Agnielly if that's what it was going to take to get me out.

I learned another key piece of information because of Sandra's visit that morning. When the guards took me back to my cell from the visitors area, I saw Rosita, a local troublemaker known to everyone in San Juan. He also happened to be the young hustler I met on my first visit to San Juan years before. I'd seen him around town since then but had never had anything more to do with him. Rosita was crouched in a tiny holding cell, shoveling rice and beans into his mouth with his bare hands as if he hadn't seen food in days. He startled me by flashing me a look of open hostility, and I knew that his being there had something to do with Doris. It made sense that he would have been picked up, as if some policeman had given the order to "round up the usual suspects." Something in Rosita's face revealed a kind of threat, as if to let me know that he held me responsible for his being in that cell and that he intended to get me back in some way. He didn't say anything, but that look rattled me.

My next visitor in the Rivas jail that Friday was a man named Michael Terry, the father of another American who was about my age and who ran one of the competing real-estate offices in Nicaragua. Michael Terry was, among other things, a defense attorney in Nashville, where my mother lived, and had been the one to phone her with the news of my arrest. He had reached her on her cell phone as she shopped in a crowded Nashville farmer's market. She collapsed on a curb as she listened to Michael and tried to absorb the news. My mom remembers this as the moment that changed her life. She in turn phoned my father, who immediately turned all his attention to seeing how he might help. In the early weeks, my parents monitored the situation closely from home, sure of my innocence and believing the situation would clear itself up quickly.

Michael Terry had immediately come to Rivas to see what help he could provide. One moment from my jailhouse conversation with Michael stands out in my memory. I remember wondering out loud about the possible motives for Doris's murder and at one point asking him if he thought it might be a possible vendetta against me or Century 21 by some unhappy real-estate competitor. Michael jumped all over this. "Put that out of your mind," he said. "This has nothing to do with real estate." Of course, there's no way a lawyer from Nashville, Tennessee, could have really known such a thing with any certainty. Michael's insistence had more to do with the nervousness of American and other foreign investors about the overall stability of Nicaragua and how my case might affect them. He might have even sensed, even that early on, how public the case would become and hoped to make sure that nothing I might say would complicate the efforts of people trying to sell Nicaragua as a hidden paradise. His reaction made it clear that there were plenty of people who cared about this situation for reasons that had nothing to do with me and even less to do with Doris Jiménez.

I now know that the one thing that was absolutely not happening on the outside was an investigation of my alibi. This simple fact lies at the heart of my entire ordeal. It would have been the easiest thing in the world for a detective to go to Managua, interview the people at the EP office, the rental car employees, Ricardo Castillo, the young woman who cut my hair—any of the people who had been with me at the time Doris was being murdered in San Juan del Sur or immediately after. And yet that never happened in the first forty-eight hours. What did happen is that the cops showed up at my house the day after my arrest and turned the place inside out and confiscated my Jeep. They didn't take statements from any of the employees.

But it isn't just that the police never checked out my story. Adam Paredes, my friend and colleague from EP, had had the sense to contact the journalist Ricardo Castillo with the news of my arrest. Ricardo, the man I'd been speaking with at our office on the day of the murder, was outraged.

He mobilized all the obvious witnesses from Managua, and on Saturday November 25th (two days after my arrest) drove everyone to Rivas, where they all volunteered to give their statements to the police. The police said it was up to the D.A., and the D.A. declined to hear them, saying it wasn't necessary. Castillo warned Adam in private that "something shady was going on and that I could potentially be in serious trouble." It has always seemed to me that nobody needs to know much more than this to understand that, from the beginning, some purpose other than finding Doris's actual killer was driving the police.

I would later learn that the police had a pretty good idea of what happened to Doris even before my arrest. After consulting many retired Nicaraguan police and government officials, there's no escaping the conclusion that a decision was made early on in the process to pin this terrible crime on me. All their actions from that point forward were part of that strategy. Furthermore, there's no way that a Rivas policeman, even the commissioner of detectives there and the local prosecutors he was working with, would have made that decision on their own. Not when the arrest of an American was involved. That had to have come down from higher up.

Late on Friday night, my second night in jail, the guards got me out of my cell and brought me into a room, where the two Managua detectives I had met in San Juan sat waiting—the chubby, oily Jorge Uriarte, who always gave me the impression that he played by his own set of rules, and the tall, nameless cop with the mustache who had winked at me during Doris's funeral. There was something about him that made me know he was the one that took care of the darkest orders. I could sense that he was dangerous.

Three local cops from Rivas and San Juan waited with them. I walked in, and someone right away pushed me up against the wall, and the cops just laid into me, yelling in my face about the desperate trouble I was in and about how I had no idea what was in store for me. The police said they were sure I had murdered Doris. They had been to my office in Managua, gone through my files and my belongings, and were sure they had their man. Then they revealed something new.

Nelson Danglas, another notorious San Juan local who had had run-ins with the law, was sitting in a chair. Cops led him through his story.

"How much did he give you?"

Danglas answered, "Oh yeah, he gave me fifty cordobas . . . and told me to put the two bags in the car. . . ."

What two bags? I thought. I got pissed because this is the first time that I was confronted with someone involved in the murder as a suspect. I told the cops that this was bullshit, that all they had to do was to verify what I told them and interview my witnesses to know that Danglas was lying.

"We've just come from Rio San Juan," they said, referring to another tourist community on the Caribbean coast. "We spoke to Armando Llanes, and he told us everything." I didn't know anyone named Armando Llanes, but I was able to piece together that he must be the guy from Miami who Doris's cousin had told me about the night I pulled him aside at the wake. In fact, a couple of weeks before she died, Doris had been talking with me about her life, as she often did. She told me about a new guy from Miami who had been pursuing her, a guy who had invited her to come live with him at the resort his father owned. In *Rio San Juan*. I knew this must be the same guy but couldn't immediately understand how the police had come to be speaking with him.

Later, I would hear a version of how the police were clued in. Doris's friend Gabi had seen a cousin of Nelson Danglas walking through San Juan del Sur wearing a new blouse that she recognized as one of the unique items from Doris's shop. She immediately told the police, which led them eventually to search Danglas's house, where they found two plastic bags filled with the goods that were found to be missing from Doris's store after the murder. From that point they rounded up Rosita as well, and that's how the two of them ended up in custody. That Thursday night they were both held and interrogated in the San Juan del Sur police jail.

Somewhere along the line, the police had gotten the name of Armando
Llanes out of them.*

The cops kept shouting at me, trying to break me, but I just squinted
my eyes and shook my head as if to say, You guys are out of your mind.
Then they took Danglas out and brought in Rosita, who looked like hell.
He always looked like hell, but this time he looked like he'd been suffering for days and days. Rosita exchanged a look with the tall, mysterious
mustached cop, who instructed Rosita to tell his story, the story he had
already given the police.

"Eric was there," he started. "Eric and Armando went into Doris's
store. Eric hit her in the mouth and then shoved her into the back room.
I was there and watched them rape and kill her."

The cop prompted Rosita, almost like he was feeding him his lines.
"Didn't they offer you money?" he asked.

Rosita looked at me. "Yeah, yeah. You offered us five thousand dollars
to help you." *Us?*

Clearly, Rosita was terrified of the men in the room. I could tell from
his manner that he was being manipulated. One moment he seemed to
be merely reciting things he had been told to say. Then the next moment
he'd be almost pleading, trying to appeal to the police, to make himself
sympathetic to them. The possibility that he was being set up, too, crossed
my mind then, although I couldn't see why.

"¡Mentiroso de mierda! ¿Porque me involucras?" I yelled at Rosita. *You're
full of shit! Why are you involving me?* He launched into a tirade about evil
gringos like me who come down to his country so we can walk all over poor
people. Rosita knew enough to know this would play well with a room full
of underpaid cops.

They took Rosita out and the tall detective with the mustache showed
me pictures on the LCD of a digital camera of all the empty rooms of the
house I rented in San Juan.

---

* We also learned later that there was at least one eyewitness interviewed the day of the murder, a girl who
worked in a pizzeria across the street, who told the police that she saw the three men—Llanes, Rosita, and
Danglas—enter Doris's store.

"We know you cleared it out," he asserted. I told him that house was always empty because we hardly ever used it. He was pissed that my answer made him look stupid in front of the others. He then yelled at me to remove my shirt and ordered me to turn around and face the wall.

He raised the camera to take a picture of my back and then blared, "Which side are the scratches on?"

"What scratches? What is it with everyone wanting to pictures of my back?" I asked. The night before, the medical forensic worker had not said anything to me when she noted "injuries . . . similar to those produced by fingernails."

Mustache cop kept at it, even more furious. "Where are the marks, goddamnit?" He moved me from side to side looking for what I later learned had been reported, but by then the bruises had almost healed. He snapped shots anyway to play his part.

I had had enough. I blew up at the detectives, screaming that they were full of shit, that they knew damn well I didn't do it, and insisting that they explain why they didn't simply go confirm the alibi I had given them. None of them responded with much more than a shrug before sending me back to my cell.

As I left the interrogation room, one policeman followed me out, a small, quiet local captain named Valerio.

"You seemed pretty upset in there, Eric," he started.

"No shit!" I began yelling, but he grabbed my arm and stopped me.

"Listen," he said, "I want to look into what you're saying about the people who were with you in Managua. Tomorrow, I'll ask for permission from my chief to investigate your alibi." I thanked him, almost begging him to follow up and help make things right.*

---

* The next morning, Saturday, Valerio did just what he promised. He had me brought to his office and took down all the information relevant to my alibi, including the names of the witnesses who had been with me in Managua. He did the legwork, tracked the people down, and was able to corroborate my story. Obviously, this caused a problem for the police who were determined to charge me with Doris's murder. They now had to decide whether to charge me as the actual murderer—which would have been difficult, given the absence of physical evidence and my solid alibi—or as the "intellectual author" of the crime, the person who planned, arranged, or financed it.

The memory of this first confrontation stayed with me for months. I simply could not understand the point of it. Why would the police put me in a room with these two guys? Were they trying to see how we'd respond to one another? More important, since they were so clearly setting me up, why would they tip their hand like that? Why would they tell me the bogus story they were preparing and give me the chance to start proving it wrong? None of it made any sense at the time, but over the many months that followed, the picture began to come clear.

The dirty cops in charge of that little face-off were the cops from the capital, the guys with the real clout. The investigator who took me aside to tell me he'd try to follow up on my story had been one of the local small-town guys. I would learn that this was one of the first moves in the game of power between the two police factions. At that point, the local cops were still actually trying to find out what really happened, but the ones who had swooped down from Managua had a different agenda. The whole scene with Rosita and Danglas had been a show for the local police, designed to convince them not just that I was guilty but that the big boys from Managua were proceeding in an honest manner and had this under control.

By Sunday night, I was still in jail, although by law in Nicaragua, nobody could be held for more than forty-eight hours without a charge made formally in a court of law. I knew this, ironically, from the poster of "prisoners' rights" displayed prominently near the entrance to the jail. It was the cleanest, shiniest thing in the whole place, "part of some gringo human-rights initiative," one old-timer told me. (What a joke that list of rights turned out to be.) Nonetheless, the police made no move to release me on Monday morning. Sandra came back that morning with a list of about a half-dozen attorneys I might use. At the top of the list was a prominent attorney who had told Sandra very simply that he would make the whole thing go away for a fee of $20,000. That may not sound like a lot of money to defend against a murder charge in the United States, but it's an outrageous sum in Nicaragua. And then Sandra mentioned one other little detail that made me rule him out. She had found the lawyer hard to

contact, and he complained to her about having to purchase phone cards
to keep his cell active and available. This thing with the cell phones in
Nicaragua had long been a pet peeve of mine and now just plain turned
me off. Even the highest-level officials in the country seemed unwilling to
buy cell-phone cards or keep their credit up. Everybody had a phone, but
nobody could actually use it. I wasn't about to hire a lawyer who couldn't
be bothered to make himself available in what could turn out to be a life-
and-death situation.

To say that turned out to be a bad decision would be a terrible under-
statement. The lawyer had all the right contacts, and it's very likely I
never even would have made it to trial if I had hired him. I passed on that
possibility over a few thousand bucks and some annoyance over his cell-
phone etiquette.

I chose to hire instead a lawyer named Ramon Rojas, who asked for only
five thousand dollars less. According to Sandra, Rojas was a well-known
defense attorney who had defended Daniel Ortega himself in the past and
who remained openly loyal to the Sandinistas. I figured that his party connections would work for me because the Sandinista party had owned the
Rivas district for a long time, but my understanding of the situation at the
time was not deep enough to realize that those connections also probably
meant that it would be easy for others to claim he was corrupt. And I was
too naïve in the ways of the Nica legal system to realize that I could be more
valuable to Rojas while I was still in custody than I would be if I were exonerated. The longer I rotted in a prison cell, still under suspicion, the more
fees he'd be able to charge. I've replayed that decision process in my head a
thousand times over.

On the plus side, Agnielly had the wisdom to hire someone to back
Rojas up. She knew that while we needed a heavy hitter like Rojas, it also
made sense to bring in someone who lived and worked around Rivas,
who knew all the local cops and legal people and where to go for information. A young attorney named Fabbrith Gomez stepped into that role.
Fabbrith knew everyone inside the local legal community, from cops and
prison guards to court clerks and judges. He had grown up with some of

them and had been to school with others and could work those contacts
for critical bits of intelligence. He would become invaluable, partly because he could keep an eye on Ramon Rojas, and I now count him as a
dear friend.

I thought that securing the right team of lawyers would change my
situation, but I quickly learned otherwise. It didn't matter much what
they said, because nobody was listening. I was furious that nobody seemed
to want to hear my side of the story, but I'd get used to that over time. I
hadn't been arraigned or formally charged and was being unlawfully detained in jail. Moreover, not once since my arrest had any policeman, government prosecutor, or investigator ever sat me down to take my official
statement. Never. Nobody ever said, "Tell us what happened, Eric. Tell
us what we need to know."

Early on the morning of Monday, November 27, five days after my arrest, two policemen got Rosita and me out of our cells and walked us
through Rivas to the courthouse for the arraignment. The streets were
relatively quiet and empty, but I felt ashamed nonetheless, being marched
through the streets with handcuffs on my wrists like the worst kind of
criminal. Being totally inexperienced and naïve about the criminal process
in my own country, I had heard that this would be my *audiencia preliminar,*
and I took the words literally. Even though I knew this was to be the government's chance to present a formal charge, I somehow believed it would
be something like an audience, and I would be able to argue my innocence.

Nothing like that happened, of course. There was an informal, almost
disorganized feel to the court that morning, and while I knew only a few
of the people who had come to witness the proceedings—Shawn and Noah
from *EP* and some of the Nica coworkers of mine from Century 21—I
could feel the intensity of their love and support. My friends made me
feel like we were in this together. *First Doris, now you, man.*

As we sat down at the defense table, my lawyer began to spread his papers out in front of him, and I saw for the first time, the official *acta,* the
formal record[EX.05] of the prosecution's case. I snatched the document and
pored over it, tuning out practically everything that was going on around

me. Here, for the first time, I could see, in horrible, bloody detail, the violence of the attack they believe Doris had experienced on the night of her
murder—how, as the prosecution contended, the four of us had gone into
the little shop; how Doris, her mouth stuffed with paper to silence her
screams, had been raped anally by Armando Llanes and by me in succes-
sion while Danglas and Rosita held her down; how we had tied her body up
in a pair of bedsheets, the knots so tight that the police had had to cut the
sheets off her; and how we saw that she had stopped moving, stopped
breathing. I saw the close-up photos of the scene[EX.06], and of her bloodied,
scraped hands and of the bruises covering her back and side. I read the
medical examiner's report[EX.07], which included, among its official conclusions:

- The cause of death is pulmonary edema caused by mechanical
  asphyxiation by suffocation and strangulation.
- Observations show a relationship exists between the neck
  injury and the cause of death.
- The deceased was tied up at her wrist and ankles before death.
- It was a violent death, characteristic of a homicide.

I also saw the list of the prosecution's witnesses, which included people
who I had once counted among my friends and many who had nothing at
all directly relevant to contribute. From my witnesses, like Noah and
Shawn, who did actually have valuable information, I heard that the police
had tried to twist their words or change the context of their statements.[EX.08]
Noah and Shawn had gone over their affidavits with extreme care before
signing. Ricardo Castillo told me that he had to go through several
rounds of corrections on the statement that Uriarte wrote up for him
and still felt the need to make a written note of typographical changes
when he added his signature. Apparently, it didn't matter that the witnesses and other alleged "evidence" I saw there in the case against me had
no legal merit. The case file was full of information that was both random and completely false. One woman claimed that I had married her

daughter and fathered a child with her. Another woman said she would
see me carrying bags of cash into my house from my car. Others claimed
to have seen me in places I could not have been or that I had given Doris
thousands of dollars with which to open another store.

The prosecutor stood up and read the charges—or rather, the prosecution's unproven theories—against me, Armando Agustín Llanes;
Julio Martín Chamorro, aka Rosita; and Nelson Antonio Lopez Danglas, aka Krusty. *Asesinato atroz.* Actually, the prosecutor *performed* more
than she read. This prim, ambitious young woman, Maria Esperanza
Peña, who made herself up like a delicate porcelain doll, gave a dramatic
reading of the charges, during which she seemed nearly to swoon and
faint, fanning herself and asking for people to fetch her cold water. I
guess Peña saw her chance to advance her career and was giving it everything she had.

For my part, it was like cramming for a final exam. I took out my notebook, which raised some eyebrows in the courtroom, and wrote down
every word. I needed my notes to be complete and correct since I didn't
even know my attorneys well enough to feel entirely comfortable trusting
them. I didn't know what kind of information was getting out of the courtroom to my family back in the States, to my friends in Nicaragua, or to
anyone in a position to help me. And the only thing I could do just then
to help myself was to absorb every possible piece of information and to
keep thinking clearly and independently.

She described the murder as a crime of passion driven by my jealous
rage over Doris's involvement with Armando Llanes. At that point, I understood that most of the case against me was based on the confession[EX.09]
the police had gotten out of Rosita. He told them that he had entered
Doris's store with Llanes and me and had stood by and watched while the
two of us robbed, raped, and strangled Doris. He added that when he
saw that Doris's body was no longer moving, he panicked and ran from
the store. To me the fact that Rosita's statement contained a million tiny
little details should have made it suspicious to anyone who heard it. He
had told the cops about the positions of the logos on our clothes and

about which rear door of my Jeep held the spare tire. (No one seemed to
care later at my trial when Danglas's testimony didn't have me in a Jeep at
all but in a white car with tinted windows.) No way could Rosita have
remembered certain things so clearly and specifically. It was even more
unlikely that he could have made it up on his own. In his own statement,
Nelson Danglas claimed that I had previously arranged for him to meet
me at 1:00 P.M. sharp. When he arrived, he said that I was opening the
door to Doris's shop and handed him two plastic bags filled with items
from the boutique.

Right off the bat, the prosecution's theory made no sense. I was jealous
of Llanes, so he and I raped Doris together? And while they referred to
the murder as a passionate crime, they also described it as premeditated
and preplanned. Other details surfaced, hinting at the ways in which
some simple actions of mine would now be used to make me look guilty.
Why did I offer to pay to have Doris's body taken to Managua for a
proper autopsy? Why did I "push" to have the funeral take place as soon
as possible? Why was I so intent on the police tracking down Doris's
missing cell phone? The prosecution twisted the perception of the things
I did to imply that I was acting suspiciously from the moment I showed
up at the crime scene. They never mentioned any of the conversations I
had had with the police before my arrest or my alibi.*

Peña was playing the moment for melodrama, but hearing the charge
read aloud for the first time made me starkly aware of the grave danger
ahead of me. For the first time, I saw clearly that these were people
who wanted to do me harm and were putting real resources into it. I felt my
future, my very life, being taken away from me. I listened to Maria Esperanza Peña recite a narrative of complete lies about my involvement in Doris's
horrible death, and suddenly the certainty I had felt that everything would

---

* In the ensuing days, when the police went to Doris's mother, Mercedes, and told her that I had confessed
the crime to them, no one seemed to make the connection that no confession or police statement affirming
that a confession existed had been offered as evidence against me at the arraignment. Also, the prosecution
mentioned at some point that they were still waiting for the results of biological tests to add to their pool of
evidence. They never bothered to point out that they still hadn't taken any blood or semen samples from me
or any of the other defendants.

get cleared up easily and quickly simply fell apart. For the first time, I sensed that my innocence no longer mattered. This prosecutor absolutely knew that I had nothing to do with the murder, but it appeared that she had an ulterior motive.

Despondent, I put my head down on my arms on the table only to feel Ramon Rojas immediately poke me and motion for me to hold my head up. Rojas explained that if I put my head down like that, the judge would think I was guilty. I couldn't believe that any properly trained judge would draw any conclusions of any kind from a gesture like that, but that was Rojas's point. It was all theater. The prosecutor had thrown herself into her part, and now I had to play mine.

Until that moment, before I had stood in a courtroom and heard the charges against me read out loud, the whole experience had felt other-worldly, like some random out-of-control dream from which I would just wake up one morning. Now, suddenly, there was no escaping the cold reality of what was happening to me. The strange thing is, the more real the situation became, the more surreal it felt to me.

Most important at that arraignment hearing, the judge, a man named Peter Palma who was a die-hard Sandinista, asked a simple and logical question: If the prosecutor was charging four men with the crime, why were only two standing in front of him that day? Where were Nelson Danglas and Armando Llanes? I didn't know it at the time—and apparently neither did the judge—but Danglas, for reasons that were never quite clear, had been released by the police the day before. Llanes's whereabouts were anybody's guess. Palma re-issued warrants[EX.10] for the two men on the spot.

When the guards brought us out of the courthouse and I found myself walking right next to the stooped frame of Rosita once more, I looked into Rosita's pockmarked, hollow-eyed face, taxed by years of drug use, and had to fight down the temptation to rip him apart. Everything I had heard in the hearing that day—including Rosita's statement—indicated that Rosita had been involved in murdering Doris. Deep inside, something compelled me to avenge Doris by hurting Rosita somehow. What stopped me? Two things. First, there was the slim chance that Rosita might be innocent—that the police were setting him up, just like me. Second, I must have known instinctively that going after Rosita would only make the situation worse for me. For the second time, I was conscious that my sadness over Doris's death and the memory of her was moving into the background. The main thing—the only thing—driving me now was my own survival.

Even though we had walked, almost casually, from the jail to the Rivas courthouse that morning, the police must have seen that the crowd situation was heating up and wanted me and Rosita driven back to the jail. Before we got outside, a friend from Century 21 came over and got my attention.

"Eric, there is press out there," she whispered. "It's important that we keep your face out of the newspapers." She draped a large shirt over my head, and the police walked me out. All I could see was my feet, but I could hear everything going on. A small crowd had gathered outside the courthouse and shouted at me, but their taunts and insults seemed tentative and uncertain, as if they still weren't quite sure who or what to believe. As we drove away from the courthouse, amazingly enough in a truck borrowed by a friend of mine and driven by another friend and with only one armed guard, the possibility of escape entered my mind for the first time. For a moment it seemed like it would be so easy—we could overpower the guard and just keep on driving—but the thought vanished as quickly as it appeared. There was no way some random, unplanned escape attempt would have ended well for me. Besides, despite all the cards stacked against me, something deep inside made me hold on to the hope that the truth would somehow come out in the end.

With the formal arraignment now public, the Nicaraguan press started to get in on the act in a big way. The first major article the morning of the arraignment was published in *El Nuevo Diario*. Entitled "North American Is Detained for *Espantoso* Murder," the article reported that Doris died of "mechanical asphyxiation" and was "sodomized and vaginally raped," although there was no evidence of this at the time. The article got my name

(Boltz) and my age (twenty-four) wrong. There was a section titled "Another North American Implicated" that said that after I raped Doris, Armando allegedly rolled her head in a sheet and raped her,* taking advantage of the fact that she was "in a state of agony as a result of the lack of oxygen." The article also said that an "extraofficial" source revealed that Danglas was given the "plastic bags plus her boom box" by me. There was no mention of money. This article was important, since it offered police and prosecution claims about the murder that would later be changed or eliminated. That first article mentioned both Armando Llanes and me as the alleged main perpetrators of the murder, although the headline spoke only of one *norte americano* charged—me. They either didn't know or didn't care that Llanes was a United States citizen who barely spoke Spanish. The reporter seemed more amazed that the notoriously incompetent police had managed to "solve" the case in only about a week.

The next day, Tuesday, saw the publication of the first newspaper piece by Lesber Quintero, a journalist who seemed determined, right from the beginning, to exploit this story in any way possible to stir up his readers. Quintero was known as working too closely with the police. He was the guy the police would call first. He'd be the first reporter to any crime scene and reported only what the police wanted the public to know. A story like this was bread and butter to Quintero, who jumped at every opportunity to bad-mouth me in the press. He'd report any outlandish rumor, any bit of hearsay in his hunger to sell papers. He printed falsehoods about me countless times, but despite my rage my attorneys advised that there was no possible way a journalist would be properly charged by the D.A. prosecutor. "The institutions are scared of the newspapers," they told me.†

His headline read, "Motivo de pasión en asesinato atroz" (*Motive of Pas-*

---

* This account of events matched past of Rosita's confession to police. (See "Ex.09.")
† At one point, he went so far as to publish a story about the "gringo" who took over the lease to Doris's store after her murder and who told Quintero that he had dreams that Doris had been "killed by a white man." Shockingly, this kind of stuff made a real impact on his readers.

sion in First-Degree Murder), and opened, as most of the articles did, by describing me not as "a suspect," but as "the murderer," at least "according to the police." The article described me as Doris's "current boyfriend" and went on to provide the police's account of how I had raped her both vaginally and anally, although no evidence of rape had been introduced. His article focused on the police's version, describing Danglas and Rosita as accomplices, men I had paid to simulate a robbery, during which things had gone way further than intended. Interestingly, the police and the prosecutors were contradicting each other concerning key elements of the story, like whether Danglas was in the store or was "just passing by." This article is the only instance in which the police publicly connected Nelson Danglas to the murder and actually placed him in Doris's shop. Quintero further related a police spokesperson's claim that Danglas and Rosita had removed bags of clothing and other articles, including Doris's cell phone, from the store on my instructions. In Quintero's version of the story, he never mentioned the name of Armando Llanes. Since Quintero's main source at the time was the police, and since Llanes was technically still under suspicion at the time, Quintero must have had a reason for leaving him out—either instruction from the police or pressure or incentives from another source, such as Llanes's family.

Also buried deep in the article was an acknowledgment that I denied having any role in the crime and claimed to have witnesses willing to support my alibi. Quintero spun even that against me, though, by stating that all of the supposed witnesses were employees of mine at Century 21. The press never spoke about *EP* magazine, where the journalistic community actually knew me from, but always cast me in the role of a greedy gringo who had come to make a bundle of cash off their real estate.

Lesber Quintero and the rest of the sensationalistic Nicaraguan press would prove to be as dangerous for me as the corrupt legal system and police or the ongoing political turmoil. His endless stream of half-truths and innuendo would eat their way into the public consciousness and eventually became what many understood to be the "truth." Adding even more fuel to the fire, the press seemed to focus on the rape element. Most

of the newspapers also ran the police photograph that was digitally en-
hanced and doctored, which the prosecution claimed were the scratch
marks on my shoulder left by Doris as she struggled to defend herself.
This was the photo taken by the cops right after I had been fingerprinted
on my first morning in jail, and in fact it was the only piece of physical
evidence ever entered against me. The awful irony, of course, was that
they were not scratch marks but rather bruises I had received from carrying Doris's coffin on my shoulders as one of the four pallbearers at her
funeral. Nonetheless, the appearance of this photo in papers all over Nicaragua helped stir up incredible hostility toward me.

   It is my belief that by this time much of the press had been contaminated, almost certainly paid off and lobbied by influential people, to do
its part in positioning public opinion against me. My attorneys had called
a press conference for newspaper journalists where they presented sworn
statements from witnesses, cell-phone records, and my rental-car receipt,
all demonstrating that I had been in Managua at the time of the murder
in San Juan del Sur, and yet not one word of that was ever reported.

   In Nicaragua, newspapers have a practice of posting comments from
readers about articles on their Web sites. With the appearance of these
first pieces, the comments reflected both the cynical attitude toward the
judicial system and the vigilantism that was so deeply rooted in the popular culture: People wrote in about the price paid by this *pobre chica* for
getting involved with a gringo or about how a rich and corrupt Americano would buy his freedom from the notoriously corrupt judges. One
even wrote that this crime made him wish the death penalty were legal in
Nicaragua. Many of my friends and supporters sent their comments in
on behalf of my defense, but none were ever posted.

Almost as soon as this nightmare began and the necessity of working
every conceivable back channel became clear I realized how lucky I was to
have a secret weapon, Agnielly Vega. The magazine had hired her away
from a miserable job in a printing company, and, as they say, she had all

the tools. Bright, educated, good looking, and highly professional, she would have been an asset to any business. In addition, Agnielly's family was connected, but only up to a point. One of the people she knew turned out to be the Rivas chief of police, and after she put in a phone call, the police moved me out of my cell in the Rivas jail and put me by myself in a small holding cell in a corner near the back of the building. The cell had no toilet—forcing me to relieve myself into plastic bags and empty gallon jugs—or even a bed, but Agnielly was able to get me a small foam mattress to sleep on. She also managed to bring me some decent food from time to time. There was a window in that cell, and even though I was generally afraid to get too close to it, it made a huge difference during the time that I was there.

On the day that I moved into that small private cell, Nelson Danglas was brought back into the jail. The judge had demanded he be returned to custody, and that morning the police dragged him in and put him in the same cell as Rosita. I watched carefully to see what would happen between them. As soon as the cell door clanged shut, Rosita walked straight up to Danglas, and without saying anything punched him hard in the stomach. Doubled him over. Whether it was because Danglas had sold him out in order to buy his own freedom or because Danglas's recapture meant things were now going to go even worse for Rosita, who could say? But, for sure, Rosita was furious.

I also had a view down the hall to the interrogation room where the policeman had taken the first photographs of my shoulder. That day, I saw them walk Nelson Danglas into the same room, where he had his pictures taken by the same cop with the same camera. He came out with his shirt still off, revealing a huge and nasty wound down one side of his rib cage. The sight of this raw and ugly gash sent electricity through me. I know it was irrational, but it struck me then that I might have been looking at a wound Doris had made as she fought for her life. I recorded the details of the wound in my notebook.

Alone in my cell for long days and longer nights, I had nothing to occupy me other than the details of the case. I convinced one of the guards to bring me even more paper and began processing all the information I had been gathering. To begin, I tried to think through every conceivable scenario for Doris's murder. I knew that the story the prosecution was telling was a lie—at least the part of it that included me—and so it made sense to try to figure out what really happened. Who else would have motive? Who else that was close to Doris might have been capable of this? Or was it possible that the crime was completely random? Among my potential theories of the murder I noted down were these:

1. Perhaps Rosita and Danglas had gone to rob Doris's shop, and things had gone badly. Maybe Doris had come in and surprised them. They must have fought, during which time they had raped her. At the end of the violent struggle, Doris was dead.

2. Doris had begun seeing Armando Llanes but hadn't made it public yet. Maybe something had triggered Llanes's jealousy, and he had hired Danglas and Rosita to scare or hurt her or to kill her and then to frame me for it. The obvious hole in this theory was that they had implicated Llanes. It occurred to me that maybe Llanes had failed to pay them and that dropping his name was their revenge. Or, more simply, Llanes could have participated with them in the crime.

3. Somebody was acting out of hatred toward Century 21, where I worked. There were certainly listing agents I knew who felt either ripped off or power played in real-estate deals, and there must have been more I didn't know about. Maybe one of them had hatched a plan that would scapegoat me and hired Rosita and Danglas to carry it out. This particular theory fell apart for a number of reasons. First, if you were devious enough to hire someone to commit a major crime as part of what was a pretty complex conspiracy, you were certainly smart enough to

hire people who had more competence than these two losers. Second, it would have been an amazingly roundabout way to get at Century 21. You could have gone after the boss of the company or paid someone off in the government to cause problems for the company or to revoke necessary licenses and papers. You could have simply burned their offices or other properties to the ground. Any of those would have been easier, safer, and more direct and effective.

4. Somebody was out to get Doris for reasons far beyond my knowledge. I had been in touch with Doris right up to the day before her death, even though we had stopped dating six months before, and I no longer knew every detail of her life the way I once did. Although I knew her well enough to conclude it was unlikely she would have been involved with anyone or anything that could have led to her being killed, at the time I really had no way of knowing for sure.

In addition to my list of theories, I filled my notes with questions about what I knew. Why was Rosita so furious with Danglas? Why did I get the feeling that Danglas was calm, as if he knew he was going to get out soon once he had fulfilled his orders? Why had Danglas been released in the first place? The police had been quoted in the press saying that he had confessed that he was in the store and that "things had gotten out of hand." What was symbolic here? Why would he and Rosita have named me, specifically, unless someone was paying them or instructing them to do so? How was it that nobody saw the killers come out of the shop, given that it was smack in the heart of San Juan's central market district in the middle of the day? If you were in prison for rape and murder for hire, why would you still be scared of the person who hired you? Why had the police declined to investigate crucial evidence, such as the source of the threatening e-mails or the whereabouts of Doris's cell phone? Armando Llanes had been formally charged, so why hadn't he been arrested? Why was I the first person arrested? Where are the pictures of my back and shoulders that Sandra took? What did the police say that upset Doris's family so much? Why was Arelis the first person to call me? It would seem that it was not a premeditated murder. If it had been planned, the murderer would surely have waited to grab Doris somewhere else or would have lured her to a beach or something rather than commit the act in broad daylight in the middle of town.

Each new question that came to me gave rise to a dozen more that would take me off into a whole different direction, until my mind was cluttered with conflicting thoughts racing back and forth. The more questions and little mysteries I thought of reminded me of how many answers I still had to uncover. The whole process made me wonder, again and again, how it was that I was in jail.

I suppose the good news was, now that we had gotten past the first hearing, the defense effort was starting to take definite shape, and there were people ready and willing to do something with the information I had been gathering and the questions I'd been formulating. I was allowed short fifteen-minute visits with my attorneys, Ramon Rojas and Fabbrith Gomez, and now was in closer touch with my family. My father told me that he was bringing in a powerful law firm based in Washington, DC, which was supposed to sound promising and hopeful but actually caused me a lot of anxiety. Not only did I worry that a U.S. firm probably had no useful experience in the regional courts of Nicaragua, but I knew how easily a move like that could backfire. In places like Rivas and San Juan del Sur, people invariably resented big self-important Americans trying to push them around and usually managed to make things even harder for such outsiders.

At the same time, I was learning how to get by in jail. Sandra was able to get some food to me sometimes, as long as she also brought food for the guard, Freddy, who was bringing me my meals. Sometimes, I'd find little notes from friends hidden in the food that Sandra brought. Freddy, a skinny young guy, became a fairly dependable asset within the jail. While most of the other guards and policemen either treated me like a faceless criminal or like some kind of exotic creature, Freddy saw me as a real person, and for that I was grateful. The personal risks Freddy took just by helping me out convinced me that he was pretty ballsy, too. Sandra would also bring cell-phone calling cards for Freddy, who would in turn let me use his phone to make quick calls while he stood by.

Among the other notable outsiders who visited me in the Rivas jail just after that first hearing were representatives of the U.S. government. First was one of the U.S. consular officials to Nicaragua, Dan Bazan. You might expect that this first contact with my own government would have been a huge relief for me, but in fact it proved to be traumatic. Whether it was a reflection of job burnout or of the insignificance of my situation to the U.S. consulate, Bazan made me feel like sitting with me in the Rivas jail was the last place he wanted to be. He quickly made it clear that if I thought the U.S. government was going to ride in and rescue me, I could forget about it. Bazan, who was at the tail end of a long career as a "Statie," wearily explained that his people were only there to "observe and monitor," not to "interfere," as if he had spent his whole career explaining the same thing to Americans who nearly always deserved whatever trouble they were in. He was my diplomatic link to the outside world, and he forgot to bring the one thing I could have used: a list of attorneys the consulate considered qualified. Fortunately, Sandra had come through on that for me.

After Bazan, I got a visit from the regional security officer, Mike Poehlitz, who initially wasn't any better. His major contribution in that first visit was to tell me that if I had anything to say to the police, I'd better say it, because, as he said, "You're in a lot of trouble." Clearly, Poehlitz was operating under the assumption that I was most likely guilty. He didn't even really want to take the time to listen to my entire side of the story.

On Wednesday, November 29, all the accused defendants (with the exception of Armando Llanes) were taken to have samples of blood, saliva, and pubic and head hair taken at the medical examiner's office in Rivas. Fabbrith was furious because I was the only one that the police handcuffed. I was extremely skeptical of the process and how easy it would be for these guys to tamper with the samples. (I remembered that, in order to establish my Nicaraguan residency status earlier that year, I had to take a legal medical exam just down the street from where I was now. I was busy with work back then so I arranged for the exam to take place without me. I paid $20 and my assistant called me when it was time to come over and sign the papers.)

The following day, I was visited by a prosecutor, who finally decided to come interview me in jail but only asked me some meaningless questions. Did I have a wife and child nearby? Of course not. Did I drink? Very rarely. Who could have been out to hurt me? How much money did I make? She didn't ask one question about my alibi. I started to tell her about it, but she stopped me and got up to leave. On her way out she said, "You seem so desperate."

The entire interview lasted maybe five minutes. It is clear to me now that the sole purpose of the interview was to have it on record that she had questioned me. The prosecutor avoided any discussion of my alibi. By then I couldn't help but suspect she had already received orders on how she was to proceed. After she left, Ramon Rojas came in and told me that she had just offered a deal to Danglas for his freedom in exchange for his testiminony against me. I asked him how he got that info.

"Everyone trusts me," he said with a wink. He also told me that she had offered the same deal to Rosita but that he had refused because "his conscience wouldn't allow it." I thought he detested me; I was confused.

In the long hours between these very infrequent visits, I spent a huge amount of time curled up on my mattress, moving in and out of sleep. I think a lot of time and the combination of hunger, nervous exhaustion, anxiety, and physical pain all but immobilized me so that even when I was awake, I was lost in my own thoughts, as if I had entered a kind of waking dream state. When I could get up the energy, I would do what I could to keep my body strong—long sets of push-ups and sit-ups, even some tai chi movements I had learned in college. The rush of physical activity would make me feel better, but never for very long. There were several small earthquakes that shook the jail that week, and it got me thinking. Often, I lay awake, staring at the two thin bars across the window of my cell, imagining my escape. In the dark, when the rest of the prisoners were supposedly asleep, I'd creep to the window and test the bars or even see if any part of my body could squeeze through them. My escape fantasies almost became an obsession, until I reluctantly accepted the fact that they were indeed only fantasies and that even if I were able to escape, at that point it would only have made things worse for me.

While I sat by myself in the Rivas jail, things were happening on the outside. At home in the United States, my father was moving ahead with the law firm in Washington, Greenberg Traurig (or GT). He was able to come down to Rivas with one of their lawyers, Jackie Becerra, a young Cuban-American woman who spoke Spanish, and a private investigator, an Englishman named Simon Strong. Jackie met with the people at the consulate, with Ramon Rojas, and with others, but, most important, was allowed to visit me one time. I didn't know anything about her then, and I had my reservations about hiring a powerful American law firm, but to have an attorney from back home sitting with me in jail, telling me about the all-star team of Latin American "specialists" they had on board, about all the contacts they had, about her plans, about all the angles she was working, brought a flood of relief. Even if some of her partners' plans had made no sense, the idea that we were finally taking some action, any action, instead of sitting around and waiting for fate to run its course gave me my first glimmer of hope. It seemed possible that once they assembled all the evidence in my favor and presented it to the press and to the court, they could still make this whole thing go away.

Even though the situation seemed more hopeful, I still told my father that investing in GT was a bad idea. Worse still, the investigator they had brought with them had left a rotten taste in my mouth. The first thing Simon Strong asked me was whether or not I was carrying on an affair with Agnielly. Somehow, he had concocted a theory that Agnielly had orchestrated Doris's murder out of jealousy. He had an alternative theory as well, that Doris was in fact working as a prostitute and her death had occurred during the making of some kind of S&M porno video. I knew instantly and instinctively how insane both these theories were, and the thought of this bald, pasty-faced, British gringo bullying his way around Nicaragua spouting his embarrassingly awful Spanish filled me with dread.

The real unknown quantity in all of this was my dad, Jan. I had always lived with my mother, and although my dad and I had grown close in recent years, he really wasn't in the picture on a day-to-day basis. Nonetheless, Jan had assumed the role of point person for my family at the outset, but in truth, as much as he loved me and meant well, he was out of his element. Dad had been all over the world but had never become a part of it. Whatever he'd seen of the world had mostly been from the inside of big hotels and tour buses. He wasn't the kind of man who liked to explore other places from the inside, to get to know people or try to absorb other cultures. He hadn't really made close friends from other countries, nor had he ever learned another language. He approached Nicaragua as some kind of broken alien place where nothing worked right. That inability to confront the reality on the ground in Nicaragua, rather than constantly fight it, was unlikely to do me any good. His animosity had shown in court at the second hearing, when he blustered around the courthouse ranting about how backward and incompetent everybody was without stopping to think about who—like the prosecution and the judge—might be hearing him.

For the time being, a team was in place, working to get me free, but there was something shaky about each piece. My father was a sort of a loose cannon, and I felt like I might have to spend more time keeping him out of trouble than vice versa. Jackie and her law firm were big guns to be sure, and as a Cuban she was able to grasp the situaion pretty quickly, but the rest of her colleagues were outsiders and likely to underestimate the system and get taken advantage of by local contacts. And as for Ramon Rojas, I didn't trust him at all. He had already started giving me a hard time about even the most trivial requests I might make, continually asking for more cash, from constant requests for "spending money" to additional chunks of salary above and beyond his retainer.

Even the best team of lawyers and advocates, in the end, could only address the legal piece of the story. I was about to get a graphic reminder that the legal case was only one small part of my problem. The Nica press was still out for my blood and had most of the population on its side by now. And there was still Doris's mother, Mercedes, on a crusade of her own.

5.

A Second Murder Attempted

After two weeks in the holding cells of the Rivas police, I was filthy and sore, and my nerves were shot. All day long, I could hear the sounds of the town coming in through the windows. One of those sounds will haunt me for a long time: the explosion of mortar shells. In late November and early December, Nicaraguans honor the Virgin Mary, their patron saint, with a festival called La Purisima. It's a happy time, almost like a carnival, with parties and celebrations. Families spill out of their homes singing and dancing and parading through the streets of every town. In Rivas, there's always a big procession, led by a float—an elaborately decorated old truck bearing a statue of Mary and blaring cracked and distorted music through old loudspeakers. The celebration always involves gunpowder, various fireworks, and firecrackers. The two weeks in jail had already nearly broken me. It wasn't just the isolation or confinement or the constant anxiety of not knowing what to expect from one day to the next. There was the endless noise from the madmen in the surrounding cells, the stench of my own waste, the deep pain in my back and limbs, and absolute physical and emotional exhaustion. And now there were bombs going off in the street just outside. With my nerves so raw and frayed, each blast sent a jolt through my aching bones and rocked me back into hyperalertness.

Prison is only partly about the locks and the bars. The other part of it is the loss of control. Jailers like to play on this, finding a thousand little ways to keep you off balance, like moving you to different cells, waking you at strange hours, or throwing you in with dangerous cell mates. Sometimes, circumstances on the outside control your fate. I was told to expect a second hearing, but I never knew when it was going to happen. Several times they told me to get ready, only to have the hearing delayed for another two, three, five days, with no explanation. On this day, the guards came in to wake me at about 6:00 A.M., but I had been awake for hours already. Since my arrest, I had been swinging back and forth between physical extremes, having to control huge surges of adrenaline one moment, then shutting down completely and escaping into long hours of deep, protective sleep.

The guards told me to get dressed and prepare for the hearing, then left me alone for an hour or two to contemplate what might happen next. I had some vague notion that this would be the day of my vindication, that the court would listen to my side of things, realize their terrible mistake, and set me free. More important, though, I kept thinking that once they saw that I wasn't their culprit, they would get serious about finding Doris's killers.

In the week between the first and the second hearings, the mood of the country had changed radically, thanks to the efforts of Mercedes and the rabid tabloid press. The police in Rivas knew this all too well. They read the papers, too, and heard the news on radio and TV. And they knew about the cars rolling through San Juan and Rivas, blaring propaganda through their loudspeakers, urging people to come to the courthouse and "bring justice to the gringo," and that others had even arranged for buses to ferry people from San Juan del Sur to Rivas on the day of the hearing.* The police knew it wasn't safe for me. The American embassy knew it, too, letting it be known that they were keeping an eye on the situation. The one helpful thing Dan Bazan had accomplished was to extract a promise from the Rivas police that I would not be taken on foot from the jail to the courthouse, only two and a half blocks away. When they finally came to put the handcuffs on me and take me to the hearing, I must have looked just like everybody's image of a common criminal. I hadn't been

---

* In fact, the hearing had been scheduled for the previous day but postponed at the prosecution's request. Unaware of the postponement, approximately three hundred residents of San Juan del Sur came to Rivas for the hearing and waited for Eric in front of the courthouse.

able to shave or wash my hair in two weeks, and I had on a pair of over-sized jeans that someone had brought me. If you had looked in my eyes you would have seen a frightening mixture of fear, exhaustion, and disorientation.

We got outside and there was no car waiting. So much for the police's promise. I'm not sure why they were deliberately putting me in potential danger. They had to have known what was waiting for us a couple blocks away. I guess it's just that these local cops saw themselves as tough and couldn't imagine anything happening that they couldn't handle. They also wanted to let me know, again, that they were in charge, that they held my fate and my safety in their hands. A few police officers surrounded me and Rosita and proceeded to march us right down the middle of the street toward the courthouse. I think the police liked keeping me next to Rosita whenever we were in public, as if they wanted to make sure everyone who saw us together would link me in their mind with the known bad guy.

It was as if everything in town just stopped at that moment and everybody turned their attention to us. There were already people waiting along the street, and the shouts of "¡Asesino!" and "¡Que te pudras en el infierno!" (*I hope you rot in hell!*) rang in my ears. At first, the crowd parted for our police escort, but, as we got to the next block, it attacked. About fifty people were waiting on the corner and swarmed over us, yelling and swinging sticks and clubs. The police fought back hard with nightsticks and with their fists, but whatever order or plan there might have been in their escort immediately fell apart. In no time at all, it turned into an ugly brawl, complete chaos. I remember one angry face in particular out of that frenzied mob. The last time I had seen that face had been at Doris's *vela*, where we had hugged and comforted each other. It was the face of Doris's uncle, and it had now become full of hate and violence, and was urging the crowd on, leading the attack.

Suddenly, one of the cops grabbed me and told me to run on ahead. I had no idea where we were going, but I did as he said. The fear must have overcome the soreness and fatigue of two weeks in a jail cell. My legs started churning and I shot out of the crowd, who chased after me, yelling and shouting while still battling the police. I ducked into a little stationery shop but immediately realized it was a dead end. If the mob caught up to me there, I would have been done for. I ran outside again, and was about to try the next shop, when, amazingly, I saw someone I knew waving at me frantically from the door of the courthouse, just a little farther down the street. I made it to the door, and he pulled me inside and took me upstairs where I burst, panting and panicked, into the very courtroom where my hearing was to take place.

There was another hearing in progress just then, so I had a little time to collect myself. I knew I had to put the chase from the police station out of my mind. I had escaped one near disaster, and the most important part of the day hadn't even begun. Soon enough, my attorneys Ramon Rojas and Fabbrith Gomez arrived and my hearing was set to start. There was one more key player in the courtroom that day: a skinny but handsome young guy with kinky black hair and light skin, Armando Llanes, whose name the police had thrown in my face when they interviewed me after the murder. Armando seemed vaguely familiar to me, and later a witness statement helped me recall an evening when Doris and a friend had asked me to pick them up from a movie in Managua. I had seen them saying good-bye to some guy in the distance before they came over to the car. Now I saw that the guy was Armando Llanes. I got my first good look at him in court that morning. It would also be my last.

People crowded into every corner of the courthouse. Doris's family and the families of all the accused except Llanes had to fight for seats with people who were there just for the spectacle. My father was there, along with Jackie from GT, but the Rivas police and court officials inexplicably banned the legal attaché from the U.S. Embassy from the hearing. Looking back on it now, I realize that the way they had us all arranged in the courtroom told us everything we needed to know about the hidden agenda. Armando Llanes and I were instructed to sit at the main defense table, separated by our attorneys. Rosita and Danglas and their lawyers were off to the side, on folding chairs against the wall. There was no doubt who the main attractions were. Facing us from the prosecution table were the district attorney, Doris's mother, and the private prosecuting attorney she had hired.

It's important to note that Llanes wasn't in custody at this point, although the rest of us were in jail. We had both been charged, and at the first hearing the judge had angrily insisted that the police execute the arrest warrant and bring Llanes in. In other words, our status under the law was equal, yet Llanes walked into the courtroom as a free man. He could not have shown up for the hearing had lines of communication not been open between the secretary of the court and Llanes's family or attorney. In fact, with an outstanding warrant for his arrest, the police could have and should have arrested him the moment he appeared at the courthouse. But there he was, sitting next to me, and apparently his father was outside. Still, Armando was visibly nervous. He was very quiet but jittery and wouldn't make eye contact with me or even look in my direction. I had thought long and hard about the key questions that needed answering at this hearing. Many of these questions were for Armando himself, and I took advantage of the fact that he was seated close to get some answers just before the hearing started.

I leaned close to my attorney and said, "Ask Llanes how he met Doris."

He turned and asked Llanes's lawyer, who himself turned and asked Llanes. The answer came back to me in the same way. Llanes said he had met Doris the year before at Semana Santa, the holy week festival before Easter.

I sent another question down the line. "When was the last time he saw Doris?"

"Why don't you just ask him yourself?" my lawyer said, and leaned forward out of the way, so I could speak to Llanes's lawyer.

"When was the last time your client saw Doris?" I asked.

"The same week he met her on spring break," the answer came back. This I knew to be a lie, based on information I had gotten from others.*

---

* Witness testimony at the trial would later confirm that he had seen her after spring break.

"When was the last time he spoke to her?" I asked.

"The Sunday before the murder," the answer came back. "And she was crying on the phone."

"Why was she crying?" I asked.

"I don't know."

Then Llanes sent a message back through his attorney to me. He said that he didn't know she had a boyfriend. And he wanted me to know that he had never had sexual relations with her.

The first order of business in the hearing was to deal with Armando Llanes. His attorney offered into evidence a single document,[EX.11] the statement of an individual claiming that Llanes was on campus at a college in Nicaragua on the day of the murder, signing up for the next semester's courses. Much later, I discovered that the woman who offered this statement was someone I knew. She told me how Llanes's father and a private investigator had come to her and urged her to make out the declaration. Llanes had, in fact, been on campus that day, but all she could confirm was that she had seen him only until about noon. That would have left him plenty of time to make the forty-five-minute drive to San Juan del Sur before the time of the murder. Nonetheless, on this statement, as weak as it was, the judge, Peter Palma, absolved Armando, acting on the prosecution's request to drop charges against him since they claimed there was no evidence tying him to the murder. After only five minutes in court, he stood and walked out the door the same free man he had been when he walked in. I don't know where Armando is today, but I heard that the judge received $3,000—to ensure Llanes's freedom.

The prosecutor next turned to the matter of Nelson Danglas and announced that Danglas, too, would be freed but in a highly irregular motion requested that he be accepted as a witness for the prosecution. Danglas was to testify specifically that he saw me at the scene of the crime. The release of Llanes and Danglas had legal significance. Both of them were implicated in the crime. The case file contained a statement from Julio Chamorro—Rosita—declaring that he and Danglas were present when Doris died and that they both witnessed me and Armando Llanes together rape and murder her. By absolving both Danglas and Llanes, the judge and prosecutor essentially nullified Rosita's statement. If they were to accept the statement as true, there is no way they could release those two. And yet, as we would learn, they considered the statement absolutely valid as it pertained to me but not relevant as it pertained to Llanes. They would use it against me throughout the legal process. This was only one of many instances of the very casual attitude toward evidence and other rules of legal procedure in my experience of the Nicaraguan judicial system.

Next, the court turned its attention to me and Rosita. My lawyer launched into a detailed explanation of my alibi, showing that overwhelming evidence existed that proved I could not have committed the murder because I was in Managua at the time. He asked the court how Armando Llanes could go free on the basis of one letter from a witness, and I, who had a stack of sworn statements, cell-phone records, rental-car records, and so on, showing my innocence, still sat in jail. Our defense effort was pointless, since these pleas fell on deaf ears. Judge Palma pretended to listen then immediately declared that both Rosita and I would stand trial for Doris's murder. I don't believe that my attorney, Rojas, expected anything different. He knew what was coming, and, what's more, he didn't seem to mind. A trial for me would mean more fees for him. He probably would have been happy for the case to continue all the way to the Supreme Court.*

I was devastated. I had started the day believing it might have been the last day of this ordeal. And then I had been chased through the streets, delivered into the hands of the mob by the Rivas police. And now this: months more in jail, at the very least, and everything I had worked so hard to develop—my career, my magazine, my friends, my entire life—all in jeopardy. I didn't know then that just making it through the day would be a near miracle.

The judge kept us in the courtroom for at least another hour, to make sure all the paperwork was in order. At one point, I asked to use a bathroom and was taken to one that had a window facing the street. Looking

---

* At the time of this writing, my case had reached the Nicaraguan Supreme Court.

out, I saw that the crowd in the street had grown since the morning (five buses were shuttling people from San Juan del Sur, and later crowd estimates put the number at well over three hundred), and even from that little window I could sense the tension in the air. Worse, I was close enough to see faces in the crowd and was stunned by how many of them I recognized. I saw many people from San Juan del Sur, people I knew and had been friendly with, to whom I'd given surfboards or who I'd helped get started in business or who had been volunteers at our magazine and so on. Yet none of these people had come to support me or to rally on my behalf. I could see that, like everyone else in that mob, they were seething with anger. They were there to see that justice was done, then and there, by whatever means necessary. I shrank back from the window, confused and very scared.

The scene back inside the courtroom had also grown more chaotic. The police insisted on staying inside, finally realizing that the crowd might be too much for them to handle. Then something even more bizarre happened. Rojas was over in the corner talking to Mercedes and called me over to her. I approached and she embraced and gave me a hug and said, "I know it wasn't you two" (referring to Rosita and myself). She also told me the prosecution knew who the true killers were. This gave me a huge relief but in retrospect was deeply troubling.

Mike Poehlitz, the regional security officer, had stayed behind, vowing not to leave until he knew I was safely back at the police station. "Don't worry, Eric," Poehlitz reassured me. "I have some guys down there." He didn't have anybody down there but wanted to make me feel better. He was probably reassuring himself as well. The crowd was getting bigger and louder, and I could tell he was nervous. I could hear the yelling from outside.

"¡Que saquen el gringo!"

"¡Aquí se va hacer justicia!"

The most terrifying were the voices of women, inflamed with fire and totally cold-blooded at the same time, egging the crowd on. Women—mothers—are central figures in Latin American culture, wielding unique power and emotional influence.

Inside, Judge Palma packed up and left. The courthouse staff wanted to close up and go home, too, since several hours had passed since the hearing ended and it was now late in the afternoon, but the police refused. The street simply was not safe. Mike Poehlitz urged the police to request additional officers to control the crowd.

Eventually, the cops decided we had no choice but to try to leave. The courthouse was surrounded, but nonetheless the police believed they could send a decoy group out the front door that would buy enough time to allow me to escape out the back door. Mike Poehlitz took of his suit jacket, shirt, and tie and gave them to me. I gave him my T-shirt and baseball cap, and we each dressed as the other, but the mob wasn't fooled in the least. The minute we left the courtroom and started down the stairs, the entire crowd fell silent, waiting to see where we would emerge. Darkness had fallen, and they could see us through the windows of the building. The moment the crowd outside saw a group heading for the front door, they ran to surround the back door.

At that moment, Agnielly, who was waiting outside for the decoy group, phoned in a panic on her cell phone to tell us not to leave the building because a man with revolver was waiting at the back door. Mike didn't need to hear anything more. He turned on the police captain, again shouting at him to call for reinforcements and refusing to step outside the building. Poehlitz was agitated, pacing nervously, as was the captain. Not knowing what else to do, he tried to organize the group, assigning one officer to be my lead man, the man whose shirt I was to grab onto and never let go of. He was to be my lifeline if security fell apart.

Then, suddenly, with no further discussion, the captain announced that the time had come; we were leaving. Just like that. Cops grabbed me by both arms and headed for the front door, now that the mob had surrounded the back door. From the door, I could see a pickup truck backed up to the corner, waiting for us. Armed police waited inside the truck, and an officer with a shotgun sat in the back. A strip of sidewalk with an iron railing stretched the short distance between the door and the truck. Straight out the front door, and much closer than the truck I was being taken to, another car waited. Rosita jumped into that car, which sped immediately away. The crowd seemed to move like a single being and in an instant was descending on the front of the building where the truck sat. Rocks came flying at the truck, at the police, at me. I didn't know whether to try to get inside the truck or simply dive into the back. I shouted, "What do I do?! What do I do?!" until one of the cops motioned for me to get in back.

I reached the truck, and, at the very instant that I laid my hand on the back of the truck bed to steady myself and leap inside, the driver gunned the engine and the truck shot out into the street, leaving me stranded. I don't know if the police planned things that way or if the driver's terror of the crowd got the better of him or if it was just horrible timing or some unimaginable mistake. All I knew was that in a heartbeat that truck was gone, and I was standing defenseless in the street.

The mob was closing in from all sides now, shouting and banging sticks or whatever they were carrying. Someone tugged at my sleeve. I turned and was face-to-face with the police captain. His men had screwed up in just about every possible way, but he was there now to protect me. He shouted, simply, "Run!"

I don't quite know how to describe the next moments. I remember it almost like a hallucination. Everything went dead silent. I was running as fast as I had ever run, yet all around me it seemed like time was standing still. I want to say that it felt as if God was moving my muscles, propelling my body forward. I know that one moment the crowd was closing in on us from all directions and rocks were whizzing by my head, and the next moment we had broken through. We had burst through to the other side of the swarm of bodies and had gotten through untouched. I have no idea how it happened. With no shoelaces, I could barely keep my shoes on my feet, and, though still in handcuffs, I had to hold up my oversized pants, but still somehow I had run through and past the murderous mob, leaving even the captain far behind.

We raced down the main street and came quickly to a doorway, really just an opening in a wall covered by an iron gate. Seeing a light inside, I ran through the door and found my way into a small office. The captain ran in right behind, pushed the door of the office shut, and shoved a desk up against it as a barricade. Outside, the police had gathered by the entrance, and again the mob rushed them as the police fought. Defending the tiny doorway proved slightly more manageable than the free-for-all in the street earlier, and the police held the mob back for a few minutes. Mike Poehlitz was out there, fighting in the riot.

Scanning the office, I found some *macate* string to tie up my shoes, a long cloth tape measure, and a fork, of all things, which I used to cut the tape measure and fashion it into a belt for my pants. I also spotted a small flag-pole that I picked up, thinking I might need it as a weapon. I kept digging through the office, emptying the drawers and cabinets, looking for anything useful—a cell phone, a gun, anything. For all I knew, I could be holed up in that office for a long time, or it could have been my last chance to supply myself before whatever came next. Once I'd turned the office completely inside out, I just crawled behind a filing cabinet and hid.

We sat there for perhaps five minutes, listening to the madness outside before the captain opened the door and went outside. A moment later, Mike Poehlitz came in and took his place. He locked the door and barricaded it again, got out his cell phone, and started calling whomever he could. I don't know who he was talking to, but I heard him yelling about the emergency we were in, about our lives being in danger. At one point he said, "These people are out for blood." The situation had gotten so extreme that at one point he had ordered someone on the other end of the line to get through to the president of Nicaragua.

Between his frenzied phone calls, he and I worked on my handcuffs, wetting my wrist with saliva and trying to slide the cuffs off. We eventually managed to slip one cuff over my hand, taking off a good bit of skin with it. I fastened the loose cuff over my other arm to get it out of the way and used my freed hands to start testing the walls. One wall seemed to be little more than a thin sheet of plywood, and I was able to kick right through it. The first thing I saw on the other side was the police. The wall opened into a large gymnasium full of exercise equipment, and some police had gathered there. Once through the wall, I grabbed a metal pole as a weapon. The police didn't even flinch at my being uncuffed and armed.

I spent the next hour in that gymnasium, making sure not to stay in any one spot very long. People seemed to be leaking through into various areas just outside of where we were hiding, finding ways to peek inside, hoping to spot me. It was far from secure, but the police could at least hold some ground there. As we huddled there, Mike kept up his efforts, barking into his phone and into the faces of the police on the scene. I can't say if something had made Mike change his mind about me, but now he was making it clear that we were in this together. He told the cops they'd have to arrest him, too, before he let them try to move me again.

Of course, that didn't stop the police from doing what they were going to do. The captain who had helped me just moments earlier had been replaced by someone higher up—Emigdio Reyes—and on his order, officers suddenly seized hold of me again, dragged me outside, and pushed me into the backseat of another pickup truck. Right away the truck took off at high speed, despite the rioters swarming all over it. I heard and felt the impact of bodies against the truck as we sped away. One man even threw himself into the back of the truck as we passed, only to get taken straight to jail.

The driver raced wildly through the streets, getting us farther than we should have been from the police station, and I could hear the other cops telling him to get there quickly because surely the mob was heading there as well. As we approached the police station, we saw that the crowd had indeed gathered and was fighting with police outside the open gate, but we were able to drive straight though to the inner courtyard. I wasn't safe, by any means, but the immediate danger was over. I never imagined that I could be so happy to be back in jail. Rosita had been there for nearly an hour already, and now there was also this man who had jumped into the truck. I had never seen this guy in my life, and yet his hatred of me, fueled by the news reports and the agitators in the streets, was beyond description. He tried to attack me again, right there in the entryway of the jail, and got roughed up by the cops as a result.

As Mike traded clothes again with me, he surveyed the situation in the jail. He saw immediately that the cell where they were holding me had a window that faced the public street. That's when he snapped, screaming at the captain of police about their incompetence that had almost got us killed. Mike was rightfully venting, letting go of all the stress and anger of the day, but at least I knew he was totally in my camp now and wasn't going to rest until he saw that I was treated properly.

I was a wreck, hysterically laughing and crying at the same time, finally losing control. Adrenaline was racing through my body like it never had before. It wasn't just that I'd survived a near-death experience. It was a near-death experience that had lasted for hours and hours. The body undergoes massive changes in times of high stress to prepare it to face danger, but it isn't designed to stay in that heightened state for so long. I think I was experiencing the comedown, the release from that stress just then, and it was like every circuit in my body had overloaded.

The worst part was that I knew I couldn't really stop to catch my breath. Even with my senses and my emotions running wild, I had to force myself to think clearly about what might happen next. I knew that they would probably move me soon to another prison and that, when that time came, I'd get no warning. I had to get back to work. I carefully went through what few things I had and stowed some essentials into a pillowcase. I separated out the books I was reading from those I had finished and made sure I had all the important papers, such as letters from my attorneys, close at hand. As it turned out, this is how I would live for the next year.

Then the police captain, Valerio, came in. He was the one that pulled on my sleeve and said "run." He was also the official that took the initiative to look into my alibi. I could see he was just as shaken as I was. He said, "That was a close call, eh, kid? Those sons of bitches almost got us." I wondered if he'd ever been through anything like that day, and by his nervous laugh between sentences, I figured he probably hadn't. As for

Mike Poehlitz, he left my cell saying he'd be right back but never returned.

My gut sense that things would change quickly turned out to be right. Word filtered down that they planned to move me to Managua later that night. Sure enough, at four o'clock in the morning, they came for me. I was able to grab the things I had stashed away earlier, and we headed out of the jail and out of Rivas, toward Managua. Our destination was the dreaded prison called Chipote. It had been used as a torture prison for decades—by both the Somoza regime and the Sandinistas—and every Nicaraguan feared the place. My experience over the next seven days proved those fears to be very well founded.

One of my last memories of the Rivas jail is the comment of the young policeman, Freddy. Just before the guards took me out of the jail, Freddy snuck into the back hallway where my cell was. He wasn't supposed to be speaking to me, but he didn't care, not after what had happened with the lynch mob. He had gotten beat up pretty badly trying to restore order, and I guess the fact he had been attacked by my enemies made him feel some sense of brotherhood. In that last stolen moment, he offered some words of solidarity.

"Eric, you must prepare yourself mentally for what is coming next."

6.

The Waiting Room to Hell

Technically, Chipote isn't a prison at all. It is the Auxilio Judicial headquarters, generally used for the same dirty tasks for which it had been built in the 1930s by the Somoza regime—chiefly, interrogation. It is a drab but chilling place, dug like a tunnel into the side of a hill outside Managua.

At first, I didn't quite understand why they had brought Rosita and me to this place, but I assumed it was because Rivas was no longer safe, at least not for me. Following the near lynching in the streets after my hearing, the police weren't sure they could protect me—or maybe themselves either—in the jailhouse and needed to get me the hell out of there. The first impression I had was that we were in some kind of underground office complex, one that hadn't been used for a long time. Reyes walked us into a large and dimly lit waiting room with crumbling plasterboard walls lit by broken and rusted light fixtures that had to have been part of the original construction. Shabby partitions along the walls broke the space up into a series of little compartments, each about the size of an old phone booth. Reyes placed Rosita and me in spaces on opposite sides of the room from each other. We saw no one else around.

A moment or two after we arrived, the door burst open again, and the dark mustached cop rushed in. For a man whose neat appearance had always seemed to reflect a cold-blooded discipline, he looked a mess, as if he had just leaped out of bed. His shirt was hanging over his belt and his hair looked like he had just licked his fingers and pasted it down. He ducked into a side office quickly, then stepped over to Rosita and began whispering into his face. I couldn't hear them, but something about the cop's body language and attitude told me that the man was reasserting his control over Rosita, either reinforcing some earlier threat or reminding him that his only hope was to do exactly as he was instructed. Mustache cop finished with Rosita and came over to me.

For a few seconds, he simply stood staring into my eyes and shaking his head. Then, with a look of pity on his face, he said, "It didn't have to be this way, you know. You should have cooperated with us. . . ." He seemed like he had more to say, but at that moment, another officer came in, and mustache cop turned and headed quickly for the door, as if he didn't want anyone to know he had been there.

The guard took away everything I had except a tank top, the boxers I was wearing, a toothbrush and toothpaste, a bar of soap, and a roll of toilet paper, then led me to a cell. Actually, *cell* is too good a word for it. We went through a door into a dark corridor puddled with water. It was like we were burrowing even deeper into the earth. We stopped in front of a heavy steel door marked number 12, but the corridor seemed to trail on forever into the blackness beyond. A box just outside the door held my shorts and a shirt, which I was to put on if and when a visitor came for me.

Veteran *reos* ("inmates") in other prisons later told me I was lucky to be thrown into number 12. It was one of the better cells in Chipote, but it was just a tiny, awful concrete box, about ten feet by eight feet with a ceiling so low I could touch it just standing on the floor. One dim light-bulb near the ceiling above the door lit only the upper parts of the walls, leaving the floor so black and mysterious I could only make things out if I stared down for several minutes, and then just barely. No natural light entered the box, but it was smoldering hot.* The heat was one of the worst parts. I never stopped sweating. A length of PVC pipe hung down from the ceiling, through which the guards would pump water once a day so I could shower and to flush out the hole in the middle of the floor into

---

* When deprived of sunlight for prolonged periods of time, the human body stops producing melatonin, which subsequently affects sleep habits.

which I had to relieve myself. There was no way for air to circulate in and out, so most of the day the box stank of shit and piss.

At first, with my wits still about me, I tried to be resourceful. I broke up the wooden planks of the bed enough to make it somewhat level. With one long splinter, I cleared the spiderwebs from the corners and scraped rat shit into the hole in the floor. Quickly, I discovered that rats were not the only creatures sharing the cell with me. Two large, black scorpions scuttled across the floor. I could also make out a large brown tarantula. Throughout my stay in Chipote, that tarantula would mysteriously disappear, only to reappear again later. That spider didn't find its way into my cell by accident. When I became a true convict, other inmates told me stories about the guards in Chipote letting coral snakes into some cells to keep prisoners in a constant state of waking terror.

Fear of what lurked on the dark floor kept me pinned to the bed. Not that the bed brought any comfort being so close to the low ceiling that I didn't even have room to sit up in it. I spent what seemed like endless days curled up on that bed, occasionally looking up through the small opening in the ceiling to see the face of a spooky white cat, of all things, staring down at me. Apparently, the guards would throw food scraps onto the roofs of the cells, deliberately hoping to attract the gangs of stray cats that hunted up there. The walls around me were smeared with shit, which prisoners before me used to scrawl messages: *Kill. Murder. God is love. I am the gun.*

Everything about the pressure box was designed to make a man go mad. There was no way to mark the passage of time, so I soon lost track of day and night. If I happened to fall asleep, I never knew how long I had been asleep. After a while I could no longer tell how long I'd even been there. The lack of food and water made me feel even more disoriented. It's not that there was no food—the guards did occasionally shove food through the little sliding panel in the door—but I would only eat it if it was in a sealed container. I had heard too many stories of prisoners eating poisoned food, allegedly delivered by "a friend." Slowly, I lapsed into a sort of dream state, hovering on the edge of consciousness, kept awake only by the constant torment of mosquitoes and flies and other insects that thrived in the festering dampness. Later, I would learn that the Chipote guards actually used hoses to fill the hallways with water, knowing that it created a breeding ground for pestilence.

I can't remember if I could think clearly enough while stuck in Chipote or if these conclusions dawned on me later, but there's no doubt that I had been put there with a very specific purpose. You don't randomly decide to hold someone over for trial in the most terrifying hellhole available. I had yet to be convicted of any crime, yet there I deteriorated in a box that couldn't even pass as a prison cell, enduring treatment that qualifies under any international guidelines as physical and psychological torture. Whether it was policemen or the prosecutors or some other unnamed political force, the people responsible for putting me in Chipote wanted me to understand something. Maybe they wanted this taste of my horrible future to make me beg for mercy, to cooperate, to confess, and to save everyone a lot of trouble. They just wanted to break me, and the longer I refused to break, the worse things would go for me.

There were other reasons perhaps more practical but no less evil. In a standard jailhouse, my attorneys and family would have had more access to me, but in Chipote, the police could effectively isolate me, cut me off from any meaningful communication. Additionally, after the Rivas police had lost control of the mob after my second hearing, they had caught major flack from their superiors in the central government.

I know that my time in Chipote, which turned out to be one week, represents the greatest challenge of endurance and concentration in my life. The heat in the box was suffocating, accelerating the process of dehydration. It was as close to hell as a man could come to on earth. As it was, I lost the ability to hold on to my sense of reality and fell into delirium. Strangely, the fantasy world I entered may actually have been what kept me sane.

In my mind, I wasn't in a filthy prison at all but had returned to my climbing days, convincing myself that the dark box of iron and concrete was in fact a small cave cut into a granite rock face. My food was gone, lost in the blizzard that had trapped me in the cave, but I knew I would survive somehow, just like so many other mountaineers before me had survived expeditions gone wrong. I think I got to the point where I actually began believing the fantasy. It couldn't have lasted long, I'm sure, but it got me through to the day when they came to take me away.*

On the morning of December 14, guards roused me and got me dressed and walked me outside into the blinding sun. The shock of it, after seven days of damp darkness, instantly made my head throb. It would take me half the day to even be able to open my eyes properly. They handcuffed me and put me into the back of a small covered pickup truck with Rosita and a lone armed guard. Rosita and I sat facing each other with our legs crossed Indian style in the cramped space, our feet and knees banging against each other. All I wanted to do was hurl myself at him and beat him to a pulp, not that I had the strength. Getting into a fight with Rosita would have been stupid for a million reasons, not least of which is that he might have whipped me. I pushed down my rage and focused on finding a way to turn these new circumstances to my advantage.

I had to get Rosita alone, not to hurt him but to probe him, to extract some information—*any* information—out of him, and amazingly I got the chance when we arrived at our next destination, the federal penitentiary at Granada. We were stuck in a holding cell alone together, just for a couple of minutes while the guards got things organized. I had rehearsed this moment a thousand times in my head and didn't waste a second. I walked straight up to Rosita and stared him in the eye.

"You get the goods?" I asked. I had sent some food and things to Rosita in Chipote, hoping to soften him a little, maybe make him think he had an ally in me.

"Yeah, brudda, *gracias, compadre*, thanks for the food." He clearly had been tensed for a confrontation, and I could see his body relax a little. "That was some fucked-up shit in Chipote, eh?"

---

* One of the few visitors I received at Chipote was Dan Bazan, the U.S. consul. I met with Bazan in the office part of the building, and he was never allowed to see the dungeons hidden deep under the hillside.

I dove right in. "Look, man, I haven't seen any hard evidence you are guilty yet, and I know that you claim to have nothing to do with this, so I'm gonna ask you. Where were you when Doris was murdered?"

"I was surfing that day at La Peña." Rosita went on to swear that he was with two buddies where a big reef created a good surfing break around a corner from the bay at San Juan del Sur. I knew instantly he was lying. The wave at La Peña only breaks in the summer when big swells come up from the south. It was nearly Christmas.

"Do you know who killed her? Was it Armando?" I didn't want to accuse Rosita directly and make him shut down, but I wanted to give him the chance to shift the blame to someone else.

"I don't know anything," he answered. "She was a good girl. The cops tortured me and punched me in the heart—like this, *boom boom*," as he pounded his fist against his chest.

"Don't lie to me, Julio." I didn't have time to let him change the subject. "I can help you get out," I bluffed. "I can protect you, but I need to know what happened. Tell me who did it and we can get out of here. Tell me about her relationship with Armando."

"Man, I'm telling you. I don't know anything. I don't know him."

That's all I was going to get out of Rosita. The guards pulled us out immediately, took us to have our heads shaved, and threw us in separate cells. I did learn one thing, though. Rosita had lied to me, which meant he had something to hide.

Granada kept its prisoners in big, dormitory-style cells, or *celdas*. In number 4, where they put me, more than fifty men had to make do with only thirty beds, only a few of which had sheets. Some *reos* slept on the floor, where there really wasn't any space for them. Others had strung makeshift hammocks from the window bars. You couldn't walk without sloshing through puddles of grimy water. The place felt like how I would imagine the cramped crew members' quarters on an old wooden slave ship.

The prison guards had assigned some inmates to act as *consejos* in each cell, unofficial leaders whose job was to keep the peace, although most just took it as an opportunity to lord their power over the other men in the cell. It turned out the head *consejo* in number 4 was someone from San Juan del Sur, and we figured out quickly that we knew people in common. I hoped that would help. I put my stuff down on his bed and went over to go to the bathroom, and that's exactly how much time it took for me to get in trouble. From the bathroom I watched some thuggish creep walk calmly over to my stuff, stick his hand in my pillowcase, and take some cookies I had in there. He knew I could see him. He wanted me to see him.

The scene unfolded as if it had been scripted. The guards knew someone was going to mess with me, the *consejos* knew, and the inmates only wondered who was going to start it. Everybody wanted to have some fun with the gringo, to test me. At the same time, I had no idea how long I might be in the cell and had no choice but to answer the challenge. I walked up to the kid and asked for the cookies back. He snickered a little with his friends and said he didn't take them.

This guy's body was covered in wounds and scars. One long slicing scar ran from his hip to his chest. I could see three ugly round scars with matching exit scars on his back—bullet wounds. If I made a move, there was a good chance I'd get hurt. If I did nothing, I'd surely suffer. Either way, I was damned. I rolled the dice and shoved the kid with both hands. The kid came back swinging, with a weird kind of happy smile on his face, and caught me with a punch on the side of my head. The cell erupted, with everybody shouting and egging us on, but the fight ended as quickly as it began. Before I could even get my balance, the *consejos* pulled me away toward the door, which one of the guards was already holding open, as if he knew I wouldn't last long enough for him to even lock the door.

I spent the night in Granada's medical wing, with the AIDS patients and the *drugos*, and the next morning found myself in the back of an open pickup truck, on the move again.

As usual, nobody said a word about where we were headed, but once we turned onto the highway toward Managua, I had a good guess, and, when we swung out past the airport there, I knew for sure: La Modelo, Nicaragua's maximum-security penitentiary.

If you've lived in Nicaragua for any amount of time, you've heard the name of La Modelo the way an American has heard of Sing Sing or Leavenworth or San Quentin. In the medical wing at Granada, some of the prisoners had described it to me. It was the nerve center of *el sistema*, since all information and intelligence eventually had to pass through La Modelo. The prison is a city unto itself, with its own internal "streets" and informal neighborhoods, and it's full of drugs and gangs and organized crime. It's also where the government houses anybody involved in political cases, which makes the warden a well-connected and important figure. Inside the walls, the warden also oversees the massive systemic corruption, deciding who gets away with what and who gets punished. The sprawling complex is situated behind high walls in a huge barren expanse outside the capital city. The main building looks like an enormous centipede, with a long, thick central body off of which shoot the individual *galerias*, or "cell blocks," like little legs.

From the moment of my arrest, everyone around me kept talking to me about how it would be over soon. *Sit tight, Eric, you'll be home in a day or two, tops. It'll all be over by Christmas, Eric, so hang in there. No way you'll still be in jail come New Year's, man.* It was already the middle of December when I was moved to La Modelo, and each one of those milestones came and went during the month that they held me there, laying open the pain in my heart each time. Deep down, I knew that my family and friends were wrong to feel so optimistic. I kept thinking that this thing was bigger than they knew, that the tentacles were longer and that my situation was more serious than anybody wanted to believe, but every time I said so out loud, somebody would always tell me to stop being paranoid and think positive.

So there I sat, in Nica's biggest and toughest prison. I had much to learn about life behind bars, but I knew enough to keep to myself as much as possible and rarely ventured beyond my cell except to get some exercise. One bright shining light broke through into my life during my time at La Modelo: My mother, Maggie, came for her first visit with me. She was spending a long week in Nica with her husband, Dane, and the warden had granted them open access to me while they were in the country. Still, we met for only a couple of hours each day, so as not to abuse the privilege. Neither of us had any clue then of the enormous role my mom would play in this story. For the moment, just having her there with me and being able to lose myself in her warm love was a gift from God. But there was more: after nearly two months surrounded by so many two-faced and devious characters, it meant the world to me to be able to talk openly to someone in whom I could put my unconditional faith and trust. We spent our time together talking through the case from every possible angle, figuring out action plans that would make sense. Somewhere in that week of discussions, our idea of incorporating the tools of the Internet into our defense strategy began to take shape.

In January 2007, the atmosphere in Nicaragua was thick with change. Daniel Ortega had won the presidential election in the fall, just two weeks before Doris's murder, and now the Sandinistas were preparing to reestablish their formal control over the country. On January 10, the day of Ortega's inauguration, the eyes of the world once again were focused on Nicaragua.

In La Modelo, the *reos* gathered around radios to listen to the ceremony. In my *galeria*, a kingpin drug dealer who had enough clout to have a TV in his cell dragged the big set out into the corridor where we could all see it. Everyone knew that Venezuela's Hugo Chávez and Evo Morales of Bolivia—both leftist agitators who were harsh and relentless critics of the United States—were slated to be guests of honor at the inaugural. Tension and anticipation filled the jail, with many of the prisoners solidly and vocally behind the new president. Sandinista banners hung from cell doors everywhere, and I could hear *reos* all over singing the old hymns from the revolution: "El Yanquí, Enemigo de la humanidad . . . nos han quitado el pan" (*The Yankee, enemy of humanity . . . have taken away our bread*). I don't think I ever felt my gringoness as strongly or as fearfully as

I did on that day. I wished I could have made myself invisible, but there was no place to hide. As I watched Daniel Ortega take his oath of office that day, all I could feel was my hole getting a lot deeper.

Amazingly, the inauguration wasn't the only memorable event of that day. Something happened in my little world, too. I had come into possession of a small digital camera with a video function. A visitor had brought me some food, including a freshly roasted chicken. I had stuck my hand into the cavity of the chicken and found the camera. The previous night, just before lockdown, I had snuck it out and snapped some quick shots[EX.12] of the *galerias* across the yard before stashing the camera in my cell. On the day of the inauguration, I took it out again to take pictures[EX.13] of my cell and to record a short video[EX.14] thank-you to all my friends and family working on my defense. The risks involved made doing this foolish enough, but I took it a step further. I showed the camera to one of the other *reos*.

I had met Jonathan (pronounced *jo-na-TAN*) at the pull-up bar at the end of the *galeria*. He approached me one day as I was doing chin-ups, and soon we had developed a kind of friendship. I could tell, just from the way that the other *reos* deferred to him, that Jonathan was a respected leader within the cell block. A good-looking twenty-five-year-old with a thick, muscular body covered in tattoos, Jonathan always dressed in slick, expensive-looking athletic gear, as if showing off his status as one of the prison boxing champs. He didn't have much formal education but was bright and articulate and socially skilled. It may be hard to understand, but most prisoners were wary of approaching me—a gringo with a high-profile case—but Jonathan had more than enough self-confidence for that. After a while, you would almost forget the crime that had landed him in La Modelo: He had stabbed his unfaithful girlfriend's lover ninety times with an icepick. Then, with the girlfriend's help, he had cut up the body and stuffed it into a car. Almost.* It seemed to me that Jonathan

---

* Jonathan's victim, I found out later, had been a psychotherapist who had at one time treated Daniel Ortega's stepdaughter in the wake of her alleged sexual abuse by Ortega, which had been a national scandal compared to Watergate. Jonathan told me he was sent to kill him by Ortega's political party. See online the exhibit[EX.15] for more details.

could be an important ally for me, but I had to find out if I could trust him, which I did by letting him in on the fact that I had the camera.

In the strange logic of prison, Jonathan, this genuine tough guy and convicted killer, thought I was a *monstro,* a "bad ass," for getting a camera in La Modelo. He excitedly took the camera from me, and we goofed around, taking snaps of each other. At one point, Jonathan held up the camera to take photos of some inmates in the *galeria* windows across the yard, and they saw the camera. I took the camera back and returned to my cell, breaking it apart into pieces small enough to dispose of safely. I saved the memory card and cut a tiny slit in the seam of my gym shorts so I could hide it.

Within minutes, guards showed up and searched Jonathan's cell. Clearly, we had been ratted out by the *reos* from across the yard. Jonathan actually covered for me, saying they must have seen him playing with the remote from his CD player. I managed to get the chip into the hands of one of the members of my team, but months later, someone from the U.S. Embassy made a comment about it. The only way word could have gotten to the embassy was through the warden of La Modelo, and the only person who could have told him was Jonathan. The guy was an informant after all, just like so many others. When I look back on it now, I realize what a stupidly naïve risk I had taken with the camera. I guess I still didn't understand how deep the shit was that I was in.

Less than a week later, on January 16, my lawyers were granted a special hearing,[EX.16] at which they moved that I be released to house arrest. The police had finally delivered the results of the biological tests taken, which showed absolutely no connection to me. In fact, although no fewer than 103 individual hairs had been collected at the scene, not one shred of physical evidence linked me to the crime. My attorneys argued that without any physical evidence, and in the light of cell-phone-triangulation records they presented demonstrating that my phone, on which I had been speaking at the time of the murder, could be traced through Managua cell antennas, there were no legal grounds for keeping me in jail. The judge, Peter Palma, agreed, but not without some insurance. Palma's collateral demands were harsh and highly unusual: $10,000 and my passport, just to start. In addition, someone I didn't even know, the aunt of one of my coworkers, put up the mortgage of her house as part of the bail. But he topped it off with the requirement of human collateral. Palma needed someone to put him or herself up. That is, someone needed to agree to take my place in prison if I were to flee the country. That someone was Agnielly. Thinking back on it now, I don't know which is more amazing— the outrageousness of Palma's demand or the depth of Agnielly's trust and sacrifice.*

Of course, nothing is ever exactly as it seems. The first startling fact about Palma's decision to release me is that the entire country of Nicaragua knew about it before I did. I heard about it when Palacios, the *reo* in the cell across from me, shouted out that he heard on the radio that the judge had approved an order to move me to house arrest. Palacios added that "some lady" was publicly protesting the decision. Mercedes. I understood there must have been a part of Mercedes that had been vulnerable to manipulation in her initial grief and pain, but, still, I could not comprehend how she could be so evil.

By noon, *El Nuevo Diario* had arrived with a front-page feature[EX.17] by Lesber Quintero. The headline screamed, "Judge Releases Gringo Who Murdered Girl in San Juan Del Sur." Not "judge releases suspect." *Gringo who murdered girl.* Worse yet, Quintero published crucial details of the order, including the location and the days on which I had to present myself twice each week as part of the deal. Only a month before, the crowd in the streets of Rivas had nearly killed me, and here for all to see were the details of where I could be found again. Since the paper clearly stated that the release order had been signed, I began to get myself ready. I gave away bits of food and clothing and bedding to Jonathan and my cell mate, Quiros, and some others. (Quiros unloaded everything in a matter of minutes, in exchange

---

* At the time of this writing, the Nicaraguan court had not released its claims on either Agnielly's liberty or the collateralized mortgage. I may be "free," but these good Nicaraguans still face legal complications because of my case. Passport and $10,000 have still not been released as well.

for cigarettes.) Within half an hour, the entire prison knew I was leaving, but still nobody had come to notify me officially. Something was not right. I didn't get out that day.

The next night, I was still in La Modelo, and what a scary night it turned out to be. The gang community inside the prison lives through cycles of truce and war. Things might stay calm for two or three months until something triggers a fight, and then suddenly *la violencia* rages for however many days it takes for the guards to clamp down again. On the night of the 17th, some screwup by the guards allowed *reos* from two rival blocks (members of the same street gang on the outside usually lived together in prison) to get too close to each other, and a riot broke out. The guards quickly lost control, and men from other *galerias* got involved, climbing over fences and roofs and charging into enemy territory. We were sure our *galeria*, which held a number of protected prisoners, would be attacked in the chaos. I ducked into Jonathan's cell, unsure whether that would offer any safety at all, and waited, convinced the rioters would come tearing through the thin sheets of the tin that formed the roof. It was perhaps the moment of greatest danger for me since coming to La Modelo, but for some reason we were passed over.

Close to three hundred prisoners were involved, many of them subjected to hideous beatings, but amazingly no one died. After order was restored, the guards removed each of the gang's leaders and beat them viciously, one at a time. They also stripped half the prison clean, searching every corner of every cell and confiscating hundreds of weapons. I watched as wheelbarrow after wheelbarrow full of rocks, shanks of metal, sharpened broom handles, and even sharpened tooth brushes rolled down the hallway.

No way I was getting out on that night. Matters hadn't even fully settled by the next morning. While in visitation with his mother a kid was stabbed fourteen times in retribution for something related to the riot. He died in her arms. The nervous tension throughout La Modelo was unbearable. Even Jonathan was scared. I sat for hours waiting in my cell, but in the afternoon the guards came for me. I remember sitting in a waiting area while they were processing me out and talking to a twenty-two-year-old kid who was being released at the same time. He was wearing practically nothing since there is a rule among prisoners from his gang that when you go free you are not allowed to leave with any belongings. Everything must stay with *el sistema*. As young as this guy was, he had spent enough time behind bars that the thought of living on the outside terrified him more than prison. He asked me questions about which bus to catch to get to the city, how to find work, food, whatever. The guy simply didn't know how to manage his life on his own. *El sistema* had destroyed him simply by institutionalizing him. At the last minute, he actually pleaded with the guards to be able to go back to his cell for another night, and he disappeared back inside.

It wasn't until the next day, after an exhausting effort by U.S. senators, the U.S. Embassy, and everyone else raising hell about the fact that the penitentiary would not release me that, at last, I found myself sitting in a car, driving out through the prison gates, with Ramon Rojas sitting next to me, bitching about a thousand things, especially about Mercedes. Here was my righteous defender, my best hope for justice at the time, telling me how he was going to "put a bullet in the head" of the woman whose daughter had just been so horribly murdered.

I spent that day trying to clear my head and get up to speed with what had been going on with my case. I remember feeling humbled by the number of people who seemed to be working on my behalf and by their dedication to the task. At the same time, though, I could see now what a huge liability Ramon Rojas represented. As soon as he told me that the judge wanted money from us, I got a strange feeling. Rojas didn't know that we had other direct lines of communication to Judge Peter Palma. Was it Rojas trying to bleed me for money the entire time? It's a terrible thing to distrust the attorney who holds your fate in his hands, but I was stuck with the guy. Firing him from the case would have caused a huge public scandal, which everybody, including Rojas, would have twisted into an admission of guilt. So we agreed that we would try to keep Rojas in line, with me playing good cop, apologizing for interference from the gringo attorneys or anything that might seem to undermine his author-ity. It annoyed me to have to pump Rojas up all the time, especially now that I understood how much good work was being done by Fabbrith Gomez and so many others.

I didn't get any better feeling from the rest of the legal crew my father had hired, who seemed to be trying to manage things from Washington, maybe to make up for their relative inability to accomplish things in Ni-caragua. In a long-distance phone call that afternoon, they kept talking about the global political ramifications of my case, bringing up everything from Venezuela to Cuba. All I could think was that if they somehow turned this into a political story for the media, it would infuriate the Ni-caraguan regime, and I would for sure be doomed.

I finally had a simple and heaven-sent moment of peaceful normalcy when I got to have dinner with my mother that first night. I cracked her up by suggesting we order in a pizza, although in the end we ate some Mexican food. Anything would have felt like a feast to me. I had terrible headaches that first night and couldn't quite calm myself after two months of the never-ending clatter and madness of jail. Whether I was awake or asleep, visions of Doris kept entering my brain.

House arrest for me meant a back bedroom in a private house where my safety would be assured. Words aren't enough to express the grati-tude I felt for the family who took me in. I rarely left the little room ex-cept to slip outside to a small patio hidden from view in back of the house, where I could sit peacefully in the fresh air. The few who visited me there had to do so with extreme caution, so as not to give away my location. Nicaragua had become, for me, a terribly dangerous place.

In the light of that danger, a security team had been brought in to pro-tect me. When I first met these former military guys, saw their weaponry, learned about their procedures and intelligence network, and received instruction on how to react in a violent crisis ("If you have to run, stay on the left rear side of your point man because he shoots right-handed . . .") I was a little shaken. I thought for sure they had all gone overboard, but I also remembered the scene in the streets of Rivas after the last hearing.

The threat was very real. The next day, when I had to show up at court, I liked knowing that escape routes and contingency plans were in place, that advance teams and short-range snipers were watching my back, and that someone had wrapped me in a bulletproof vest.

When Judge Palma let me out of jail and into house arrest, the press went nuts. In the days since the arraignment, the articles had been growing more and more sensational, focusing almost exclusively on me, the gringo, and dealing in increasingly wild half truths and false claims. Now the media could use my new detention status as an opportunity to pump life back into the story and provide an outlet for the outrage of the people. Worse, this was the excuse that Mercedes, Doris's mother, used to speak directly to the press for the first time, giving birth to a malicious partnership that would stop at nothing to see me punished. Mercedes had two claims that she aired. First, that there was no way Palma would have released me unless he had been bribed. The papers always stopped short of saying explicitly that he had received money from me or my family, but they hinted at it every which way, going so far as to call him a *capón*, slang for an organized-crime boss. (I'd later learn that this wasn't all that far from the truth when he was disbarred for having taken bribes from drug traffickers.) They even ran a front-page headline, "Crimen dolarizado"— *Dollarized Crime.* Second, and more problematic for me, Mercedes made the outrageous claim that my family had offered her a million dollars to back off.

The fact that my family didn't have a million dollars to offer or anything even close is beside the point. Mercedes's claim was nonsense to anyone who bothered to pay attention. What did Mercedes have to sell me? This was a criminal case, brought on by the state. Even as the victim's mother, Mercedes had no way of dropping charges or of calling off the prosecution.

Mercedes and Judge Palma each became overnight media sensations. Mercedes, the heartbroken mother crusading for justice, and Palma, the slick, street-smart judge who stank of corruption. The papers went after

Peter Palma with such ferocity, bringing so much attention to my case, that the Supreme Court of Nicaragua eventually stepped in to review his decision to release me to house arrest. Despite the obvious relevance, the result of the highest court's review received only minimal coverage in the press. In fact it was so marginalized that it seemed to reveal that the press wanted to actively avoid reporting anything in my favor for fear that the lucrative story would come to an end. But to me and anyone who understood due process, it had huge significance. The court found that Peter Palma had "acted correctly" by releasing me because the case against me was "full of deficiencies and anomalies." Here was the Nicaraguan Supreme Court examining my case file and concluding that the prosecution's case was weak long before my trial ever began, but it was like nobody ever heard them.

For a moment it seemed like the tide had finally turned. Not only was I out of jail, but the Supreme Court had publicly stated[EX.18] that the prosecution's case was insufficient. Even though I wasn't out of the woods—my fleeing at that point would have made me a fugitive and have jeopardized the people who had risked so much for my bail, not to mention confirming my guilt in the court of public opinion—everybody connected to my defense, from my family to people within the U.S. government, relaxed their efforts just a little, believing that this was the first step on the road to my ultimate exoneration. That proved to be a devastating miscalculation. Palma, and by extension the Nicaraguan government, had turned the heat down, and we played right into their hand.

For her part, Mercedes seemed not just to like the spotlight but to know how to work it to her advantage. Maybe these were skills she had picked up working as an organizer for the Sandinistas as a young woman. Between Mercedes and the Nicaraguan press, which was thrilled to have this ready-made heroine to set up against me, the villain, it's hard to say who was manipulating whom, but certainly each got something they wanted out of the other. You couldn't open a newspaper anymore and not see a picture of her indignant face. Mercedes took her campaign beyond the tabloid media, exploiting the willing voices of women's-rights groups and others looking for some mainstream exposure. As the case took over the attention of the media and the public, all respect for the tragedy of Doris's death was crushed by the spectacle of Mercedes's crusade against Eric.

Mercedes's comments actually started to get pretty bizarre. She was casting about in every direction, venting at everyone, accusing anyone, keeping her message alive. She began demanding, through Lesber Quintero, an investigation into Judge Peter Palma. Palma may have given the order to release me to house arrest, but we can't forget that it was also Palma who held me over for trial, who set Armando Llanes and Nelson Danglas free, and who had sent me to rot in stinking prisons for nearly two months.

My team got down to the hard work of preparing for trial over the next few weeks. We endured postponements and denials of every request, whether for a change of venue, a subpoena for Doris's cell-phone records, or a simple scheduling adjustment in response to a report of armed men lying in wait for me at the courthouse. At one point, we were actually on our way to Rivas on the day the trial was to begin, having executed our complex security plans and organized our witnesses, only to be turned away just outside of town. The judge who had been assigned to oversee the trial (unlike in the United States, in Nicaragua arraignments and trials are handled by separate judges) had apparently "called in sick," and no other judge was available. At the same time, we were told that she had returned the case file to Peter Palma because he hadn't prepared it properly. (She claimed that the pages were not correctly numbered and some were out of order!) Clearly, whoever was behind this insane scheme needed more time.

To read the Nicaraguan papers in those weeks, you would have thought that nothing else was happening in the country. The stories grew more numerous and more fantastical. At one point, Rosita's mother got into the act, claiming in one story that someone had approached her son after the second hearing and offered him a big chunk of money to take the blame. This could have been a tactic she picked up from watching Mercedes, or maybe someone actually did try to buy Rosita off, but no offer ever came from anyone connected with me. *La Prensa*, the most sober newspaper in the country, especially in comparison to Lesber Quintero's *El Nuevo Diario*, ran a story in which Mercedes went off about a toxicology report from Doris's autopsy that found traces of alcohol in her blood. Mercedes and the prosecutor together used this as "proof" that I was the killer, by claiming that Doris only drank when she was with me, so I had to have been with her when she died. I was being tried—maybe I had already been convicted—in the Nicaraguan popular press, and looking back on it all any judge would have been scared to acquit me in the actual trial. It seemed as if a verdict of not guilty would set the whole country on fire.

At one point in early February, as we awaited trial, I remember seeing an article in one of the many newspapers the doña of the safe house slid under my door. It wasn't in *El Nuevo Diario* or *La Prensa* but *The Washington Post*, and it wasn't about me at all. The headline ran, "U.S. Wants Nicaraguan Missiles Destroyed." The piece opened as follows:

> The United States insisted Monday that Nicaragua destroy hundreds of Soviet made surface-to-air missiles after President Daniel Ortega said the weapons were needed for the country's defense.
>
> Ortega, a former revolutionary who returned to the presidency on Jan. 10, said Friday it would be "absurd" to destroy Nicaragua's SAM-7 missiles while neighboring Honduras is adding U.S. planes to its military fleet. Nicaragua has been in a dispute with Honduras since 1999. . . .

The piece stuck in my mind, though I had no idea at the time that it would become a part of my story.

On February 13, the day before Valentine's Day, which turned out to be the eve of my trial, Lesber Quintero published an incendiary article comparing my trial to that of a man who raped and murdered a three-year-old girl in Rivas a few years before. That man had confessed and received the maximum sentence allowable under Nicaraguan law, thirty years in prison. A vigilante mob had been waiting for that defendant at the courthouse, Lesber pointed out, as if to remind readers of the role they needed to play. He closed by describing my upcoming trial as the highest-profile case in the history of the Rivas courts.

The name of Eric Volz—sadly and tellingly no longer the name of Doris Jiménez—was in the mouths of everyone across Nicaragua that night. Rivas was like a smoldering volcano, moments away from disaster. I see these words in my own journal:

> I know this is not my time to go. I believe it is possible that someone else could get hurt, though. My life is speaking to me, but I still don't understand the language. . . . So many people are getting drug into this because of me . . . I am the son of the most beautiful woman on earth. I realize that I learned my strength from her.
>
> Dios Primero.

It was out of my hands now.

7.

Justicia

Rivas was ready to blow. The threat of uncontrollable violence was so severe by the time my trial opened on February 14, Valentines Day, that even the Rivas police had asked the judge for a change of venue. They had concluded they couldn't guarantee anyone's safety. Not mine, not that of the witnesses or the lawyers or the judge, and not that of the seething crowd of onlookers in the street. Nobody, from the Nicaraguan chief of police to the U.S. ambassador to my own security team, believed the situation could be reasonably controlled. Rivas was a powder keg, ready to be set off by the smallest spark. The trial judge, Ivette Toruño, denied the police's request. The last thing she needed was for people to think she had done anything to grant me "special treatment."

The central area of Rivas came to a standstill. Shop owners closed down and shuttered their businesses, and the police sealed off several blocks surrounding the courthouse. Anyone going through the police cordon had to show ID, and just outside the perimeter crowds armed with sticks and other weapons waited anxiously for news. The cops had sent in eighty helmeted riot police with shields and body armor, who formed a human barricade by the doors, and word was that police in at least two other cities had been placed on alert, ready to descend on Rivas if things got out of hand. According to the papers that day, no Nicaraguan trial had ever received such a high level of police protection.

Just about everyone connected with the case, no matter how remotely, was living in fear. Someone in the crowd outside my second hearing had been observed carrying a gun. Witnesses had been directly threatened; the EP office in Managua had been so harassed and menaced by gangs of men in trucks and on motorcycles that several employees had simply picked up and left the country entirely. A number of foreign journalists had been threatened, and one American reporter had his windows smashed and his tires slashed in San Juan del Sur. Peter Palma, the judge who had released me from La Modelo, had felt the need to hire his own private security. Jackie and the rest of the American legal team stayed out of Nicaragua altogether, and my own family knew better than to go anywhere near the courthouse. Americans were advised by the U.S. Embassy to stay out of Rivas.

All those people were what the security guards around us refered to as "secondary targets," and it tore me up to think that the risks they faced all started with me. It was me the crowd was after. I felt it in the air the night the mob chased me after the hearing in Rivas. I felt it all around me. Three times in prison the guards had brought me a fresh meal delivered by a "friend" who never left her name—meals that I didn't dare eat. Mercedes had tasked rotating men out front of the Rivas courthouse on surveillance. Armed civilians had shown up at the Managua courts looking for me. Even Mercedes allegedly was found one day at the trial to have gotten a .38 past the police perimeter. The police didn't press charges. With this record of violence and the resources that had been put into the campaign against me, we were expecting a shooter or some sort of organized attempt on my life. When one of our agents reported that he had information that men in Doris's family had vowed to sacrifice their own lives to avenge Doris's death, the threat was even more realistic. So our security team planned the transit of me and my witnesses to the court with the care and precision of a sensitive military operation. In the twisted, surreal logic of that day, I guess that's exactly what it was like—a commando unit penetrating the armed territory of Rivas. In fact the only difference in the structure of our security detail and that of a diplomat or politico was the number of men and our lack of snipers. I awoke before sunrise and went with a small unit of armed men, first to pick up our defense witnesses at a rendezvous point, and then to conceal a cache of extra weapons in the cane fields outside Rivas. We had plotted multiple escape routes, choreographed and rehearsed action plans for a number of different potential emergencies, developed signals and communications. Everyone but me wore earbuds. In a totally unpredictable situation, we were leaving as little to chance as possible.

Inside the courtroom, the scene was much the same. Riot cops in black armor blocked the door, and six other armed policemen stood in strategic positions around the small, cramped room. My own bodyguard, forbidden from carrying a weapon into the courtroom, stood as close to me as physically possible. The frigid air blasting noisily out of the air conditioners made the atmosphere feel all the more brittle. The moment I entered, the room exploded in a dizzying attack of camera lights, accompanied by the buzz of dozens of hushed conversations. Judge Toruño brought the room under control, and I got myself ready for what was to come.*

The months of anxiety and anguish spent enduring everything from slander to torture had finally brought me to this moment of truth. For the first time since my arrest in November, I could look into the eyes of people who, whether through the press, the legal system, or their own secret networks of evil, had turned my life into a waking nightmare. Finally, I had to face them. All their plotting and strategizing, the games these people had been playing with my life, transformed from some kind of horrible abstract puzzle into something I could almost touch, something I could drink in through my senses. It was as if some piece of understanding had been missing until that moment. Even if I still wasn't able to fit all the pieces together, this new, tangible sensation of their animosity helped me understand what it meant to have real enemies in ways words could not.

For the next three days, I would become another set of eyes and ears for my attorneys, observing witnesses on the stand, scanning the courtroom for whatever subtle transactions might be taking place behind us,

---

* The entire trial plus specific portions of the trial testimonies are available in audio form at the Exhibit Hall at www.grinonightmare.com.

listening to every word uttered and scrutinizing every inflection and every hint of body language, trying to make sure we didn't miss anything. It's hard to say whether I was trying to *help* Ramon Rojas or just cover his back. My distrust of him had intensified in recent weeks, when he started demanding full payment *before* the trial. In fact, I had had to slip an envelope filled with cash under the table while people were distracted by the judge's entrance into the courtroom. I waited until the last possible moment to give him the money, to make certain that, if nothing else, he'd at least show up for the first day of trial.

I studied Ivette Toruño as she took her place on the judge's bench at the head of the room. She was elegantly turned out, with black hair falling neatly to her shoulders and her black judicial robe left open to reveal her stylish outfit and plenty of cleavage. An educated, prosperous professional woman is more unusual still in Nicaragua than in the United States, but it is more common there than in other Central American countries. Ivette Toruño, from a powerful and influential family strongly tied to the Sandinistas, had become used to her position of authority. She was known as something of a champion of feminist issues and women's rights, even if her advocacy came at the expense of justice: The word in legal circles was she had a controversial approach to evidence when convicting accused rapists and molesters.* On many levels, she commanded and deserved respect, but if you studied her closely on that day, as I did, you could see telltale signs of the enormous pressure she was under. I can't imagine that any judge would have been happy to draw my case.

Judge Toruño opened the trial by reading the formal charge, reminding a nation of people who didn't need to be reminded that Eric Stanley Volz and Julio Martin Chamorro Lopez stood accused of the rape and first-degree murder of Doris Ivania Jiménez Alvarado. Although it sent a chill

---

* Coincidentally, one of Toruño's secretaries was the girlfriend of a young man who worked for me. She not only shared insights about the judge's temperament but provided our team with inside information throughout the trial and other proceedings. However, Toruño's ultimate plan was kept secret even from her most trusted assistants.

through me to hear the words *asesinato atroz*, I thought it was good to bring Doris's name back into people's minds.

At the prosecution table sat Isolda Ibarra Aguello, the chief prosecutor for the Rivas district, and Allan Velasquez Martinez, the prosecutor who would actually try the case. Although she never spoke, Isolda remained there throughout the trial, to ensure that their case unfolded exactly as planned. The prosecution opened its case by calling to the witness stand a police detective, Silvio Aguirre, who described the crime scene[EX.19] and introduced Rosita's confession. Visibly shaking with nervousness, Silvio walked everyone through what seemed to be a totally routine investigation. Never mind Rosita's claim that the confession had been beaten out of him. I had seen Rosita with my own eyes in the days after the police had gotten his statement, and there was no mistaking the pressure he was feeling or the physical pain in his body. Silvio told his story slowly and carefully, as if he was terrified of making a mistake. This is how it would be for virtually all the government witnesses.

Nelson "Krusty" Danglas took the stand next and offered the *only direct evidence against me* that ever came into the trial. And yet his testimony[EX.20] was just about all anyone needed to understand the travesty being acted out. It's not just that Danglas wasn't credible; he was nearly incoherent. The district attorney gently led him through what appeared to be carefully rehearsed testimony, and still Danglas couldn't give consistent information. I could see him searching his memory after each question, yet he generally seemed confused, giving halting answers that weren't clear until the prosecutor did everything but put the words in his mouth. It was unsettling to hear people snickering in the courtroom, but Krusty did provide a bizarre kind of comic relief to the grim proceedings. What the testimony eventually got across was that I had spoken with him at 10 A.M. the morning of the murder and arranged for him to meet me in front of Doris's shop at 1 P.M. He claimed he showed up at 1 P.M. and that I was standing in the door. He approached, and I gave him two plastic bags and payed him fifty cordobas (USD $2.50). After that, I had skidded away in a white car that had tinted windows partially down. Danglas had caught a glimpse of another man in the car as well but could not offer any positive identification, only that he was "resio"—*stocky*.

Ramon Rojas cross-examined Danglas in a manner that on the surface seemed very delicate, but was actually, if you were paying close attention, and to my lawyer's credit, a devastating assault. Rojas politely quizzed him on simple details—what the car looked like or how many steps it was from the store to the car—just enough to make it clear that Danglas's story was false. Rojas's simple questions were too much, and Danglas finally stood up from the witness chair to tell him, "I may be an alcoholic, but I'm no liar!"

Ramon Rojas caught a fair amount of flack for his handling of the trial. For sure, he could have gone after Danglas harder and could have easily discredited every bit of his testimony. During this stage of the trial, Rojas never even mentioned the fact that Danglas had been arrested soon after Doris's murder, which would have allowed him to get Danglas's injuries, especially the lesions on his penis that were noted in the medical examiner's report[EX.21] and the fact that despite blood having been taken there were no blood test results for Danglas in the case file, on the official court record. These aren't the cutthroat, win-at-all-costs lawyers we're used to in the United States. Rojas had to tread softly. After all, my ultimate fate was of little consequence to Rojas, but there were official people on all sides of the case who were important for his long-term career. He made it obvious that Danglas was lying on the stand but stopped short of completely taking him apart, which would have been easy. Rojas had to at least look like he was trying to get me acquitted, but he couldn't do anything that would expose the people who were pulling Danglas's strings. It would have been like tugging on a loose thread on your sleeve and having the whole shirt unravel.

When Rojas finished with Krusty, the stage was set for the headline act. All eyes were on Doris's mother, Doña Mercedes Alvarado, as she walked to the witness stand in her finest clothes, stacked with bad gold jewelry, and with heavy makeup on her face, ready for the biggest performance of her life. Mercedes had already become famous throughout

Nicaragua, and everyone knew her story, at least in part, but like a broken record, she dramatically recounted the story of the million-dollar offer she had allegedly received. Mercedes told the court that Cesar Baltodano, Danglas's attorney, had been the one to convey the offer, allegedly on behalf of my family, as they ate together in a restaurant. In her testimony,[EX.22] she quoted or paraphrased Baltodano as saying, "Look, this gringo could walk because he has the U.S. Embassy on his side, so take advantage of what I'm about to offer you. . . . In the United States, the average wage is fifty dollars a day, but since Doris was a professional, she would earn seventy to eighty dollars a day. So by the time she was forty, her life would be worth a million dollars." She added that he specified that 20 percent would be for her lawyer. Mercedes claimed that she was offended by the outrageous offer, and then popped the restaurant receipt out from her purse as if to prove the truth of her story, proclaiming, "I don't need a million dollars! I need my daughter!"

No such offer ever came from my family or from anyone connected to me, and the prosecution's promoting Mercedes's claim had absolutely no relevance to my alleged participation in the crime. The "facts" that we learned later about this alleged offer reveal how lies and fabrication schemes were being used by the police behind the scenes in a campaign to convince Mercedes and the public that I was guilty.

Shortly before the special hearing at which Judge Palma released me to house arrest, Jackie, the attorney from Washington, had gone with the English investigator Simon Strong and Ramon Rojas to meet with Eduardo Hollmann, the mayor of San Juan del Sur. They wanted to lay out the evidence of my innocence and hopefully enlist him in my support. At the time, Hollmann seemed like he could be tremendously influential, not only because his open support of me could change the way people in San Juan del Sur felt about me and the case but also because of his connections beyond the town. His family had company shares in both major newspapers, *La Prensa* and *El Nuevo Diario*, and our team fully understood the role of public opinion in the outcome of the case. They were surprised when they showed up, to say the least, to see that Hollmann had invited Danglas's attorney Cesar Baltodano and a Rivas police official to that meeting.

Baltodano had no business in that meeting, but, as we learned, he and Hollmann were very tight. Baltodano had also served in the past as San Juan's police chief, and, without doubt, Nica police were driving the push to hang Doris's murder on me. He was also married to Nelson Danglas's aunt, and his presence at the meeting was in fact useful to the police strategy to sink me, a strategy which it seemed possible that Hollmann was supporting.*

The day after the special hearing, Baltodano arranged to meet Mercedes at a restaurant. Not only could he credibly tell her that he had met with my representatives, but there would be proof that he had met her. At the restaurant, he had told Mercedes that we had authorized him to make her an offer of money—the million dollars—if she would stop her public attacks against me. There are different versions of how Mercedes responded to his offer—which as far as she knew was absolutely real. What we do know is she was never paid one million dollars and she went to the press with the story.

Mercedes was just getting warmed up. She went on to talk about what an oppressive boyfriend I had been to Doris, both callous and controlling at the same time. Mercedes claimed that Doris had told her how jealous I could be and how I'd threatened to kill Doris if she ever started dating anyone else. One very telling moment came when she told an outrageous lie about how she had read my lips from across the courtroom as I whispered into my lawyer's ear during the first hearing. She had seen me telling him to "send Mercedes a note and offer her money." I was practically jumping out of my chair, urging my lawyers to take her on, and giving them ways to expose her lies, but they just tried to calm me down. One of

---

* There were indications that Hollmann resented my defense effort. Tim Rogers reported on the *Time.com* Web site on January 24, 2007, that "San Juan del Sur's Sandinista Mayor, Eduardo Hollmann, had a heated phone exchange with U.S. Ambassador Paul Trivelli" regarding the lynch-mob incident. Rogers quotes Hollmann as saying, "He (Trivelli) told me 'You don't have lynch mobs in a civilized country?' and I told him, 'Yeah, didn't you used to lynch blacks in the United States?'"

my attorneys, Fabbrith, simply said, "La señora está loca." Mercedes was far from crazy, though. She knew her audience well, and she knew exactly how to press their buttons. A natural ringleader with genuine powers of persuasion, she knew how to play to the crowd and had an instinct for stirring things up.

When Mercedes finished, the prosecution called a young woman who occasionally worked in the shop for Doris. She also claimed[EX.23] that Doris had told her the same thing she had told Mercedes—that I would kill her if she ever cheated on me. I have no idea where she got this. She also, to the prosecution's dismay, offered that, "Eric didn't show signs of jealousy."

When the prosecution was done with its parade of lies and innuendo, none of which, with the exception of Danglas's testimony, was actually connected to the specific crime, they put Dr. Oscar Flores, the forensic expert who performed the autopsy on Doris's body when it was taken to Managua, on the stand. Flores was a respected authority and handled himself with calm professionalism, unlike most of the other prosecution witnesses. The cause of death, he explained, was pulmonary edema caused by mechanical asphyxiation from suffocation or strangulation. Doris had signs of violent defensive struggle all over her body. She had a busted lip, a bruise on her right cheekbone, scrapes on the outside of her knuckles, friction wounds on both wrists where she had been tied up, bruises and scrapes on both knees, and a large bruise on the front of her right thigh. Her neck in particular had friction wounds she had sustained before she died and that Flores concluded were related to the cause of death.

When asked by the prosecutor if the victim had been raped, Flores answered[EX.24] that he had not observed signs of rape. He saw no lesions in the vaginal area, for example. In a surprising twist, one possible reason he suggested for the inability to detect signs of rape was that Doris's body had already been embalmed by the time it arrived in Managua for postmortem examination. The embalming process, especially the introduction of formalin and the sealing of all body openings, rendered his findings and observations all but useless.

Later in the morning, the testimony[EX.25] of Vanesa Arcia Juarez, the medical examiner who had inspected Doris at the crime scene in San Juan del Sur and who had examined me and Rosita—*and* Danglas—brought a little more clarity to the matter. Juarez confirmed all the defensive injuries that Doris had sustained and also collected samples of material from under her fingernails, which were sent for testing immediately.[EX.26] (Those test results, like so many other important documents, either disappeared from or never even made it into the case file.*) She removed bloody cardboard that had been shoved into Doris's throat and also observed that Doris had been penetrated anally and that her vagina contained a "creamy white substance" with a "characteristic smell," although she never actually identified it.

The prosecutor led Juarez through testimony about the parallel bruises she found on my shoulder—the only marks present on my body—which she believed had been caused by fingernails. In fact, she could imagine no other cause for them. She observed scratches on Rosita's body, as well as scratches on his knuckles, forearms, and other bruises. Juarez never mentioned the third person she had examined after the murder—Nelson Danglas—because the prosecutor never asked her.

Oscar Flores had the authority of an accomplished veteran medical examiner. By contrast, Vanesa Juarez wasn't even a fully trained doctor but a licensed medic from a tiny little island in the middle of Lake Nicaragua. The same naïveté and inexperience that made it possible for someone to influence Vanesa Juarez's report made it easy for Ramon Rojas to blow huge holes in her testimony. He got her to admit to examining Danglas, reminding the court that he, too, had been a solid suspect early on. Rojas further discredited her professional opinions by asking how she knew that clothes were missing from the shop (something she says she

---

* The case-file documents that the results from Doris's fingernail tests were returned to the police just three days after the murder. When questioned by the press, the police said simply that the prosecution never asked for the results, and the prosecution claimed that the police never informed them they had results. They blamed each other. I believe that the results were omitted from the case since they would have had either blood or skin samples of Doris's true killers, who were being protected by the cops. Those samples should still be in police evidence today and could be subpoenaed. See the receipt document.[EX.26]

observed when she arrived at the crime scene). How could she know such a thing if that had been her first and only time in the shop? And he tripped her up by asking how it was that fingernails could bruise without scratching. Backed into an uncomfortable corner, she ultimately suggested that fingernails aren't generally sharp.

Several other witnesses came to the stand that morning as part of the prosecution's case, including Doris's friend, Gabi, who had been the one to call me with the news. She seemed to be willing to say whatever it took to make me look like a killer, at least until Rojas flipped her testimony to support the defense. She admitted that she had called me at my phone number to inform me of Doris's death at 2:43 P.M. the day of the murder. The prosecution was arguing that the records proved the location of the phone but not of Eric Volz. Gabi's testimony,[EX.27] combined with the cell-phone-triangulation records, proved that I had been in Managua.* Some other neighbors and townspeople offered inconclusive testimony about who or what they remembered seeing on the street that day. One final prosecution witness created a moment of high drama and tension in the courtroom and for a moment had me thinking he was about to set a torch to the prosecution's case and tell the court what really happened. If anybody knew, it was this guy.

Jose Juarquin Herrera lived next door to Doris's shop and acted like he knew more about her comings and goings than anyone else on earth. He claimed he knew her daily habits down to the most minute details. He knew, for instance, that she never closed herself in her shop with the door shut unless she was with someone she trusted completely. (He added that he had only seen her do that with me.) On that day, his daughter saw Doris leave for lunch but stop when she ran into "someone she trusted," with whom she went back into the store and shut the door. Juarquin had never seen the wooden door to the shop closed without the metal gate closed over it. That day, the gate remained open. Intrigued, he tried peeking into the

---

* The police or prosecution could have subpoenaed the other people with whom I had spoken from my phone that morning up to the time I got Gabi's call to verify my location. They did not.

shop but claimed that he couldn't see anything through Doris's tinted windows. The windows of Sol Fashion were not tinted.

Jose Herrera had told the press that he "was haunted by Doris" because he had not saved her and that he had to seek help from a mental-health professional. That alone had made me wonder if he knew more than he was letting on, but his uncertain manner on the witness stand strengthened my suspicions. Moments later, his testimony took a shockingly dramatic detour. He seemed to switch gears in the middle of a sentence. His voice grew weak and shaky and tears welled up in his eyes. He turned his gaze directly at Rosita and spoke through his sobs.

"I know you can talk," Juarquin began. "You can talk because San Juan knows you are a good person, and I know you know what happened. You have to tell the judge because your mom is suffering, my daughters are suffering. . . ." Herrera's quivering voice trailed off and suddenly there was only stunned silence in the courtroom.[EX.28] I know that everyone was thinking what I was thinking: *How could he say "I know you know" unless he was there and saw something and he knew, too?* A flicker of hope sprang up in me. Maybe the truth was about to come bubbling out of this man. For a few moments, it was as if nobody knew what to do. The prosecutor didn't dare proceed with his questioning, for fear that the dam would break and Herrera would sink their case. Finally, Judge Toruño broke the tension.

"Bien," she said. "Pass him some water."

When his turn came, Ramon Rojas stood in front of Jose Herrera. "You have told the court that you have recently found God's word and that you are a Christian, right?" Herrera nodded in agreement. "We are all Christians here," Rojas continued. "I have only one question for you. Did you see Eric Volz inside the store on November 21?"

Juarquin answered simply: "No."

So ended the first day. Only one prosecution witness—Nelson Danglas—had offered testimony directly incriminating me in the crime, and virtually everyone watching the trial agreed that his testimony had been laughable. The rest of the prosecution's case consisted of either pure hearsay or testimony that was essentially irrelevant to me or to the actual crime. Even Ramon Rojas had handled himself well that morning, taking apart more than one prosecution witness and laying open the ridiculous holes in the case against me.

Of course, it was too much to ask that Rojas would get through the day without pissing me off. At 1:00 in the afternoon, when the prosecution had wrapped up, he packed up to leave, saying he had another trial that afternoon in Managua. *Another trial*. I was furious. Leave it to Ramon Rojas to make sure this trial dragged on for another day or two. Each day meant more anguish for me and my family, not to mention adding to the enormous expense of our team, but it also meant more time on center stage for Rojas. It didn't seem to concern him that my future hung in the balance.

As soon as court adjourned, Mercedes ran outside to join the crowd of protesters who had come to Rivas from San Juan del Sur. It seemed that the mob was just waiting for their ringleader, and Mercedes jumped right in. The police closed their perimeter tighter in the face of the increasingly agitated crowd, who responded by screaming in their faces, "You all are whores of the gringo!" When I met up outside with Frank, the head of my security team, he told me how a car full of uniformed men had pulled up next to our convoy and waved a gun, trying to pull our car over, but bailed when our guys produced a shotgun. I'm not sure if this story was supposed to make me feel better or safer, but it turned out that the presence of my security team actually backfired on that first day. *El Nuevo Diario* published an article the next day describing Frank carrying an AR-15 machine gun and asking how it was possible that foreigners were walking around in Rivas with military weapons. After that, the security team was no longer allowed within the trial perimeter.

By day two of the trail, the dangerous mood had only intensified, thanks largely to the efforts of *El Nuevo Diario* and the rest of the Nica press. Lesber Quintero manipulated the reports of the testimony and evidence so that it appeared damning to me. He claimed Danglas's testimony "Sunk Volz." Another headline read, "If You Cheat on Me, I Will Kill You." Reader

Exploring the self. Ropeless ascent of a 500-foot cliff,
Sierra Nevada, California, 1998. *Chris Wellhausen*

Eric and John "JT" Thompson in San Juan del Sur, Nicaragua,
in 2000 when they first met. They would return four years later
to launch the bilingual *El Puente* magazine. *Eric V. Archive*

EP magazine, issue #3. *EP Magazine S.A*

Doris Jiménez as she appeared in *EP* magazine's Mujeres de Centro America campaign. *EP Magazine S.A*

Sol Fashion, Doris's clothing boutique and the place of her murder. *Eric V. Archive*

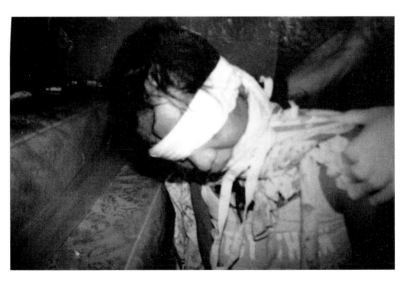

Crime scene photo #9, from case file #02480535. *Eric V. Archive*

Individuals originally accused of Doris Jiménez's murder:
(top) Armando Agustín Llanes Navarro
(middle) Nelson Lopez Danglas. *Eric V. Archive*
(bottom) Julio Martín Chamorro. *Eric V. Archive*

Heavily armed escort was common throughout Eric's imprisonment.
This photo is from immediately after his conviction. *Miguel Molina*

Maximum security prison, "Carcel La Modelo."
Awaiting trial, January 2007. *Eric V. Archive*

"Celda #21" January 2007. *Eric V. Archive*

Mother and son reunited. *Ben Pearson*

Interviews Eric did in New York City a couple of weeks after his release were broadcast worldwide, including this one with Anderson Cooper. *Eric V. Archive*

Eric in January 2008, two weeks after his release.
Ben Pearson

Doris Jiménez, 2005. *Eric Volz*

comments posted online revealed the power of the public's hatred. One reader wanted me shot, another suggested lynching for me and Rosita—and the *judge*—should we be declared innocent. Another paper, *Hoy*, published a full-page photo of me that had red brushed in around my eyes, creating an evil impression. The piece expressed outrage that I should be wearing "armor" and be protected by a squad of "Guatemalan mercenaries."

The *fiscal*, or "prosecutor," continued his presentation on the second morning. The key witnesses were two employees of Hertz, the agency from who I had rented a car in Managua to drive to San Juan del Sur on the afternoon I learned of Doris's death. Both witnesses offered testimony that differed from the original statements they had given to the police in the days following the murder. Both also seemed nervous and uncertain on the stand, but that was nothing new.

Victor, who had delivered the Hertz car to the EP house, spoke first. Victor had originally told the police that two women from my office had gone to him and asked him to sign a statement that he had "seen me" while dropping off the car. He hadn't seen me, and they had never asked him to say that he had. They only asked him to confirm that I had signed the credit-card voucher, which I had done. The police had his statement, though, and the prosecution and Lesber used it whenever they could to make it look like people in my office were working to cover my tracks. Victor's original statement[EX.29] also specified that Indira, the other Hertz witness, had called him at 3:00 p.m. to ask Victor to get a car ready, but now, three months later, he testified that he got the call "sometime after noon." Victor grew more visibly nervous under cross-examination from Rojas, who got him to admit that he couldn't even remember the color of the car he brought over or whether the people he saw at the house were male or female.

Indira hedged also when she took the stand. Originally she had told the police in a sworn and written declaration[EX.30] that Leidy, my assistant, had called at around 2:50 because I needed a car urgently. That made sense, since Gabi had phoned me with the news of Doris's death just five or ten minutes before. And yet now she told the court in her oral testimony[EX.31] that she had received the call from our office sometime between 1:00 and 2:00, adding that it took thirty minutes to make a car available.* If you believed her testimony now, you could deduce that I had knowledge of the murder *before* I ordered the rental car, which would make Indira a golden witness. Or you could ask yourself why she had said one thing in the days immediately following Doris's murder and now, three months later and finding herself in the eye of the storm, was changing her story the way so many others had.

The simple fact was that the time stamped on the rental contract was 3:11 P.M. and that Indira testified that it was about thirty minutes from the time she received the call from my assistant until the time she sent the car. That would put Leidy's call at around 2:45 P.M. In addition she asserted that my signature on the voucher matched signatures on previous contracts and vouchers from the many times I had rented from that Hertz office. That alone confirmed my presence in Managua on the afternoon of the murder and should have been a fatal blow to the prosecution's case. Then again, I had already lost count of the things that should have been fatal blows to their case.

The final significant witness for the prosecution was Noel Martin Corea, a blood sampling expert from the forensic crime lab in Managua. The fact that traces of type O blood had been found on the sheets used to tie up Doris and that Corea had found me to be type O had contributed in the judge's justification to bring me to trial. Corea testified that he had done lab tests on the swabs from my fingernails. One hand showed no traces of blood, he said, while the other tested positive for the presence of blood, but that the sample was too "scarce" to identify a blood type.†

---

* It would have been obvious to produce the phone records from the office phone, but our landlady refused to turn them over to me, claiming she "didn't want to get involved." We pressed for Judge Palma to subpoena the phone records from the telephone company, but he declined. Of equal value would have been a subpoena of the Hertz records to verify the incoming call time, but again our request for a subpoena was denied.

† DNA testing is available in Nicaragua, although it is not widely used. My defense team considered requesting DNA evidence, but we had seen so many underhanded moves by the police that we decided we simply couldn't trust them not to manipulate the results or mess with the records or documents in some way. It was too big a risk to take. Ironically, not soliciting evidence was a defense move.

On cross-examination, Rojas brought Corea down hard, using Fabbrith's discovery the previous night that the case file listed my blood as type A in one place and type O in another.

Corea testified[EX.32] that the two different blood types had been a simple typing error and that he had faxed the correction to . . . he couldn't say to whom. The frigid air pouring out of the courtroom air conditioners couldn't keep Corea from breaking out into a mad sweat as Rojas did away with him. He was so agitated that his hands were shaking. He was fired from his position after the trial.

My blood is in fact type A, not O. O is the most common blood type, so even if the report had been accurate and conclusive, by itself it could not have proved that I was present at the crime. At the time, it seemed not only like the defense had scored a major victory but also that we had exposed either horrendous police incompetence or calculated tampering with the case file—possibly both.

The prosecution wrapped up its case around noon. I remember actually feeling pretty confident once the *fiscal* was finished. I couldn't imagine that anybody could have sat in the courtroom for the last day and a half and think for even a second that I could have had anything to do with Doris's murder. It was simply inconceivable to me. There's a little hand-held video recording of me talking with Nick Purdy as he waited in the visitors room for his turn to testify, in which I tell him how the prosecution's case was unraveling.

The last memory I have of that morning doesn't actually have anything to do with the *fiscal* or any of the particulars of the case. What I remember is the sound of a cell phone ringing in the courtroom as the last prosecution witness was speaking. It was Judge Ivette Toruño's phone, and not only did she answer it in the middle of the trial, but we could all hear her whispering, "Perame . . . perame . . ." (*hold on a sec . . .*), before ducking her head down under the bench so that she could take the call. This particular bizarre scene would repeat itself several times over the course of the three-day trial. On the afternoon of the second day, Ramon Rojas presented our defense. Of the ten eyewitnesses able to testify that they were with me in Managua at the time of the murder in San Juan del Sur, the judge had rejected, on the grounds that they were "redundant," all but three. Most important, of course, were Nick Purdy and Ricardo Castillo, the two men with whom I was having a conference call at the time of the murder. I was also simultaneously conversing with Nick by an instant-message service at the precise time the police and prosecution claimed I was murdering Doris. Despite leaving behind a wife, four small children, and countless friends who counseled him not to come because of the potential danger, Nick had courageously come to Rivas from the United States in order to testify, and everything about the scene in Rivas, both inside and outside the courthouse, had left him in stunned disbelief.

Nick testified[EX.33] regarding the exact times that the phone call with me and Ricardo Castillo had begun and ended—basic facts supported by phone records but that the prosecution managed to get wrong anyway, or at least to deliberately confuse. To begin with, the clerk entered the wrong time into the trial transcript (2:19 P.M. instead of 12:19 P.M.). When my attorney pointed this out, Judge Toruño acknowledged the mistake but let the record stand uncorrected and incorporated the incorrect time as a linchpin in her verdict. In addition, the *fiscal* brought up the issue of different time zones during Nick's testimony and later, during closing arguments, made the completely false assertion that Nicaragua was an hour *ahead* of Virginia (where Nick was at the time of the call) rather than an hour behind, claiming that the call actually occurred two hours later than it had. This supposedly made it possible for me to be somewhere other than Managua at the time of the murder and so discredited my alibi. The prosecution's claim was shown to be inaccurate, but, again, was never stricken from the record. Even after his testimony concluded, Nick Purdy wasn't feeling any better about the situation he was in. He took one look at the door and said, "I ain't going out on the street."*

As nervous as all the prosecution witnesses had appeared, none of

---

* Reported by Tony D'Souza, *Outside* magazine, June 2007.

them were quite as freaked out about being in the witness box as Rosy Lopez, the young woman who had cut my hair that afternoon. Rosy testified[EX.34] that she had cut my hair and then I left the house before she did. She also said that she had seen a white car outside the house when she arrived. Although this was actually the silver car of an *EP* staffer, the prosecution managed to slip in a hint that it was the same white car in which Danglas had claimed to see me in San Juan del Sur.

When Ricardo Castillo's turn came, he confirmed[EX.35] the actual time of the phone call, but that isn't what I remember most about his testimony. At one point, the questioning veered away from telephones and times of day, and Ricardo was asked to elaborate on the content of our conversation that day. For a few minutes, he talked with both affection and enthusiasm about the dream of *EP* magazine, now a thing of the past, a forgotten footnote to this whole ugly drama. It was heartbreaking for me to sit in that totally surreal courtroom, to be reminded of the big ideas that had brought me to Nicaragua in the beginning, and to think that all of it was now gone forever. Instead of trying to trip him up on the facts, the prosecution went after Castillo by reminding the court that he had a genuine interest in my staying out of jail and in my continuing to run my business. The same point had been argued in relation to Nick Purdy.

Then, without real warning, and certainly without preparation, I found myself sitting in the witness chair. I finally had a chance to speak out in my own defense, and Ramon Rojas had not given one word of legal guidance to get me ready to testify. My head was spinning; there was so much I wanted to say, so many scores to settle, so much anger and frustration to vent. At the same time, I heard a voice of reason from deep within, telling me to be careful, not to take any unnecessary risks. This was neither the time nor place for me to go off on Nelson Danglas or anybody else whose falsehoods or incompetence could bury me. My team had begged me to focus on proving my innocence, not to solve Doris's murder from inside the courtroom.

Over the previous three months, whenever I had been in any public setting, I had grown used to the glare of attention. I had grown used to crowds of people watching my every move, scrutinizing me. As I took the stand, I felt everyone's eyes on me, but the attention had a different quality. For the first time in a very long time, I felt the interest was something more than just voyeurism, like the crowd's genuine curiosity for what I would say from the witness chair had finally trumped whatever other feeling they had about me. But those onlookers didn't matter to me much right then. When the questioning began and I was able to tell my story [EX.36] through my answers, I turned and spoke directly to Ivette Toruño, the judge who would decide my fate.

I had no bombshells to drop, no new information to change the course of the trial. I simply recounted exactly what had happened—*again*. I went through the events of that day and provided relevant information from the subsequent days before my arrest, including the fact that the bruises the medical examiner claimed were caused by fingernails had been made by the weight of Doris's coffin on my shoulder. I looked only at Toruño; she was the only one I needed to hear the truth. Even as I gave my testimony, something in me still believed in the process. I suppose I still somehow naïvely imagined myself in a real court, a place where facts, logic, testifying under oath, and the rule of law were the only things that mattered and where a legitimate verdict was possible.

The hardest part was holding my tongue, especially about how Llanes and Danglas were exonerated. The prosecutor gave me the opportunity to make the judicial system look bad by asking me why I thought Danglas would lie. To this day, a part of me regrets not letting loose about how he had plenty of motive to cooperate with the prosecution and offer a false statement in exchange for freedom. He'd been locked up. He felt the fear; he had felt the hunger; he had even been assaulted in jail. I couldn't do it, though. I couldn't attack the *fiscalia*, a part of the judicial system. From my perspective in that moment, it was unwise to publicly make the government look bad. I had to allow the system a way to save face. A way out of the mess they had created. The most strategic answer I could give was, "I don't know."

Our defense didn't take up that much time. The truth wasn't complicated. Applying the conventional rules of law, the prosecution had blown its case, presenting not one shred of meaningful evidence against me. When Rojas wrapped up, Giovani Ruiz, the attorney representing Rosita, took over. He proceeded to present an alibi that was completely different than what Rosita had sworn to me during our short conversation in the holding cells of Granada. Ruiz claimed that his client was eating lunch with some friends in the market just a couple of doors down from Doris's shop. I have no doubt in my mind that Rosita was present when she was murdered and in one way or another contributed to her death. I have no warm feelings for the man, and I don't feel bad for him in any way, but a part of me understands the ways in which the guy never had a chance. Rosita had gotten himself caught up in something huge and didn't have the means to weasel his way out of this one. He had a lawyer who was way out of his depth and a codefendant who had become the focus of popular hatred. Three out of the four defense witnesses he had supposedly lined up never even showed up at the trial, and Rosita chose to exercise his right to remain silent rather than take the witness stand in his own defense. Ruiz's entire presentation took less than forty-five minutes. Rosita would surely go down.

The third morning of the trial brought a flood of new press, including one of the most damaging articles published about me throughout this ordeal. Again, *El Nuevo Diario* was the culprit. "Que Corona Tiene Volz?" (*What Crown Does Volz Have?*) the front page screamed. The article described a squadron of mercenaries armed with AR-15 machine guns with an accompanying photograph (only one member of the security team carried such a weapon) and decried the presence of what was depicted as a private army on Nicaraguan soil. Other papers picked up the story, all asking how such an insult to the competency of their own police and

security people, not to mention to Nicaraguan sovereignty and national
security, could have ever been allowed. The papers' only intention was to
fan the flames of anti-Volz sentiment across the country. Now not only
was I killer, but they even reported that I was the privileged "son of
an important U.S. politician" bringing in my own soldiers to cover my
back. There was only one reference to the fact that every last thing our
security team did had been carefully negotiated and approved with the
Nicaraguan authorities in the presence of Mike Poehlitz, the regional
security officer from the embassy. It did come out in the *El Nuevo Diario*
that a police commissioner had approved the use of properly registered
military-style weapons, but the paper wanted to use that to add to their
argument, asking if that meant that now all private citizens were allowed
to carry machine guns through the middle of town. All the advance planning and efforts at cooperation; all the high-level government meetings,
phone calls from no less important a person than the U.S. ambassador,
and approvals; all the hoops the team had jumped through—they all
blew up in our faces. It seemed that we'd never be able to undo the damage caused.

Other newspapers contributed their own brands of poison. *Hoy* ran
a piece about the support network that was growing on my behalf, since now
I had become an American "martyr." It took a lot to make me laugh that
morning, but I at least had to shake my head at the irony of an article that
appeared in *USA Today*: "Nicaragua Rising: War-Torn Image Gets a Tourist Makeover." That very day the paper ran a gorgeous color photo of the
bay at San Juan del Sur and spoke glowingly about the exciting growth
and stable investment opportunities in Nicaragua.

The opposing attorneys each made their closing arguments that morning. The prosecution offered their list of conclusions: The fact that
Doris's body was dressed showed a sentimental attachment between the
victim and the killer; the marks on my shoulder could not have been caused
by the coffin and were obviously fingernail scratches; Nelson Danglas must
have been telling the truth, because he was courageous enough to tell it "to
my face," a gesture that carries enormous weight in their culture; three

witnesses claimed I had threatened to kill Doris if she ever cheated on me; and the two Hertz employees, who had no interest of any kind in the case, must have been telling the truth about my ordering the car earlier in the day than was indicated by every single piece of evidence; and finally, cell-phone records are meaningless because they cannot prove my location.

The prosecution's conclusions proved nothing, of course, but they were highly dramatic and played into the emotions that had so contaminated the trial.

Ramon Rojas rose to the occasion, delivering an impassioned closing. He picked apart each point in the prosecution's case: It made no sense that I would risk turning Danglas into a witness by asking him to dispose of the two bags; the prosecution claims my motive was jealousy, but, non-sensically, I had been arrested on the suspicion that I had gone with Armando Llanes, possibly Doris's current lover, to rape her. It's remarkable that the only way Llanes's name was brought into the trial was by Rojas's reminding the court that the prosecution had only made use of a portion of Rosita's original confession. The part they had left out is the part where Rosita implicated Armando Llanes. Rojas explained how finger-nails would have left an entirely different kind of mark on my shoulder and questioned how the prosecution could conclude she scratched me if it had not presented test results from under her nails. He reminded the court that Danglas had originally been one of the men accused of the crime and had been jailed and that the record showed that he had abrasions on his penis when examined after the murder. He went through the evidence regarding the rental car to show that I had absolutely requested the car well after the murder had taken place, and he blasted the police over the outrageous "inhumanity," as he called it, of a typing error in the report on blood types in one the highest-profile murder cases the country had ever seen. Rojas made sure to emphasize the fact that not one shred of physical evidence, including the more than a hundred hair samples taken at the crime scene, showed any link to me.

In these final moments of the trial, when tension and drama was at its greatest intensity, I noticed Mercedes, seated at the prosecution's counsel table, take out her cell phone. She appeared to start sending a text message with her thumbs. Within a few moments, gunshots rang out from the street. One of the court clerks began shouting about the shooting outside, and, as if we all couldn't hear the sudden commotion for ourselves, Mercedes held up her cell phone, trying to broadcast the sounds of the impending riot to the live cameras. Judge Toruño immediately ordered that nobody leave the courtroom. We were all thinking it at the time: Mercedes had been orchestrating the actions of the mob outside. On the street, the observers—many of whom, as it turned out, had actually been paid to show up outside the trial—were taking orders from a woman who only issued instructions after receiving them herself by cell phone, presumably from Mercedes. The timing of the shooting outburst, at exactly the moment that Rojas was picking apart the prosecution case in his summation, was no accident. The little piece of theater did exactly what Mercedes and her gang had wanted. It distracted every last person in the courtroom to such a degree that Ramon Rojas's brilliant and powerful arguments immediately took a backseat in everyone's mind.

The crowd outside the courthouse was not quieting down, and from that point on Toruño rushed everything. I was stunned to see that the prosecution, having already delivered its summation, was allowed a final opportunity to address Rojas's closing statement and offer rebuttals to his arguments. At last, the judge asked Rosita and me to make final statements to the court. I spoke from my heart:

"I want to say before all of those who are present, to the people of San Juan and to you, Your Honor, here, that I am not a killer. I am innocent. God knows it. Nicaragua is a country with a great heart, and I trust in her justice."

Even that simple statement got mangled by the press. "God knows it" became "*only* God knows it," changing the meaning and intent of my last declaration. Despite everything that had happened; despite all the ominous signs; despite all the dirty tricks used by the police, the prosecutors, and the judge herself; despite the relentless campaign of lies and propaganda in the Nicaraguan press, the members of my defense team felt good about the verdict to come. We were sure the prosecution's case had been blown apart, sure that all the hard evidence, not to mention simple common sense, led to the inescapable conclusion that I had absolutely nothing to do with the death of Doris Jiménez. The U.S. embassy staff believed that. Fabbrith believed it. I believed it. We would have to wait a little longer, though. Ivette Toruño stood and excused herself and announced that she would return with her verdict in two hours.

It was a bad sign when Toruño ordered the police not to allow the U.S. Embassy personnel into the courtroom for the reading of the verdict. Something was about to go down if she was prepared to implement that kind of diplomatic insult. At about 4:15 in the afternoon, she came back into the courtroom and took her place at the judge's bench. All were to be seated with the exception of Rosita and me. She began reading—slowly, solemnly, theatrically—drawing out her speech in a way that seemed calculated to prolong the drama and leave us drowning in the anxiety for just a little while longer. She was also very conscious of the cameras, knowing that her performance would soon be televised.

I remember her verdict[EX.37] almost as a montage of little symbolic phrases, each one like a boxer's quick jab: *Justice is the supreme ideal. . . . What one affirms, it is proved. . . . It is proven that the death of the young woman . . . happens of a violent form . . . that in the moments before her death she was violated. . . . The defense centers its unproved statements. . . .* And then the final blow: *. . . The accusing witnesses, Nelson Lopez Danglas and Pedro Joaquin Narváez have the whole necessary credibility. . . .*

There was no need to listen to the rest. I knew then what was coming. If she declared Danglas credible, the verdict had to be guilty. I began assembling the few belongings I had—my watch, cash, cell phone, and the little handheld digital recorder I carried—and consolidating them into the pockets of my jacket. When I took off the jacket and handed it to

Fabbrith to give to my mother, the room instantly burst with camera flashes. The press had been waiting for a photo of the gringo in his bulletproof vest.

As Toruño kept up her recitation, I spoke to Fabbrith. "Tell my mother I love her."

"Be strong, Eric," he consoled, while he was in shock himself. "We are going to fight this in appeal right away."

Judge Ivette Toruño went on. Nick Purdy and Ricardo Castillo had no credibility, but Nelson Danglas—*Krusty*—had plenty. The cell-phone records did not prove that I was the one on the phone and thus meant nothing. The Hertz employees' new testimony showed that I rented the car before I had been told about the murder. The fact that I drove to San Juan from Managua so quickly once I had learned of Doris's death demonstrated that I could have been there at the moment of the crime and still raced back to Managua to establish my alibi. And so it went. Every outrageous hypothesis, every calculated lie, every rejection of logic and science offered up by the prosecution had been accepted as gospel and was now offered up as administration of justice. Toruño did take the time to express her outrage at the miserable screwups in the police crime lab, but she didn't let the problems they caused affect her decision. Finally, after ten minutes of this, she pronounced judgment.

"The accused, Eric Stanley Volz and Julio Martín Chamorro, are found guilty for being the perpetrators of the crime of first-degree murder in harming the young Doris Ivania Jiménez Alvarado, may she rest in peace."

Toruño thumped her gavel down, and, instantly, policemen grabbed me by the arms and hustled me out of the court into a dark little side room. As I was leaving, I could see the people hurrying out into the street, as if afraid to miss whatever drama might unfold when they brought me outside to the crowd. For ten minutes, I waited under guard until Captain Valerio gave the order to bring me outside. The police walked me through a back hallway, empty except for one person standing in the doorway of an office—Ivette Toruño. She was leaning, almost casually, with one shoulder against the doorjamb. Her legs were crossed at the ankles and her arms were folded across her chest. I looked up to meet her cold stare, but she said nothing. The cops quickly moved to get themselves between her and me.

At the time, I was so stunned, so scared, and so disoriented that I didn't know what to think about what this woman had just done to me or about why she had done it.

I do now.

8.

30 Años

"Ya llegó el gringo!"

The shrieks and banging on the bars by the *reos* stuck me like knives. I had just survived the terror of being detoured through the sugarcane only to be thrown back into the Granada prison. On the one hand, the place was familiar, although I had only spent one night there before the trial. In another sense, everything was different. Even if I had known every inch of the place and the names of every single prisoner, my mind still needed to make the shift from biding time to *doing time*. For all I knew, I was here to stay. Mike Poehlitz, who came to visit with Dan Bazan a couple of days after the conviction, drove the point home with unintended force: "Eric," he said, "up till now, this was a sprint, but now you have to adjust your mind for a marathon."

There was, in fact, no end in sight. At the very least, I was looking at a significant chunk of my life, a very real part of my short time on earth, spent in a filthy and dangerous prison far from home. That was hard to deal with, but the fact is that Mike did me a favor. His stark statement forced me to change my thinking, and it did the same for the team helping me. We had to get ourselves beyond the moment and start planning for the long term. This was going to be about strategy, about holding on, and about seeing through to the end, whenever that was going to be.

As it happened, I remained in Granada for only about a week, confined for security reasons to a large room in the medical wing, where blood literally flowed in the hallways. All day and all night, prisoners would be dragged in with blood spurting like geysers out of hideous wounds, their flesh sliced open in knife fights or their wrists slashed by their own hand.

One stumbled in with some of his intestines in his hands as he pressed against his belly to keep his guts from spilling out onto the floor. The doctor—another inmate called El Brujo, or "the Shaman," who had demonstrated his taste for gore by chopping off a man's head with a machete—would stitch them up.

That first week back in Granada turned out to be critical because of what my defense team was doing during the same time. The guilty verdict confirmed beyond any doubt that I had been set up according to a plan and that many, many people were involved in carrying out that plan. I knew enough about Nicaragua to know that a scheme like that could only have come down from the highest levels of government, which meant there was a powerful enemy facing us.

Developments of all kinds both deepened our understanding of the situation and helped us prepare for the long effort ahead. First, Frank, the American who was the owner and manager of the company providing my security, was literally forced to leave Nicaragua. He received a call from a police contact who told him to get out of the country immediately because they were coming to arrest him. He grabbed his wife and kids and fled that same day. Later that evening his house was ransacked and his three dogs were shot through the head. The Nica bodyguards and administrative personnel from his company were ordered by the police not to talk to me or anyone from my defense team. The sheer audacity of such a move against a respected American who ran a company with close ties to the Nicaraguan military sector was another strong indication that powerful people were calling the shots around my case. Those associated with me were at risk. The fight had come out into the open.

A week after the trial ended, Maggie and Dane traveled to Nicaragua for the formal sentencing. The embassy had suggested they stay away from the trial, because of concerns for their safety, but now things were different. From this moment forward, my mother was to be the public face of our heartbreak and our outrage, our fear and our fury. We never planned it this way, but nobody could have missed the imagery of Doña Maggie, the proud heartsick mother of a son she knew to be innocent, standing across the great divide from the outrageous Doña Mercedes, urging the *pueblo* to condemn me.

I can't imagine what it was like for my mother to see me ill and hungry and hopeless in the Granada pen, but we managed to talk about a few important issues when she and Dane were granted their visit. We agreed that day to change our previous approach of holding back with the press and the media. We would use them aggressively and to our advantage. It would be a delicate and tricky matter. We had to go on the attack, but while the police and prosecution were fair game, we knew we had to hold back our criticism of Judge Toruño and the court system, since my fate still lay directly in their hands, and they could turn up the misery for me in prison whenever they chose. In fact, using the press in any way would be a huge gamble. Embarrass the wrong people, and things would only get worse for me.

My conviction had consumed the Nica press, and readers from around the country were joining in the celebration, posting hateful comments on newspaper Web sites like "Kill that gringo!" or "Hopefully, he'll get raped in La Modelo." Clearly, it would be quite some time before we could think about making any cracks in what appeared to be a wall of hatred. Maybe it would never happen, but my mother had had at least one conversation with a journalist, leading her to believe that working the Nica press to our benefit might someday be possible. A producer for *Esta Semana*, a television news program like *60 Minutes* and hosted by Carlos Fernando Chamorro, the son of the former president Violetta Chamorro, actually seemed to be investigating the facts and ran the most objective piece at that time, just before the trial. Carlos Fernando is one of the most trusted journalists in Nicaragua. He had abandoned the politics of his parents more than twenty years before and joined the Sandinistas. But in recent years he had grown profoundly disillusioned with Ortega and his form of governing and had become an outspoken critic. Chamorro's producer took my mom aside and explained a basic principle to her.

"The problem is that Eric doesn't have a *padrino* ("godfather"), to say, 'Don't fuck with my godson.' . . . This is a land of guns and money." In the largest sense, he was reinforcing the point that the moves we needed to make were not the ones that might seem obvious from an American perspective. We needed someone pulling strings and applying pressure in the right places. We had to play the game the way Nicas played it. No option was perfect. It had come down to a choice between the lesser of the two evils.

The first step—and in the end the most important step we ever took—was adding a new member to the team, a *fixer*, a consultant who brought knowledge, experience, and sheer heroic commitment to the job of helping me. This man was Bob Lady, a former CIA operative who came recommended by Simon Strong, the investigator hired by Greenburg Traurig. For the previous few months, Simon, although he meant well in my opinion, had done more harm than good, wasting both invaluable time and resources chasing down his harebrained theories and managing to alienate many people on all sides of the case in the process. Even in his reason for bowing out to Bob, Simon was misguided. He had been hired to help prevent my conviction. Now that I was convicted, he conveniently claimed that only bribery would ever get me out of prison and that his company could have nothing to do with illicit maneuvers. Instead, he referred us to Bob, "the man that could make sure money changed hands in the right way."

The fact that Simon introduced him as the "bribe guy" made Bob furious. Bob was totally against bribes, and he made that clear from the start. Bob explained that paying bribes would only establish me as an easy target for extortion—it would never get me out. The case was already too high profile for one. If I had gotten caught trying to buy my freedom, no honest person of influence in Nicaragua would ever step up to the plate for me. (Evidence of that was how radioactive the $1 million rumor had become.)

Bob Lady came to us with some heavy baggage, and he began our relationship by laying that on the table for us. There would be no secrets. He had retired from the CIA but was wanted in Europe as a result of the capture (rendition) of a suspected Islamic terrorist in Milan, where Bob had been station chief. The suspect was turned over to authorities in Egypt, where he was imprisoned and allegedly tortured, and when details of the case came to light, the CIA and the U.S. government found themselves in the middle of an international scandal.[EX.38] The agency chose to make Bob—a career officer who had done nothing more than carry out his instructions—the fall guy and allowed him to be publicly disgraced.

Bob, who I came to love and trust like an uncle (in fact, I still call him Tío Bob), agreed to become part of the team, but not in the way that Simon Strong had anticipated. Bob began by redefining the game for us. He got my family and me once and for all to stop thinking about the case as a miscarriage of justice or a legal railroading and to understand it as an organized, institutional kidnapping by the Sandinista government. This wasn't about evidence or the lack of it; it wasn't about incompetent lawyers or judges or slimy police captains. It was a political hostage taking, pure and simple. We are dealing with an anti-American regime, and this is what such regimes do. It is a mistake, Bob said, to solely focus on the courts and legal process. Focus on the centers of power at the highest levels of government. Find out who's benefiting from this and how. We had to understand the true nature of the situation before we could change it. Bob added candidly that in his twenty-five years of experience, this was the most complicated case he had even seen.

And Bob started making things happen. Even as he counseled us to be patient, preparing us for a long process, he started mining the network of contacts he had developed over his years working in the region. He spoke to judges and bureaucrats and all kinds of people with influence. He developed an ally in Adolfo Calero, a noble man who had served as the longest standing general of the Contra army. Calero had the respect of leaders throughout Central America and in Washington and gave Bob both credibility and political currency, eventually helping him strengthen our connection with an important figure, ex-president Arnoldo Alemán.

Alemán is the head of the Liberal Constitution Party (PLC), the largest political opposition to Ortega. After serving as mayor of Managua and then president of Nicaragua from 1997 to 2002, Alemán stands at the front of a vast network of Nicas who hold key posts in the government bureaucracy while remaining deeply loyal to him. Although he was under "country arrest" (meaning he was free to move about the country but not allowed to leave it's borders) at the time, serving a twenty-year sentence stemming from a conviction on alleged corruption charges, Alemán still wielded tremendous power throughout the country and will likely be president again in the not-too-distant future.

It would be reasonable to ask why a figure of such stature would bother getting involved in the plight of a young American stuck in jail. There were two reasons, and they are both important to understanding the rest of this story. The first was a humanitarian one. He and his wife took the time to hear the facts, and, after they looked over the case file and did some investigating on their own, they saw that I was clearly innocent and wanted to help. The second reason was political. The level of attention my case drew from all levels of Nica and U.S. society had turned this into so much more than the murder of young woman and a framed gringo. If people now saw the case through the lens of anti-Americanism or as a showcase for vengeance against the Yankee empire, it had legitimately become a political and cultural touchstone worthy of the involvement of a player as powerful as Alemán. Helping an American in the clutches of the Sandinistas was also helping the U.S. Embassy solve its own problem, and doing so would be a substantial step to rebuilding his reputation in Washington.

In any event, with Tio Bob and Alemán—or El Gordo ("Fat Man"), as he is popularly known—in place, my family and I were set to confront the next phase of our ordeal.

Inside the Granada pen, another event of real significance took place, and that was a second face-to-face encounter with Rosita. The encounter was no accident. I used every trick I could think of to arrange it. I found out that every morning pills were taken to Rosita's cell for his stomach ulcers by the prison nurse. So I paid two guards with a pack of Marlboros to make sure that Rosita would not get his medication at the regular time, knowing that he would be asking for it later. The guards would then conveniently have a justifiable reason to bring him down to the medical wing that afternoon. And sure enough, as planned, a guard brought Rosita right to me and sat him next to my door. I got right to the point, speaking Spanish, but he responded in broken English he had picked up from hanging with traveling surfers to create a sense of privacy. I told him that I knew he got dragged into this mess just like I had but that I was going to get out. He could rot there all by himself or he could talk to me and I could try to help him. None of it was true, but I had to get him on my side.

"I'm walking," I told him. "You're gonna take the blame for this unless you talk to me. The way you get out of this hellhole is if you bring the main person into the picture, to replace you. Who was it?"

Rosita would not look at me. "Man, I wasn't there. I can't say anything. Doris was my friend. I would never have wanted to hurt her."

"Thirty years is a long time, brother," I went on. "I'm your only chance. Now tell me, or I will do everything in my power to make sure you complete every day of this sentence."

Rosita stiffened. He realized I was trying to probe him, and suddenly he went off, shouting in Spanish so that anyone could hear him. "These gringos think they own the world and can just walk all over us poor Nicas. . . ."

That was it. I had failed utterly. The guards took Rosita away, and I knew I'd never get another chance with him. Even if I did, I doubted he'd ever tell me anything. Either he was going to maintain his innocence forever and had figured out that giving up anyone else would be the same as admitting he had been there at the murder, or somebody somewhere was holding something over him. If that were the case, it had to be someone with a very powerful threat for Rosita to bear the burden of a thirty-year sentence in that horrific place rather than simply speak the truth.

The next day, after receiving intel that Doris's family might be trying to plan some sort of attack on me in the Granada prison, the director of the National Penitentiary System (SPN) ordered me to be moved. I was squeezed into the back of a small unmarked car full of guards and driven away from Granada. I knew the destination, La Modelo. Hard time.

There is no "department of corrections" in the Nicaraguan justice system. There is no real institutional interest in rehabilitating prisoners or reintegrating them as productive members of society. There is only *el sistema*. In other neighboring countries, even the maximum-security prisons have names like Renacer ("Rebirth") or Esperanza ("Hope"). Not in Nica. The big max-security prison is simply La Modelo—"The Model"—so named because its architecture, which has become the template for other Central American prisons, maximizes the ability of the authorities to control the prison population. It is as if they want only to lock prisoners away, to give them no more than the barest necessities, and maybe a little less. The mentality seems to be that if you survive, then good for you. Prison is for punishment, and it should hurt. It does.

It felt like the whole prison had been waiting for me. Guards would flash wicked little smirks and make comments like, "We've been wondering if you'd return" or, "Lookee who we have here!" As soon as I arrived, I picked up a very clear vibe: *You're ours now, boy.* The prisoners, too. As soon as I got to know my new cell mate, Leonardo, he told me that the entire prison population had celebrated my conviction when it was announced in the news. Everyone had been excited to see the gringo go down. Now that I'm a little more familiar with their worldview, I think most of them saw it as simple payback for all the trials and tribulations they had faced in life, regardless of whether or not any of it had anything to do with Americans. It didn't help that I got put in a cell just a few doors down from the one that had held Eugene Hasenfus, the American pilot who had survived a plane crash while ferrying in supplies to the Contras and whose capture had helped expose the Iran-Contra affair and triggered the resentment toward Americans that still pervades the collective consciousness in Nicaragua. Some inmates were drawn to me out of simple self-interest, thinking maybe a guy who had the attention of the press could shine a light on the sickening conditions or the corruption of *el sistema*. Leo even told me about the *reos* who had been begging to get me assigned as their cell mate, thinking it would give them access to all the luxuries they assumed I would have in prison. Two of them had even gotten into a fight about it.

Leo and I shared a cell at the end of the long block known as *dos alta*, the second floor of *galeria* 2. As filthy and broke-down as it was, *dos alta* was as good a place as I could ask for in La Modelo. Most of the men in *dos alta* were former cops, military guys, or other government officials, along with some high-profile drug traffickers, although our end of the hallway had its share of drug addicts and petty thieves, too. Whenever someone from the outside would visit, such as representatives from human-rights commissions or a church making a donation, the warden only showed them our *galeria*, and only after we'd been forced to quickly mop the floors and make ourselves presentable. The visitors were never taken to the block below us on the first floor, *dos baja*, the most dangerous *galeria* in the entire prison. Gangs ruled the *dos baja* without mercy.

Even in this "healthiest" of *galerias* there was still plenty of violence. I quickly learned from watching others that when you are not hustling out in the *galeria* for the provisions you need to survive, the safest thing to do is to remain locked behind the heavy steel door of your cell, but even then you could be targeted. During my time in La Modelo, two inmates who had been confined to their cell had actually chipped through the concrete wall and broken into the adjacent cell, just so they could rape a new young *reo*. Recently, some journalists and experts have condemned solitary confinement as a form of torture in and of itself. It doesn't really matter if a prisoner is placed in solitary for his own safety or punishment or if he imposes it on himself for some reason. It's still unbearable. Nonetheless, I didn't come out of the cell unless I had to. I rarely even got off the bed.

The space that I would have to call home consisted of a tiny cell with a tile floor and greasy live electrical wires sticking out of the walls and the ceiling (a syringe connecting two wires served as the light switch). It had a concrete toilet with no water pressure, where the urine would accumulate until it got too full and unmanageable and we'd have to flush it by pouring water from gallon buckets we kept stored. Plastic bags were woven through the bars at the bottom of the doors to keep out the disgusting cats, and there were lines of homemade string for drying clothes, a hot plate and some plastic cups and dishes, a wooden cabinet that Leo had scored but that only he used, and an old school desk that was more than a desk. Leo showed me how one leg could come off and serve as a weapon and where one of the hollow metal tubes hid a homemade stabbing knife. We shared our cell with swarms of flies and mosquitoes so thick you could swipe your hand through the air and grab a fistful of them. They were everywhere—on your food, your coffee cup—landing on your face every second, covering your body when you got out of the shower. The air in the prison felt like a thick, wet, ferociously hot blanket of air and insects. After all, this is a prison in the tropics. Moisture settled on every surface, and any place you put your body quickly became a nasty puddle of stinking sweat, a breeding ground that ensured the cycle of filth and infestation never ended. Secondhand smoke from the *bañados*, weed joints laced with crack cocaine that *reos* consantly smoked, turned the already-oppressive atmosphere poisonous. When you add the rot and mold created by the penetrating moisture, it's no surprise that I quickly developed severe respiratory problems. It would be a miracle if I escaped the more serious diseases that were common there, like hepatitis B and tuberculosis.

As for Leonardo, I could have done worse. A dropout from a rural town, Leo was in for having "accidentally" shot his pregnant wife in the shoulder during a drunken rampage. He could drive me crazy with his constant complaining, but he was never any kind of a physical threat. Leo kept a little radio, which he listened to literally all the time, cradling it on his chest like a baby. The radio provided companionship, much like the volleyball, Wilson, did for Tom Hanks's character in the film *Cast Away*. Lots of prisoners developed unusual attachments to objects this way; treating things almost like pets was a survival instinct. Any kind of relationship helps someone escape the solitude of prison. Given that he was a former Sandinista soldier and at one point had worked as a guard in the prison and that I was at the center of the most-high-profile case in the country at the time, it was a pretty safe bet that Leo was some kind of informer, but he also had useful inside information to share.

For the two and a half months since my arrest in November, I had totally occupied my brain with trying to figure a way out. I was consumed, either by analyzing theories of Doris's murder or by attempting to comprehend the incomprehensible puzzle of the Nicaraguan legal system or by trying to uncover the hidden forces that had snatched me out of my life. Now it was time to set all that to one side. I had to put my faith in Maggie and Dane, in Tio Bob, in Fabbrith, and in so many people on the outside working for my freedom. I could have only one primary mission now: survival.

I had spent just a few weeks in La Modelo before the trial, but during that short time there had been too many fights to count, multiple stabbings, two deaths, suicides, and a bloody gang riot that involved three hundred *reos*. Then I had just come from the smaller Granada prison, where I saw more blood in a single week in the medical wing than in my entire life before that. There's no such thing as absolute safety inside those prisons, and at that point I had yet to figure out whether the people who wanted me there had any interest in my staying alive. The wardens and guards could try to keep me safe from harm, if that suited them, but they could just as easily arrange for me to be killed.

And, of course, the threat of rape is everywhere. Since coming home, I've learned that prison rape is the question that everybody wants to ask and nobody does. I will say that fortunately I was spared, but the ugliness of rape was part of daily life in La Modelo. Even when the sex between the *reos* was consensual—and it often was—situations could turn violent in a heartbeat. Even on the less chaotic *dos alta* level of La Modelo, lovers were likely to settle their quarrels with a shank.

Beyond the obvious physical danger was the bigger challenge of staying sane. In fact I already understood that my old standards for sanity and madness were meaningless in prison. Almost everyone here was crazy, each in his own way, and it was very possible that this assessment would come to include me someday. To survive, the smart *reos* find a way to blend in. You have to know the demented codes of prison life and the criminal way of thinking well enough to avoid trouble, to fade into invisibility. In order to truly make the transition into the rhythms of the pen, you have to leave the rules and rhythms of the free world behind. One elder *reo* liked to say, "I'm in prison, but the prison is not in me."

During my first stay in La Modelo, I hadn't let myself really become part of the place. I was just counting the days until the trial then, and I wouldn't allow myself to consider the possibility that I'd be coming back here for thirty years. I had a lot to figure out now, and quickly. It's not like you get a training period. In Nicaragua, the prisons don't provide for basic needs, so every inmate has to improvise. I'd need systems and networks and allies just to get edible food and supplies. I'd need something to barter with, whether money or cigarettes or something else on a consistent basis. I would have little time to learn who I could trust and who I had to fear among the prisoners and the guards. Who could be bribed and with what? Who had a supply chain into which I could tap? I had to learn the unwritten rules of the gang conflicts that had infiltrated *el sistema* from the streets of Managua and other towns so that I could understand the hidden loyalties and deadly grudges. In other words, survival meant hustling. You hear stories about men in U.S. penitentiaries who make it through by holing up in their cell or in the prison library or something. Maybe that's possible if you don't have to worry about food in your belly or shoes on your feet. But you can't sit back in La Modelo. A man who doesn't make moves, who doesn't take action and set things up for himself—that's a man who will simply waste away and die, if he doesn't get himself killed first.

9.

Breakfast with the President

My attorneys moved ahead with the appeals process. We knew now that my captivity had nothing to do with the legal process, but we had to go along with it nonetheless, even as we began working the back channels of power. Nicaraguan law requires an appeal to be filed almost immediately after a verdict, but the Sandinistas were putting obstacles in our way. Judge Toruño ordered the Rivas court *not* to release the trial tapes to us, so our appeal would have to be drafted from notes and memory and from the incomplete recordings we had made with my handheld digital recorder during the trial.

After my conviction, Ramon Rojas had all but disappeared from the scene, so the burden of the legal work fell to Fabbrith Gomez. Joe Reeder and Greenburg Traurig in Washington made a lot of noise about wanting to be involved but were able to contribute very little beyond editing documents. Fabbrith, with assistance from Jackie, managed to draft a solid appeal[EX.39] though and submitted it on time. The prosecution paid far less attention to the time requirements for their response, if they even were aware of them. (Most lawyers and judges have conflicting opinions about these procedural details.) Again, Toruño took an active role in delaying justice. Even when she received the appeal[EX.40] from the prosecutors in late March, she sat on it for several weeks, despite the law. Her political bosses, the Sandinistas, had a problem on their hands.

The only way to assure I would not be released was if the Sandinista *bancada*, or "bench" (judicial bench loyal to the Sandinista leaders) had one of their own to handle the appeal, but there was only one justice on the panel who had the experience to actually elaborate and type up a ruling in such a complicated case, Judge Roberto Rodriguez, and he was not a Sandinista; Rodriguez was a liberal sympathetic to the country's liberal party (the PLC) but steadfastly remained politically neutral in his administration of the law. The president of the appeals court, Ángela Gross (a Sandinista), knew only about civil, not criminal law. And, a third justice, Alejandro Estrada, a purely political appointee of Alemán's, had so little competence that the court rarely gave him the responsibility of drafting rulings. At this point, the cast of characters involved in my case—at least those on whom we put names and faces—started to grow out of control. Worse, the cast kept changing. In fact, the final makeup of the appeals panel wasn't even decided for several more months.

Several key players surfaced around this time. First was Julio Centeno, the *fiscal general* for the entire country. Centeno's role is that of an attorney general. We learned from a source inside the Rivas prosecutor's office that all the orders to Isolda Ibarra and other prosecutors in my case came directly from Centeno in Managua. To understand Centeno's background is to understand the shifting sands of political allegiance in Nicaragua. He was actually a liberal and had been appointed to his position by Arnoldo Alemán, to whom he remained loyal. Centeno still held his position when Ortega came back to power just before my arrest, so now he was subject to pressure from two opposing masters.

Alba Luz Ramos, a chief justice of the Nica Supreme Court and a long-time operator of the Sandinista party, had entrenched influence. It is commonly known, even reported in the local press, that she is one of the bosses of the mafia of judges loyal to the Sandinistas, known collectively as the Sandinista *bancada*. She controls several district-level judges, including Ivette Toruño. According to what we were told by senior politicians, Toruño would have never been the one to make the decision on how to rule on a case as high profile as mine. Fabbrith and Tio Bob had to learn who those players were and what to expect from them.

When you peel back the layers of politicos in Nicaragua, you inevitably get to the round, pockmarked face of Lenin Cerna. You only need to hear his first name to know where his loyalties lie. Lenin Cerna headed the

Seguridad del Estado, the intelligence agency of the Sandinista government in the 1980s. He was trained by the Cubans and Russians, operating with the structure and techniques similar to that of the KGB.* He keeps a low public profile, but, in fact, his hands touch just about everything in the country through a deep network of operators and former agents that remain loyal to the party. Lenin Cerna is the embodiment of the "Russian shadow" in Nicaragua, but his role in my story demonstrates how personal agendas often make interactions and relationships so unpredictable and unmanageable.

Soon after arriving at La Modelo, I met Tio Bob face-to-face for the first time, on a family visit day with Maggie and Dane. There's something about Bob that inspires confidence. Maybe it's the calm clarity of his mind or the way he gently takes command of any situation. Maybe it's his solid, slightly imposing physical presence or his surprising charm and sense of humor. Maybe it was simply knowing what he had been through in his life and career. Whatever the case, I felt right away that his presence was a blessing.

I remember that I dove right into telling Bob every detail of the prison that might be relevant to an escape plan, from the physical layout to the positions and schedules of the guards. Now that I fully understood that I was a political prisoner, I believed it was both my right and duty to escape, but Bob immediately made me think otherwise. He showed me why any attempt at escape could be something I'd regret. To begin with, it would never happen like in the movies, with some commando team sneaking in at night and smuggling me out. It would require a full-scale assault with as many as a hundred men. Apart from the prohibitive expense, the potential human costs were too great. There would surely be some kind of exchange of bullets. After that, I no longer considered escape from La Modelo a possibility. No way could I ask another person to put himself or herself into that type of danger to rescue my skin.

---

* After the civil war ended in 1990, the Seguridad del Estado was formally dissolved and faded into various sectors of society. The Sandinistas sent hundreds of their agents to law school to become judges. Today, many of these former Sandinista intelligence officers are presently licensed judges.

Either we'd find a way or we wouldn't, but I would not have blood on my hands.

Tio Bob's position on escape was reinforced by the fact that La Modelo had recently become something of a fortress. Nica authorities had made a huge drug bust, nabbing members of Mexico's notorious Sinaloa cartel, which had recently established a corridor for transporting northbound product. The traffickers, including some high-ranking members of the cartel, had been brought to La Modelo to await trial. In fact, the brother of El Chapo, who is the head boss of the entire cartel and is considered to be one the most powerful narcos in the history of cocaine, was locked in a cell just fifty feet from mine. It is estimated that he is worth over $1 billion. The authorities were so worried about an extraction attempt that prison security was fortified with military soldiers and police SWAT teams. No one was getting in or out of that pen unless by formal proclamation or all-out war.

On the opposite side of the spectrum from Tio Bob sat Dan Bazan from the U.S. Embassy. Bazan had told me to expect visits from embassy personnel only once every three months or so, which was standard. My team, with the help of senators in DC, reminded him that there was nothing standard about my conviction. The embassy knew it, and eventually they agreed to visit me weekly. Those visits were invaluable to me, not because the embassy ever had much of an impact but because their mere presence on a regular basis prevented the guards from beating me like they did the other *reos*. At that point in my story it would have been counterproductive to present a bruised and beaten U.S. citizen to representatives of his own government.

While we waited on the appeals process, we began to see our gloves-off approach with the media start to bear fruit. Up to that point, nothing had broken in any of the internationally influential media outlets, but on March 19, a month after my conviction, *The Wall Street Journal* ran a lengthy front-page feature[EX.41] that changed everything. Two days later, friends of mine made it a one-two punch by releasing a short documentary[EX.42] about my case on YouTube, which they promoted through MySpace and other Internet sites. The video went viral within days, and suddenly the case became a lightning rod.

Everyone in Washington is aware of what makes the front page of the *Journal*, as is just about everyone in positions of real power throughout the world. The paper is a leader in online journalism. Even more important, having the *Journal* cover a story represents a stamp of approval for journalists in all other outlets. The *Journal*'s coverage of a story requires other papers and news organizations to pay attention as well and serves as the catalyst for their own investigations and stories. The article they ran on March 19 was the first major story to take a hard and critical look at the flaws and mistakes and suspected misconduct that had led to my conviction, giving our appeal efforts and our pleas for public and governmental support much-needed weight and credibility.

In the next week, segments about my case began to appear on nightly news broadcasts in the United States. Major metropolitan dailies around the country picked up the story, as did wire services and the big online players, including AOL, MSNBC, and CNN. By the end of the week, two investigative magazine reporters came to Managua and were allowed to interview me in La Modelo. Tony D'Souza's long and detailed piece eventually ran in *Outside* magazine, and Dean La Tourette's was featured in *Men's Journal*.

The story was reaching a tipping point in the public consciousness, which meant that the informal support network around the world was also growing at amazing speed, in both size and strength with an average of 140,000 monthly visitors to the "Friends of Eric Volz" Web site. I supposed then that the honest portrayal of my situation was gaining traction in terms of public awareness and thought that all the press attention from then on was going to work to my benefit. So when we heard that NBC's *Dateline* wanted to send a crew down and that the director of the pentitiary system had approved the interview, we figured it could only be good news. The result, however, turned out to be something of a mixed blessing.

Imagine walking out of a disgusting cell, out of the infested bowels of the prison, and being confronted by an American television crew—L.A. hipsters lugging around millions of dollars' worth of equipment, a blow-dried correspondent in designer jeans in the middle of an elaborate tropical-island set they had put up right in the prison meeting hall. They interviewed me for a long time, covering the case in real depth and detail. I felt great afterward, and people on the crew gave me fantastic feedback. The anchor on the set said something about the program reaching an audience of around fifteen million viewers, and I thought for sure we were on the way to some kind of breakthrough.

Until then, my only experience as the subject of a big media story had been through the rabid Nica press, which didn't always place a high value on truth and objectivity. A story on a primetime network program in the U.S. seemed like a chance for the real story to come out. What I didn't understand is that the story that I had been living and breathing for so long had grown—at least in my mind—into something far more complex and nuanced than could ever fit into a compact newsmagazine segment. A piece on a show like *Dateline* can't really go into the level of detail—and take into account the huge number of characters and narrative threads— that my case involved. The natural tendency is to fall back on much simpler story lines in which people are either good or bad, happy or sad, victim or offender. That perspective helped shape the questions posed by the reporters and producers.

The story that aired was not the legal and political story I had conveyed. It was more of a thriller or a soap opera, centered on the question of how much I really cared about Doris, and whether or not I might have murdered her. One narrative technique upset me greatly. The producers could have titled the piece something like "An Innocent American" or "American Hostage in Nicaragua?" but chose "Murder by the Sea." The idea was to keep the viewer in suspense about my guilt or innocence for as long as possible. The few snippets of my interview that made the final cut seemed carefully chosen to prolong that sense of suspense. In particular, the sound bites about Doris made me look not necessarily like a guilty man but, at the very least, like an uncompassionate jerk. Just at the time when the support network was blossoming, I started getting letters, mostly from women, calling me an arrogant asshole. Not what I needed.

I felt the impact of the piece much more harshly inside the prison. There was one Nicaraguan on the crew, a local news correspondent and production assistant named Rosemary Thornton. Rosemary would commonly get hired by foreign news groups, helping them with logistics and contacts inside the country. After the main interview, Rosemary wanted to bring cameras into the *galeria* and pushed the warden to allow it. Amazingly, the warden left the decision up to me, and I said no. I wanted so badly to have the conditions of the prison documented and revealed to the world, but I also knew that many of the *reos* already resented my "wealthy gringo" status, and I knew it would only agitate them further if I showed up on the block with a film crew. I also thought I could send a message to the warden that I was willing to play ball in this way and keep the spotlight off him and his prison.

Rosemary didn't like that I turned her down. She threw a fit, ranting at the guards and officers, and angered a lot of people. What did I care about Rosemary's tantrum? The next day, an order came down that I was to be handcuffed whenever I left the cell block. The only prisoners who were put in restraints were the ones being punished in solitary confinement. Out of three thousand prisoners, I was the only one not serving a punishment regimen who was being cuffed. I had no misconduct reports, but, despite numerous formal complaints, I never got an explanation. Those handcuffs stayed on for two and a half months.

Rosemary became an intense troublemaker in fact, and it became clear that she was more than just a journalist. She was an infiltrated operator carrying out someone else's agenda. We would learn that her husband had been the former national police chief with close ties to the boys of the Auxilio Judicial. They were able to work together to contaminate the opinions of many influential people, including those from the international press, with varying degress of success. It also turned out that one of her best friends was the wife of the journalist Ricardo Castillo, who had testified in my defense at the trial. Rosemary told stories about my being involved in drug trafficking and money laundering. By the time she was through, Ricardo had convinced himself that, even if I were innocent, he shouldn't get his hands dirty for me and declined to help the defense any longer. She also told Mercedes that I was guilty because I had been planning on leaving the country the week of Doris's murder. And, later, Rosemary went as far as contacting one of the justices on the appeals panel and pumping him with controversial questions, even though her job was merely to schedule interviews. He shut the press out after that.*

Nonetheless, the media attention kept rolling forward. The *Today* show on NBC aired a long segment. MSNBC, largely through the efforts of Kerry Sanders, a deeply motivated and experienced reporter, covered the case regularly and in careful detail. At home, the tenacious Melissa Campbell, a media-relations expert who worked with my mother and Dane, saw to it that more newspaper and magazine articles appeared while protecting my family from the hungry and less-ethical media sharks. I was learning to grit my teeth through inevitable nonsense about my being a surfer dude in search of island paradise, believing that the increased awareness in the United States and elsewhere could help put pressure on the Nica government, perhaps still too optimistic to understand that the attention would make the important Sandinistas in power just dig their heels in even deeper. We were, however, able to make use of all the ink and airplay my case was getting to fuel the Internet efforts. More and more people were visiting the Friends of Eric Volz Web site and were sending letters of support, encouragement, and advice, and even much-needed donations toward my defense. Momentum was building.

Tio Bob and Adolfo Calero had initiated a relationship with Arnoldo Alemán, but it was actually through an admirer of *EP* magazine that the first meeting with the ex-president was facilitated. An arrangement was made to bring my mother and Dane to a breakfast with Alemán and his

---

* Rosemary Thornton was fired and blacklisted by NBC, CNN, and A&E.

wife. Like most powerful people in Nicaragua, Alemán was a controversial figure. In a classically *pais de maravillas*—"country of marvels"—story, his own vice president helped bring him down politically. Enrique Bolaños had come into office with Alemán and had won the presidency when Alemán's term ended, switching party allegiance literally the moment after he was sworn into office. He dramatically removed his red shirt— red being the color of the Liberal party—to reveal the shirt of the Conservative party's blue underneath. Bolaños, working closely with a small group out of Washington, went after the former president, and Alemán was tried on charges of corruption and embezzlement and sentenced to twenty years. He spent less than a year in prison and quickly maneuvered to be able to serve his term under house arrest. The facts of his case are epically complex. No doubt, Alemán become an extremely wealthy man while in office. He explains that the money never came to him illegally, that it was gifted by the Taiwanese government in order to maintain and lubricate trade relations. Perhaps he did nothing criminal, but his actions weren't considered ethical by many observers. What most people may not know is that such arrangements are common and effective in many parts of the world.

Alemán's big personality matched his bulk. El Gordo is a master politician, charming and charismatic, big hearted and funny, and a great talker. He's the kind of man who would rather crush you in a bear hug than give you a firm, businesslike handshake. Underneath his plainspoken, common-man exterior, though, was a brilliant political strategist who could not just understand all the angles in any situation but knew how to work them. Even if you had unlimited money to pay legal experts or to bribe officials, you couldn't accomplish what Alemán could with a single phone call. I could not have asked for a better godfather to have in my corner.

I first met El Gordo in a secret meeting in the office of the SPN director, El Prefecto or chief officer, Carols Sobalvarro, at La Modelo. Just getting me through the interior security gate to the administration building and back again became an elaborate hush-hush operation. He came to the meeting with his wife and a man named Rene Herrera, a respected political advisor who would serve as the go-between for Alemán and our people. Although the meeting was legal, it was highly risky—a former president coming to talk with the radioactive figure Eric Volz in a backroom meeting. El Prefecto was extremely nervous and made sure that I was clear that the press was not to find out. My being embraced by a man more powerful than he must have made El Prefecto feel somewhat smaller. It changed the power dynamic, and he treated me with more respect after that.

El Gordo hugged me and made a polite inquiry into how I was doing. When I answered, his eyes widened, and, with a big grin, he turned to his wife. "The son of a bitch speaks perfect Spanish!" The ice was broken, and we quickly developed a rapport.

"These sons of bitches [the Sandinistas] don't value human life or the rule law. You and I have the same adversaries, Eric," Alemán said, after I had filled him in on some of the details about my situation, and, I think, given him the sense that I was both levelheaded and sympathetic. It was important to get on the table the understanding that we had mutual interests and that his helping me made political sense for him.

"With all due respect, Mr. President," I responded, "the difference is I'm locked up, and you're free to roam the country."

10.

Chew Your Rice

It sounds strange to say it now, but the most important thing I had to do was figure out who I was going to be in prison. In life your identity evolves slowly, but when you come into the closed, contained, and completely alien world of prison as a kind of blank slate, you have to establish your place in the social order quickly. At least that's how it was for me, and, even worse, I was locked up in a foreign country. I had no history in common with other prisoners—no same hometown, no distant relatives, no gang loyalty, no similar accent, nothing. I would have to establish an identity for myself.

Ultimately, it's about respect. The saying in prison is "ni amigos, ni enemigos"—*neither friends nor enemies*. I didn't need anyone to fear me or follow me; I only wanted to be left alone. It was important that I demonstrated that I wasn't an easy mark, that hassling me just wouldn't be worth the trouble. No doubt, the political notoriety surrounding my case helped, but I could never stop posturing.

The fact is that I was fighting for respect constantly, not just with the other prisoners but with the guards, the warden, the whole system. I came in with so many strikes against me. Aside from the obvious, I wasn't prepared to find myself part of a minority. For the first time in my life, I felt irrational hatred directed toward me based not on who I was but on my nationality and background. It's not that a middle-class white American has any place complaining about blatant discrimination, but it's painful and demeaning to feel that kind of prejudice and disdain. Part of me is grateful for the experience. Walking in those shoes for a time deepened my understanding of a much more profound level of injustice.

I had to "train" the guards, which I did by asserting the rights I knew I had as an inmate. They hadn't seen much of that before and were used to doing pretty much whatever they wanted with little chance of getting into any trouble. I'm sure that standing up for myself mostly just pissed them off, but really I didn't care. Fighting for my rights kept me grounded. It gave me purpose and preserved my dignity.

The guards were all over me though. One day they came in and tore my cell apart, looking for a cell phone they suspected me of having based on a tip from another inmate—a guy named Fierro who had killed an elderly woman while holding up a bus with an AK-47. When I had landed in La Modelo, I made it my business to read and learn the constitutional rights of an inmate and asserted those rights at all times. The guards never quite knew what to make of a prisoner who refers to laws and international conventions to stick up for himself. Mostly my formal letters to the warden and the block supervisors just annoyed them and rarely yielded results. When they searched our cell that day, I insisted on exercising my right to stay in there with them, knowing their regular practice of planting contraband in a cell and then "discovering" it. I tried to keep track as they went through every scrap of paper, including the used toilet paper sitting in the trashcan. (Flushing of toilet paper is not allowed, although it is sometimes done as a form of protest.) When they shook out my books, they came across twenty cordobas in cash (the equivalent of not much more than a U.S. dollar). When you think about all the crazy stuff that goes down every hour of every day, you have to wonder how that little bit of money earned me a trip to the warden's office, but that's where I found myself a half hour later, facing the prison's entire chain of command. I got the explanation when I caught a glimpse of the contents of a folder that fell to the floor during the meeting. It was my file, and, in addition to the usual forms and paperwork you'd find in any prisoner's file, there were printed downloads from my Web site, my MySpace page, documents I recognized from my legal case file, photographs of my family and friends, and so on. It was unusual, to say the least, for the prison warden to have that material.

I got spooked by the level of surveillance on me. I'd see them hovering at my door at all hours of the night, silhouetted by the dim light outside our dark cell, peering in to check on me. Sometimes, high-ranking guards would pass by—very unusual for the interior blocks. One finally whispered to me that they had word that I wanted to kill myself. It took a while, but I figured out that another inmate—Fierro again—had told the guards I planned on hanging myself. As awful as my life in prison was, even at the earliest stages suicide had not crossed my mind. No way. It was Fierro screwing with me and my cell mate Leo. It wasn't just that the constant surveillance was preventing sleep night after night. The real problem was that the presence of extra guards on the block was jamming up the other *reos* there, especially the druggies who needed privacy to do their thing. I had so little cred to begin with and couldn't bear the idea of giving them another reason to resent me. It took me weeks to convince the warden that I had no intention of harming myself, and, finally, those night watchers disappeared.

Currency takes many different forms inside the multilayered economy of La Modelo. It's forbidden to have actual money—although there was plenty of it floating around—so the *reos'* economy runs on cigarettes, food, newspapers, drugs, construction, prostitution, taco stands, appliances, homemade antennas, taxes on the warden's authorization to bring in furniture—anything that might have value to prisoners. There are unwritten rules, too. For example, you never give anything away. Do it once and they'll expect you to give away free stuff forever. If you have something somebody else wants, you have to get something in return for it, even if you have no use for what you receive in the barter. Whatever it might be, it represents an asset in the bank. Eventually you'll be able to unload just about anything.

I did manage to have cash smuggled in. It would come in a box of fifty packets of instant coffee, five of which would actually contain a few bills rolled up into a tight cylinder. Possession of cash, however, as I had learned, is a punishable offense, so I made sure the money never stayed in my hands for long. Besides, I wanted people to know that I never had much cash on me so nobody would be tempted to rob me. Cigarettes, too, were like gold, especially the Marlboros people brought me. I could trade or sell off a few cigarettes or a pack at a time, getting only the money I needed for another transaction. Sometimes I never even saw the money. For example, I tried to keep a stockpile of limes. Limes, of all things, are a useful commodity in prison. They make a good disinfectant, but more important you could easily resell them to people who make jailhouse liquor—*chicha*—which itself could be sold or bartered. I'd give a runner a pack of cigarettes, and then he'd sell it to someone else and use the money to buy limes, and get to keep some cash as part of the deal. Or something like that. It seemed like everything would happen real quickly, almost with a little sleight of hand, like a game of three-card monte on the streets of New York.

For instance, one day a kid from *dos baja* managed to get up to our second-story window, reach through the bars, and snatch a pair of Leo's pants off the clothesline. He had pulled them through the bars of the window before Leo even realized what was happening. As the kid leapt down to the dirt two floors below, Leo jumped up to go after him. By the time Leo chased him down, the kid had already sold the pants for a dollar and half, bought some weed with the money—and smoked it—while the Colombian who bought the pants turned around and sold them for twice the profit to someone in another block. The whole thing happened in a matter of minutes.

The kid had taken a risk because stealing like that could just as easily get you killed. Just two or three weeks after I got to La Modelo, two guys had ripped off another, older inmate and then made a show of mocking him about it. The *reo* who had gotten robbed just snapped and stabbed both of them brutally, sparking another shakedown in which the guards confiscated hundreds more weapons.

That was the same day that the two inmates had broken through the wall of their cell to rape a newcomer. Proving the point that anything could be fashioned into a weapon or a tool, these guys had broken off a piece of their concrete sink and used that to slowly break a hole in their cell wall. I had examined the walls very closely—whenever the fantasy of escape overtook me—and knew that the effort involved in chipping through them was unimaginable. It took them a week, but they were so high on crack cocaine that they probably didn't even notice the pain of the labor.

One of the rapists, a man named Campana who had spent some time illegally in California and liked to talk to me in Spanglish about places we had both been, ended up on lockdown in a cell across from me. *Lockdown*, or a punishment regimen, is when the guards replace the normal lock on the door of the cell with a bolt sealed with crescent wrenches. You are bound to your cell and are only let out to visit the doctor. The length of the punishment can vary from a couple of weeks to several years. There is no running water in the cells and the guys who bring the prison chow usually don't voluntarily go to the cells of those on lockdown. As a result, there is an unspoken code that you lend a hand to another prisoner in that situation. They need stuff brought to them and other favors. I would give Campana soap, but only tiny little pieces of it—nothing large enough that he could trade it for drugs. I wasn't the only one, but, when he saw that I was willing to help him, he started asking for more and more stuff, until I eventually just cut him off. He got all vexed, swearing he'd make me pay.

It could have gone worse for Campana, but the victim refused to press any formal charges. That's usually how it went. Shame and fear on the victim's part usually meant only minor consequences for the most dangerous offenders in the prison. Rape and sexuality are a part of the life, but prison has its own codes and rules about it. The rape victim was ashamed, but the rapists were not. You are only considered gay if you are the one being penetrated. You can violate another man and not be gay. For this reason men who were constantly having sex with other men had no problem mocking the men they considered "faggots."

One day the guards put a *reo* named Alex in the cell next to me that they often used as a lockdown cell. Alex had stabbed a guy to death in the hallway of his block for stealing a little hand mirror. He was considered so dangerous and violent that the guards warned me to stay clear of his cell, but he was still allowed some privileges and received regular visits from a girlfriend. There also happened to be on our block a seventeen-year-old kid whose name was Ronald but who was know by everyone as La Kimberly. With his feminine face and flamboyantly gay manner, La Kimberly had been raped so often in the juvenile pen that the guards had given up the impossible task of keeping him safe. He had been moved to *dos alta* for his own protection, since it was the place he was least likely to find trouble—unless, of course, he went looking for it, which is exactly what he did. He set his sights on the murderous Alex, and I watched him carry out his seduction over the course of one week. It moved from flirtation to hand-holding to putting makeup on Alex's face through the bars, and, before anyone knew it, La Kimberly was regularly giving oral sex to Alex, again through the bars. Right out in the open where the whole block could watch. As soon as the guards opened La Kimberly's cell in the morning, he'd be at Alex's door, while Alex would slip money to the guards to let him spend time in La Kimberly's cell on the way back from a visit to the doctor. The thing is that when Alex got called "faggot" by his own brother, the two of them got into a fight, with Alex insisting that because he was using La Kimberly like a woman, he was the *marido* of the couple and was absolutely not gay.

Campana, Alex, Fierro, La Kimberly. These were just a few of the *reos* who made up the world of *dos alta*, but there were so many others, each one with his own personal story of tragedy and violence. Now, when I think that I spent months and months with these men in the most ungodly circumstances, it makes my heart start to pound.

Fat, piggish Polanco was an ex-cop who would tell me that his life was already over. They called him Polanco after the name of the man he killed, a mob kingpin. The word on the block was that he had carried out the hit on orders from his ranking superiors and would most likely be taken out himself before he ever left La Modelo. There was El Pelon, a member of the Council of the Catholic Church, who appeared to be one of the most trusted inmates in the pen. The warden and guards thought so, anyway, and even gave him keys to certain rooms and offices. I wonder how much his current girlfriend, a woman with a young daughter, knew about the crime that landed El Pelon in prison—the two small children he had viciously hacked to death, the children of his former girlfriend whom he suspected of cheating on him. El Pelon's perfect behavior had the prison staff fooled, but those of us who lived with him saw his vicious insanity every day.

It was actually hard to tell the sane from the insane at times. Miniku- chi, a tall, skinny guy with a pencil mustache and the name "Antonio" tattooed across his back, acted as the block's street vendor. He could and would get you anything you needed, for a commission. Each time his mom came to visit, he'd sell the provisions she brought the moment she had left so that he could buy drugs. One day, Minikuchi got totally jacked up on crack rock, covered himself in his own feces, came out into the *gale- ria*, and tried to hug the other inmates. The guy was just putting on a show, hoping to get labeled insane and transferred off the block, but all he got was a beating from the guards. It seemed to me you'd have to be some- what insane just to try something like that.

There was Pablito, one of the late Pablo Escobar's drug pilots, who would insist—in his clear, elegant, unmistakably Colombian accent— that he was actually from Guatemala and that the police had mistaken him for someone else. Poison, so named because of the album cover from the band of that name he had tattooed across his back, had carried on a sexual relationship with his own teenage daughter for three years. He was the *galeria's* mutt, doing any job for anybody. Poison spun outrageous stories for us—lying about how he had been in the Iraq war or was a world-champion motocross racer. One day in his cell I found the maga- zines that contained all the stories that he had told as his own.

Rapists, child abusers, witch doctors, and cold-blooded killers. These were my constant companions. I also found some *reos* with whom I could be—and I hesitate to use the word—friends. It started with my cell mate Leonardo. As hideous as the situation was, I can't imagine the added misery of a permanent cell mate you can't get along with. Leo could bug the shit out of me with his radio, but most of the time he was chill, and we managed to avoid any serious problems.

I also found Jonathan again, the boxer with the tattooed and muscled body—who had stabbed his victim ninety times with an icepick—whom I'd met in La Modelo before the trial. I could hang with Jonathan, sometimes just sitting in his cell and escaping into some music. The funny thing about my relationships with both Jonathan and Leo is the very fact that the closer we got, the more carefully I had to watch them and watch myself around them. I could never forget about the "Russian shadow," the culture of suspicion that had turned Nicaragua into a nation of informers, and nowhere was that as intense as it was in prison. I quickly trained myself to always operate on the assumption that anything I did or said, if it could be used against me in some way, would get reported back to intelligence agents and possibly beyond. Who better to provide that kind of information than my closest prison companions? I didn't necessarily like these guys, but I needed them. They helped make the time slightly bearable. But despite the unique bonding that happens behind bars, I couldn't trust them as far as I could spit.

There was a guy named Walter who had gotten busted on some minor drug-possession charge while in Nicaragua visiting family. He had lived in the United States for a few years, spoke perfect English, and could talk about a lot of things that mattered. Walter's education alone made him unique, but he was likable as well and someone else I could hang with. There were other "good guys," each of whom helped me in his own way to get through my time at La Modelo. Mostly I learned a lot from hearing the details of their cases. Some were innocent like me. Some are still there. One guy in particular made a deeper, spiritual contribution. That was Pastor Mario, a true agent of grace.

Once a kidnapper and a drug pilot, Pastor Mario held a daily Bible-study gathering at the end of our hallway. I realize that stories of men turning to God in prison go back as far as written history will take us. The phenomenon turns up so often in memoirs that some have even called it cliché. But there is a reason why. Prison is a journey to the furthest reaches of suffering, loneliness, and danger. When you face the reality of death, you are forced to ask big questions. Inevitably, you arrive at the issue of what happens when your life ends. For me personally, I started to feel like there has to be more to this than *I'm just screwed*. In the Bible study I came to understand that the possibility of life after death allows one to maintain hope even in the depths of pain.

For my part, I was raised with a Christian faith. Not in-your-face fundamentalism but a simple, everyday Christian consciousness and lifestyle. My family felt comfortable with a Christianity that made room for all kinds of people and all shades of believers. In La Modelo, where I was thrust into emotional and psychological solitude, my relationship with God took on much more significance and so played a greater role in my life. The daily sessions with Pastor Mario did not "bring me to God," but they certainly gave me a map. Study, writing, and prayer gave structure to my previously vague feelings of faith and provided logical purpose and direction for the battle I was fighting.

In the first months of my sentence, I occupied myself with the practicalities of survival—learning the ropes, setting up my systems, mentally lining up my allies and enemies, establishing my rank, and so on. I had not yet arrived at the understanding that my spiritual faith would itself become the most significant practical element of survival, that God would make it possible to survive, but I was starting to get small indications. I had never in my life felt so completely alone, but really I hadn't even glimpsed the far reaches of despair I would experience later. I still hadn't gotten used to the complete absence of all the things in life that provided the feedback one uses to define oneself. Magazines, job, Internet, clothing style, friends, lovers, family, community—all the stuff we use to help us manufacture our illusion of joy, importance, success—it was all gone, so far out of reach. The human resources had run out. It was like being stripped bare, with no one even there to see you exposed. In those studies with Pastor Mario I began to grasp what it meant to be saved and to feel the fullness of God's grace rushing in to fill the void.

Very soon after I came to *dos alta* I began receiving letters of support written to the Web site, which were printed and brought to me. I can't count the times some letter, even just a quick note of encouragement from a complete stranger, brought me back from the edge of desperation. People I knew I'd never meet would take the time to write down their prayers, share with me their stories, tell me of their love or even of their own pain. The letters became my own private epistles, almost like a bible edited just for my situation. Some letters had practical advice—"chew your food until it is like soup to extract the maximum amount of nutrients possible"—others held spiritual insight: "God is kind but not soft."

When possible, I would draft a letter back, not to any specific individual but to everybody. The letters appeared on the Web site like blog posts. They would briefly describe my life in prison, my health, my surroundings and offer thanks and praise for the compassion these people shared in their letters. Usually, the truth painted a horribly bleak picture; in one letter I compared the experience of wrongful imprisonment to being buried alive. In the same letter, however, I shared the lessons that these letters from the support community had given me the strength to see:

> Despite the hardship and loss of freedom, I am developing. I'm developing in ways that would not be possible unless I was walking this path. I see this as a test; a rite of passage on a spiritual journey. I will not be defeated and I will see each and every one of you on the free side.

I went on to say that I pulled all my strength from these unseen but deeply felt supporters:

> The prayers, the campaigns, the letters, the movement . . . Without you, I'd be lost.

It seems inappropriate to point out that while I was pouring my emotions out on the page for this great network of support to read, my cell mate was laying on his bunk watching porn on a portable DVD player.

II.

The Missile Deal

In the steamy heat of April, it pays to keep your body as still as possible. In my cell, consumed by books and journals, my thoughts would often turn to those two eerily frigid nights in December—recorded as some of the lowest temperatures of the last fifty years in Nicaragua—when we gathered to mourn Doris and prepared to bury her. I imagined her smiling at the customers in her shop or how she would always take food to the struggling family a couple of houses down. Images like that would break my heart, but they actually kept my mind clear. So many people had been focused for so many months on winning my freedom; it wasn't surprising that the atrocity that ended Doris's life—the act that had triggered my own ordeal—tended to fade from consciousness. I would like to think that I never forgot about Doris for a moment, but truthfully I'm sure there were many moments where my focus on survival crowded out all other thoughts. But when my thoughts returned to Doris, often just when I would start to wallow in self-pity, the memories and images of her put my own problems back into perspective and helped keep me moving forward.

It was healthy for me to remember that all the legal efforts and behind-the-scenes maneuvering had a purpose beyond my release. I hoped—we all hoped—that clearing my name would bring us one step closer to real justice for Doris. The words were printed boldly across a T-shirt I had made for the day I was released: *Justicia para Doris.* If I ever got out, I knew there might be cameras around, and I wanted to start to rechannel the focus onto the original crime immediately. So now, in April, two months into my sentence, the tireless Fabbrith was still pushing the appeal up a very steep hill.

The appellate court in Granada received our appeal in mid-April, after Judge Toruño had sat on it for two months. Ángela Gross, the Sandinista *presidenta* of the appeals court, had run out of options and eventually passed the appeal to Judge Roberto Rodriguez, telling him, "El gringo es más culpable que el Diablo." *More guilty than the devil.* Rodriguez told us that he asked Gross how she could have known that and that she responded by quoting Ivette Toruño: "Porque así es y eso le basta." *Because that's how it is. Enough said.* The Sandinista *bancada* comforted themselves with the assumption that if Rodriguez didn't vote to uphold the guilty verdict, they would be able to recruit the two votes needed to keep me locked up. Rodriguez himself later admitted that before reading the case file, he shared Gross's opinion of the case. Even as an experienced judge, he couldn't escape the influence of the lopsided press coverage.

Judge Rodriguez has a fascinating story. Early in life he grew disenchanted with the politics of his father, who, although he was a first cousin to Somoza and served as one of his generals, had grown estranged from the power base. Rodriguez's father never considered himself a true Somozista and later earned the respect of the Sandinistas, although he eventually angered them by representing the wrong side in a court case. Rodriguez himself survived three bullet wounds when his car was shot up by the *guardia*, and, having no friends left on either side of the Nicaraguan political divide, was forced to flee the country in a private plane one night. He spent eighteen years working odd jobs in Miami before returning to his homeland and becoming a magistrate. During the agonizingly long appeals process, we got to know Robert Rodriguez very well, and I know how much I owe my freedom to his deep moral sense and his absolute unwillingness to compromise on the law.

Although Nicaraguan penal code requires an appeals hearing to take place within six days of receipt of the case file, Rodriguez told Ángela Gross that the backlog of pending cases would prevent him from even starting review of the case until mid-May. In the intervening time, Ángela Gross would come to the end of her term as president of the court and someone would have to fill her position.

We were still uncertain about the third justice on the panel, Alejandro Estrada. Although Estrada toed the party line, we uncovered that he was reputedly part of a little mafia of judicial *bandidos* who found ways to profit from their positions on the bench. He could be easily enticed, which made him a wild card.

The appeal we filed[EX.43] pointed, again, to the mountain of evidence supporting my alibi, not only calling into question the conflicting testimony of Danglas and Rosita but also raising the issue of Armando Llanes's release based on a single, highly questionable document[EX.44] and despite the fact that Llanes had never been tested for comparison with any of the forensic evidence uncovered at the scene. The appeal provided a comprehensive analysis of what the document referred to as the "mistakes" and "misinterpretations" made regarding testimony and evidence and spelled out the airtight argument for overturning the guilty verdict. The appeal cited numerous errors of law, and, while we had to take care not to attack Ivette Toruño directly, Fabbrith hammered home the point that in the presence of reasonable doubt a judge or jury is *obligated* by law to acquit. Indicative of the culture of Spanish language was a comment in the document—"If you have a judge who acts like a prosecutor, look to God for defense"—and a bit of sarcasm aimed at Toruño, "Eric doesn't have an arm long enough to land deadly blows all the way from Managua. He does not possess that ability to be at two places at the same time."

Finally, and as it turns out most important, an appeal by a defendant must specifically seek either a reversal of the original verdict, a reduction of the charges and sentence, or a retrial. The ruling of the appeals court must answer to the specific request made. Obviously, my attorneys requested a reversal of the original verdict. They did not seek a retrial, a new judge, a chance to introduce new evidence, or any other remedies. The appeal sought only a verdict of not guilty. The appeals panel could either grant the request or deny it. No other legal choices were on the table.

In Washington, the "big-time" law firm my parents had hired was spinning its wheels. They spent very little time on the ground in Nica, but, since they knew so little about how things worked there, we weren't sure what they could have accomplished if they had. From their office in Washington they worked on a press strategy that involved planting stories that featured a photo of my carrying Doris's coffin, intended to get equal coverage for the evidence of my innocence. Joe Reeder, the partner heading the team of lawyers on my case, is a notable figure in DC and could get in to see the right people, including a number of influential U.S. senators, as well as staffers of the assistant secretary of state for the Western Hemisphere and Arturo Cruz, the Nicaraguan ambassador to the United States, who at one point had guaranteed Reeder that I would get a "fair trial."

For all his clout, Reeder turned out to be rather naïve about a lot of things. It was Tio Bob who actually unearthed some critical information about Ambassador Cruz and the Nicaraguan agenda—a piece of the puzzle that nobody at the DC law firm Greenberg Traurig figured out. One day in early May, Tio Bob came to see me in La Modelo. He brought with him a fast-food cheeseburger and some onion rings, which I inhaled, despite the intestinal problems that had started to develop, and he told me a story.

During the 1980s, after the Sandinistas had established their hold on Nicaragua, the Soviets had provided them with a cache of weapons. Among those weapons were SAM-7 missiles—shoulder-borne surface-to-air missiles of the kind so feared by Homeland Security in Washington today. With one of these missiles a single individual can shoot a plane out of the sky. In the hands of a terrorist with a passenger airliner in his sights, a SAM-7 would be a terrible instrument of death. According to Tio's sources, Nicaragua had about 1,700 of these missiles in its possession at the time of my arrest and trial.

One of the first diplomatic moves of Ortega when he took office was to sever the U.S. Embassy's access to the Nicaraguan immigration registry.[EX.45] After 9/11, the United States became adamant about having access to these records as part of the effort to track the movement of suspected terrorist networks. Simultaneously, Ortega aligned himself with Iran and started allowing Iranians and third-world nationals to enter Nicaragua with little to no screening process. Washington had been negotiating with the Nicas for some time, with the goal of seeing the missiles destroyed, but now, when they added into the equation the newly perceived risk that the SAM-7s could fall into the wrong hands, the matter rose to the top of the State Department's agenda with Ortega.

The talks had progressed to the point where the United States had offered a substantial mix of cash and targeted aid in exchange for the destruction of the missiles, but that progress stalled when Ortega returned to power. Insisting that the SAM-7s constituted Nicaragua's only credible air defense at a time of increasing tension with its neighbor, Colombia, Ortega upped the ante. He wanted cash and less aid.

Talks were at an impasse, and it had been made clear to Tio Bob that Arturo Cruz had been appointed ambassador with the sole mission of closing the missile deal. Joe Reeder could wine and dine Cruz all he wanted; he could plead my innocence until he ran out of ways to say it, but unless he found a way to advance Cruz's real agenda, Joe would just be wasting his breath.

Ironically, Cruz's counterpart, Paul Trivelli, the U.S. ambassador to Nicaragua, had been sent to his post with a mission as well. The Americans openly supported a particular candidate in the 2006 presidential elections, and it was no secret that Trivelli was working to ensure his victory. That entailed orchestrating press conferences and public statements against the other candidate, who was from Alemán's party. In the process, Trivelli's efforts left the opposition to Ortega divided and in disarray, effectively doing Ortega's political dirty work for him and clearing his path to the presidency. Trivelli's campaign to discredit Alemán and his party was not just bad politics, it was bad for me personally. My mother wrote him a letter at one point asking if he had forgotten that two of the three appellate justices who held my future in their hands were from Alemán's party.

Nonetheless, the momentum was real. The press attention in the United States had forced Washington to take a more active stance on my case. Officials at the highest levels in the State Department had discussed it directly with both Ambassador Cruz and the foreign minister, although as far as I could tell those discussions accomplished pretty much nothing. In fact, every time the guards slapped the handcuffs on me for a simple walk from one part of the prison to another, I remembered that too much attention or the wrong kind attention could do as much harm as good. It was a nasty catch-22. I needed as many people as possible to know about my situation, but the more the story spread, the more the Nica authorities felt the heat of international scrutiny, which they didn't like. And they had no one to take their annoyance out on but me. The vice president said in an interview that "the Volz family has done a good job with technology and resources to the point of manipulating some of the media outlets in the U.S. with the objective of freeing the prisoner. Although it insults Nicaraguan justice, this is the reason that we are having to listen to the mother in seeking liberty for her son."*

I realized that being at the complete mercy of the prison authorities left me in this kind of bind on other fronts as well. For instance, while I was incarcerated, I had the clout and notoriety to expose the routine human-rights abuses in the Nica penal system. But if I did that—if I contacted the right agency, provided testimony, or somehow arranged for some kind of secret inspection—I would surely face dangerous blowback. If I were released from prison, I wondered if any of the big human-rights groups would even take my call. And yet there was virtually no protest about my case from any of the major international watchdog agencies on human rights. You have to look behind their supposedly altruistic principles to find the explanation.

---

* *El Nuevo Diario*, May 11, 2007.

Throughout college and when I began to spend extended amounts of time in Latin America, I instinctively aligned myself with the ideologies of the political left. I had been schooled by founders of the revolution, had lived among the undocumented and the underprivileged, and had the chance to see America through the eyes of people who, although they live right next door, might as well be on the other side of the planet. I was initially attracted to the left because it stood in opposition to the right-wing politics represented by the "Bush doctrine." I never felt anything but awe and admiration for the men and women throughout Central America who had fought or were still fighting to take back their countries from colonial powers or for the puppet dictators their labor and money supported. But living and working in Nicaragua tested my left-leaning perspective. Thirty years of Somoza rule had not benefited the poorer class of Nicaraguas, even while Americans enjoyed their bananas and their sugar. The Sandinista revolution created hope and pride, for sure, and triggered improvements in education and elsewhere, but in the years of Ortega's rule what little infrastructure there was crumbled even further, while food and other basic goods grew more scarce than ever. Corruption and oppression may have been less prominent for a little while, but pretty soon they were thriving again, only they had a new name and a new ideology.

With the end of the cold war and pressure from neighboring republics, the Sandinistas were gradually choked out and forced to hold elections. In 1990, when Ortega was unseated by Violetta Chamorro, she turned to a neoliberal model, and over time foreign capital and visitors started flowing once again. There was an increase in privatization and the development of general economic stability. Communism was no more. Nicaraguans' lives started to change, and it seemed like the world and Nicaragua were possibly reconnecting. I was a prime example of that change. I went there to start a magazine intended to bridge communities and promote responsible, sustainable development, and I also found myself helping to fund that project by becoming part of the development process.

The longer I spent in Nicaragua—especially in the Nica prison system—

the more the labels of left and right, or liberal and conservative, lost their meaning for me. By the time Doris was murdered and I arrested, ideology was barely relevant. All that mattered was whose side you were on now, who owed who a favor, or who bore some ancient grudge. I discovered that the United States wasn't much better, but that's another story for another time.

To the outside world, however, Ortega's return to power meant a new foothold for the left. On paper, anyway, Ortega had once stood for the same great and noble "leftist" principles that drove the founders of the global human-rights groups. For them to challenge Ortega in any serious way would have meant embarrassing one of their ideological brothers, and most of the agencies just didn't want to go there. Besides, the human-rights crusaders didn't like to give Washington credit for being on the right side of anything. Tio believed that the central agenda for the major human-rights organizations was to create problems for "right-wing" governments allied with or sympathetic to the United States. Even within the U.S. government, my most vocal advocates and supporters in the Senate came from the political right.

The media attention grew much more intense in early May. One day I was lying in my cell shaking and shivering from the various ailments that would soon take over my life when I was called to the telephone.* Someone on the other line said something about being from CNN and that the network was going to "put me through to broadcast." The next thing I knew, a correspondent named Rick Sanchez was peppering me with questions that I was almost too dizzy and feverish to answer. I did my best, knowing that my mom believed CNN to be sympathetic. The story aired that same night, accompanied by a live interview of my mother by Anderson Cooper, and received a huge outpouring of responses.

On May 7, *The Washington Post* ran their first story about my case, a big

---

* On occasion a battery-operated cell phone would be bought into the *dos alta*, and the *reos* could receive calls from outsiders. It was not a "courtesy" as the warden marketed it. It was a tactic to "ear hustle" (eavesdrop) and document the names and phone numbers of incoming callers and those suspected of gang activity. None of the veteran *reos* ever used that phone.

front-page article entitled "An American's Kafkaesque Encounter with Nicaragua's Justice System." The story used language like "a highly politicized judicial system" and had a major impact in the United States and around the world and especially in Nicaragua, where the *Post* is read and respected even more than *The Wall Street Journal*.

The coverage by two news organizations of international stature made the one-sided Nica press look bad and set the stage for Nicaragua's few responsible journalists to begin examining my case from a less-sensationalist point of view, and they were allowed into La Modelo to interview me. These would be the first and last Nica interviews allowed while I was imprisoned. Guards dragged me out of my cell with no warning. They were obviously angry, and I felt sure they were taking me somewhere for a beating, but instead we went to the administration building, where the interviewers waited. I looked horrible—sick, dirty, exhausted—but that didn't matter if they really intended to give me a chance to speak. On that day I spoke to the producer for *Esta Semana*, the news-magazine program hosted by Violetta Chamorro's son, Carlos Fernando, and to the deeply respected journalist Xavier Reyes Alba, from a smaller but very influential paper called *La Trinchera*. The next day, I gave another interview to the semi-well-regarded newspaper *La Prensa*. Although the interview went well overall, I must say that I was taken aback by the first question: "Eric, your government has been very involved in your case and there is speculation that you are an agent from the CIA. Tell me, is this true?" Though the assertion has not one shred of truth, it would be repeated many times over in the coming months.

Half a year had passed since Doris's murder and my arrest, yet this was my first real opportunity to tell my side of the story to the audience that really mattered—the people of Nicaragua—and I made the most of it. I explained in detail how so many of the "facts" about the case that had seeped into the popular consciousness were nothing more than outrageous lies. For instance, I posed simple questions: If Doris had really gone to her family fearing that I would kill her out of jealousy, as her mother and two friends claimed, why didn't any of them go to the police at that time? Why did Mercedes confide in me and ask for my help in the days after the murder? How was it that Nelson Danglas was the only person out of 23,000 residents who managed to see me in the heart of San Juan del Sur's central shopping district in the middle of the day? What about Rosita's original confession? According to a policeman, Rosita and Danglas had sold Doris's cell phone. How did that escape the case file? I believe not only that I came across as logical and assertive but also that, for the first time, people saw me as a complete person with real feelings, particularly about Doris.

I also think that one very important reason these interviews hit the mark was that I spoke in Spanish. My fluency surprised many readers and television viewers and made me that much more sympathetic. The interviews caused many Nicas to begin to rethink my case. Any thoughtful person who was paying attention would have to at least consider the possibility that I was telling the truth. In addition, once the press gave a public airing to this new perspective on my case, people who had already believed in my innocence but out of fear had to keep quiet about it now felt more comfortable speaking out.

It amazed me that the stories had such an immediate effect, because in truth not all of them were that well done. *La Prensa* edited my comments more than I would have liked, giving my story a spin I wouldn't exactly call objective, but the main message got through, just as it did on *Esta Semana*, even though it actually aired a lukewarm and noncommittal piece. The program, the most prominent voice of independent journalism in Nicaraguan TV, aired two stories about my case over the time of my imprisonment, neither of which went as deep as one would expect, given the show's reputation and history for uncovering corruption. Since Ortega's return to power they had covered all the scandals in which he was allegedly involved. My case was right up their alley, but mysteriously they didn't jump at the opportunity.

Overall, my interviews really heated things up by airing, for the first time, powerful and credible criticisms of the police and the prosecution and by dropping enormous hints about the Sandinista involvement. The embassy was extremely pleased with my interviews, which it said would make its job easier, but it was surprised that I wasn't more aggressive. In fact, I had been extremely aggressive, but the most incendiary stuff had gotten edited out. Even so, fellow prisoners told me that I was crazy to go on the record saying the things I did. They advised me to be careful and that I was surely gaining enemies. Some of my well-connected Nica friends shared deep concern as well, but they didn't understand that I had no choice.

I knew that my speaking out would create blowback from some institutions, but I needed to plant some doubt in the public's consciousness to assist my defense effort, and it worked. A couple of very influential Nicaraguans, an economist and a political analyst, went on prime-time TV advising that if my case wasn't resolved quickly Nica would lose hundreds of millions of dollars, getting the Sandinistas started off on the wrong foot. The interviews also put a lot of heat on Rosita to talk because of my suggestion that things like his confession and his possession of Doris's cell phone confirmed his involvement in the crime. He wanted to hold a press conference, but the prison wouldn't let him. The word in San Juan del Sur and Managua was that my interviews changed a lot of public opinion and that people started asking themselves, If it wasn't Eric, then who was it? San Juaneños were frightened.

Around the same time Nica friends started an awareness campaign in Nicaragua. They passed out fifteen thousand flyers at churches and at major intersections, printed and distributed T-shirts, and hung twenty-eight huge banners in the most congested parts of the country's roadways. The banners read, *"Justicia para Eric Volz. Visite: amigosdeeric.com."* Large numbers of Nicas started visiting our Spanish Web site, where they could finally learn the facts that the local media had not reported. The campaign, combined with the new tenor in the press coverage, helped to rebalance public opinion.*

---

* None of the Nicaraguan press (with the exception of the newsletter, *La Trinchera*) gave any coverage to the "Justicia" campaign—not even one line in print, TV, or radio.

It felt like the truth was pushing its way out into the open with the force of inevitability. One day, in the visitors room for my weekly phone call, a woman came up and slipped a card into my hand. I looked down to see that it was her business card (she was an attorney), and on the back she had written, "Estoy contigo, como muchos mas. No preguntes a nadie por mi" (*I'm with you, as are many others. Don't ask around about me.*). Clearly, the woman didn't want her sympathy or support for me to get out, but those three words—*I'm with you*—from a complete stranger, a Nica, meant everything to me.

Judge Rodriguez had told everyone not to expect any action on the appeal until May, and true to his word he dropped a bombshell at the end of the month. Ángela Gross had to have been shocked to read the opinion that Rodriguez passed to her: He had decided that my conviction should be overturned. With only a week left in Ángela Gross's term on the court, the Sandinista *bancada*—at this point, our working assumption was that the Sandinista administration was effectively holding me hostage—had a real problem on its hands. The Sandinistas needed to get someone they felt like they could manipulate on the appeals panel and settled on a judge named Norman Miranda.

Miranda is quite a character. Twenty years ago he had been a deeply committed Sandinista but had fallen out with the party when it confiscated his father's house. A liberal attorney later recovered his father's house, and Miranda became a liberal with sworn allegiance to the PLC. At one point he had even received the sponsorship of Arnoldo Alemán in a campaign securing himself a new term as a magistrate in Granada. When Ortega came back to power in early 2007, many suspected that Norman Miranda's loyalties were shifting back again. In Nicaragua, people call someone like Miranda a chameleon. Our team saw him as unpredictable in the extreme, someone they would have to study until they could figure out what hidden dynamics made up his agenda.

Spring passed into sweltering summer. The tireless effort by my defense team—the legal moves, the press campaign, the endless phone calls and closed-door meetings in Washington and Managua—turned up the heat all around me. La Modela itself was a furnace. I, too, was on fire, for an entirely different reason. I now had to face the reality that in just a few short months in prison, surrounded by disease and bacteria and deprived of legitimate nourishment, my body was breaking down. I was literally burning up with fever.

12.

La Violencia

I couldn't remember a time in my life when I hadn't worked hard to keep myself near peak physical condition. From the time I started playing soccer and through my climbing years when I could scale up sheer rock faces, I had kept myself fit and strong. By the time I finished school in California and had left such sports behind, running and working out and remaining careful about what I ate had become second nature to me. It had simply become part of who I was.

I established a workout routine as soon as I got to La Modelo, including rigging up some strips of cloth through the bars at the bottom of our cell door to slide my feet under so I could do sit-ups. If I spent any time with *reos* other than my cell mate, Leo, it was most likely because we worked out together, meeting in the yard or challenging each other in the hall. That's how I had met Jonathan before the trial, and it was the main way he and I socialized after my return to prison.

I had even gotten involved in playing soccer in the yard, which turned out to be an surprise blessing, not only because of the exercise but also because it helped me earn some unexpected respect inside the prison— not with the Nicas, who overwhelmingly favored baseball, but with the foreign prisoners, the men from all over Latin America and the Caribbean who had found their way to La Modelo. It was funny: the soccer skills I had developed as a kid had provided social access for me throughout my travels, but this was the first time they seemed critical to my very survival.

But now, of all bizarre things that I had experienced so far in prison, nothing felt as alien as the sudden collapse of my health. After only a

195

couple of months, my body felt like it was no longer my own. The first and most severe blow came from the simple lack of sleep. Although I spent nearly all of my time in my cell, curled up around myself on my mattress, I could never really rest. The shouting and banging and clatter filled the prison all day and all night, and my perpetual state of hyper-vigilance kept an insanely high volume of adrenaline and cortisol pumping through me constantly. The short and infrequent moments of sleep that did come were plagued with nightmares, which I'd never had before in my life. Often, I was woken by my own muscles twitching in uncontrollable spasm.

My belly was on fire, as if my body was eating itself from the inside. The digestive juices of my stomach were corroding the lining so it felt like food would come into contact with my bloodstream before it was properly digested. First, the prison doctor told me I had gastritis, caused primarily from starvation; as a result, eating food at all triggered sharp, burning pain. Then the doctor also diagnosed stomach ulcers and prescribed medicine that the prison pharmacy did not have. And since lying down only intensified the pain, it was impossible to find relief.

I began to have trouble breathing as well. The dank, moldy atmosphere of the prison all by itself was hard on the lungs, but the inmates poisoned it further every day just by going about their lives. Weed and crack smoke filtered out of nearly every cell, not to mention the smoke from thousands of cigarettes each day. Worse, men would burn anything they could get their hands on, even in the heat, to cook or to boil water or sometimes just to try to keep the mosquitoes away. Plastic bags and rags, food waste, tattered clothing, newspapers and magazines—whatever could be used as fuel. It didn't take long for me to develop an asthmatic condition requiring treatment. The respiratory therapy, involving inhaling medicated vapor from a nebulizer for a few minutes each day, would cause its own problems.

Other lesser conditions surfaced—loss of sense of taste and smell, muscle spasms, torturous fiery itching—but the point is not to offer a litany of ailments. Rather, if readers learn nothing else about La Modelo than the speed with which the conditions destroyed the health of a well-conditioned twenty-seven-year-old man, it would be reason enough for outrage.

Before April was over, after my abdominal problems grew worse, arrangements "were made" for me to leave the prison to visit a private clinic for an ultrasound scan of my stomach. Allegedly nobody knew about this plan except for Fabbrith, Marc Meznar, the warden of La Modelo, and the national director of SPN, El Prefecto, and yet at 8:00 that morning, Doris's mother, Mercedes, appeared on Rivas radio, breaking the news that I was to be "taken out" of prison that day. Protesters soon crowded the gates, making the visit impossible without jeopardizing my safety. They never even came to get me from my cell. I know that neither Fabbrith nor Meznar leaked the information, so there's no question that it was someone within the SPN or the Nicaraguan Government.

The longer I sat in La Modelo, the more the meaning of "doing time" revealed itself to me. Everyone's experience of prison is utterly unique, of course, and hinges in part on what your life was like before you got locked up. If you've lived your entire life in deadening poverty, with inadequate education, starving, and with no work, maybe prison feels similar to life outside. If you grow up fighting in street gangs, doing or selling drugs, or stealing and hustling for money, maybe day-to-day life in prison doesn't seem all that different to you.

For me, there were times when my faith in God's unforeseen plans eased the pain, but for the most part it was still excruciating. I simply couldn't bear my existence in prison. What seemed to be the complete absence of purpose left nothing to keep me moving forward through time. Every last part of my heart and soul ached for freedom. I saw all the different ways that people cope with this phenomenon. Some retreated into drug abuse or troublemaking. Others would just sleep or gorge themselves with whatever food they could find. But most would just wander aimlessly around, rambling about anything to anyone or just mumbling to themselves, trapped inside their own heads. The *reos* even had a name for this phenomenon: *quemando cable* ("burning cable"). It was like being surrounded by real-life zombies, and I could sense that with time it would happen to me, too. I knew that the symptoms of trauma and depression were already setting in.

I continued to occupy myself with reading the books that circulated around the prison or that my lawyers occasionally brought me and with writing. Whenever they could, my lawyers would bring me copies of some of the thousands of letters that came in to me and my family from the vast support network that had been born on the Internet. Sometimes they'd bring me a stack, other times just a handful, but it didn't matter. I would read them over and over, feeling the love and prayers of so many intimate strangers filling me up like nourishing food. Like air. It was as if all those people, all over the world, were breathing for me. In the most literal sense, those letters and the deep and genuine caring they conveyed kept me alive.

I also suppose that I was fortunate to have my own case on which to keep my mind focused. I wrote down facts, every memory, every bit of conversation that might have some use or relevance and turned it over to my team. I think this set me apart from the other inmates, the over-whelming majority of whom take their conviction as just one more step on some kind of inevitable path. If they are waiting on appeal, most have simply left the work in the hands of their attorneys. Then again, most of them deserve to be there.

So I kept to myself as much as I could, but nobody can be alone all the time. In the relative safety of my cell I could at least talk to Leo. Really, Leo did most of the talking, and he had a lot to tell me. He had actually worked as a guard in La Modelo more than fifteen years before after fighting for the Sandinista Army, and he had seen some heavy shit. He explained that while prison officials and guards might turn their back on violations of prisoners' rights or international conventions, those con-cepts didn't even exist in 1990. Guards beat and killed prisoners regu-larly. Leo even told me that one time, when he was on post in a gun tower, he was ordered to shoot—shoot to kill—two prisoners who were shouting obscenities at him. He did as he was told, but he missed. Leo knew from an uncle of his who had also worked as a guard how the wardens and other administrators regularly skimmed money from prison budgets or from money that came through charities and aid organizations and how one of the reasons the food was either awful or completely nonexistent was that people were stealing from the kitchens as well, not just money but the food itself.

Slowly I began to venture out more, to make connections beyond Leo. I tried to be careful, but you can't really be in prison without hearing stuff—stuff that you probably don't want to know about organized crime activity, drug trafficking, even classified government information. Occasionally, I would hear some of the older inmates speaking to one another or on the pay phone in Russian, a vivid reminder of Nicaragua's recent past. Sometimes I wondered if I had learned too much—worrying that certain kinds of knowledge could actually be dangerous.

Nonetheless, information was still the only tool that I could contribute, and inside La Modelo I unearthed things that nobody else on my team could know. Leo helped me establish a network of informants, using cigarettes as payment. This presented its own risk. I had to always remind myself that my cell mate not only had fought with the Sandinistas but also had once been a prison guard. I was already working under the assumption that Leo was most likely an informer, funneling information about me back to an intelligence handler, who then passed it back up the chain. I watched what I said to him, telling him just enough to make it seem like I had taken him into my confidence but never sharing anything that could come back to hurt me. At the same time, I had to evaluate anything I learned from him with deep suspicion and be careful how much of it I repeated.

Call it suspicion, call it paranoia, but I had to be alert to informers and the web of whispers at all times. People can end up rolling on their best friends if they think it might ease their own situation in prison even a little. A few of them were pretty stealthy, but most of them didn't have enough sense even to be subtle about it. One guy, who had been part of an elite military unit trained by the CIA for Somoza, was doing time for attempted murder and for having escaped from Chipote. Through Leo, he sent me a folder of clippings about the crimes he had committed against Sandinistas, in an effort to gain my trust. With the file, he sent a slip of paper with the phone number of "an agency that wants information" that he had. His request was that I make the call for him. This was so obvious that it made me laugh. Someone somewhere must have thought that if I made the call for him, it would prove that I was an intelligence agent interested in recruiting people who had issues with the Sandinistas. I gave the guy a neutral response I had learned from the real-estate scene. I told him, "Let me think about it."

Other encounters were more heartrending. One older man, nearly broken by his time in prison, took me aside and told me his story. He and his two sons had stepped in to stop a man from attacking his daughter and their sister. The armed assailant had turned on them, and they had killed him in self-defense. All four family members had been locked up until the father stepped up and claimed responsibility for the man's death, allowing his two sons and daughter to go free. I think this man sensed that I would end up going free—perhaps sooner rather than later—and made me promise to speak out for men like him, good men caught up in random circumstances now wasting away their lives in prison

The more time I spent outside my cell, the keener my prison sense became. I learned to read the tiny changes in expressions or attitudes that signaled tension or conflict. It was eerie, almost like a kind of internal early-warning system. I got to the point where I could just feel trouble coming and was lucky enough to pick myself up and get back to my cell before fights broke out or guards started busting heads.

By summer, the entire prison seemed to be gripped by a whole new kind of madness. The militarization of the prison after the capture and conviction of the Mexican Sinaloa crew had cranked up the tension. On one level, the prison authorities were panicked that the Sinaloans would attempt some bloody operation to break their guys out of La Modelo. On a more subtle level, the mistrust and suspicion that defined the prison culture grew significantly more intense. So many undercover cops infiltrated the prisons to keep a close eye on the Sinaloans that even the wardens and guards didn't know who was a real prisoner and who wasn't.

The sudden presence of a huge number of undercover policemen inside La Modelo would inevitably spell trouble for the warden and his boss, El Prefecto. Sure enough, in early June, Ana Morales, the minister of government, ordered an end to the massive corruption. She put an end to extra privileges for inmates, bribery, and favors for food or money. She insisted on better search procedures before and after visits and all kinds of other increased restrictions. Men who enjoyed power in prison—whether they were inmates or jailers—pissed and moaned loudly about the new crackdown. Me, I welcomed the leveling of the playing field. The minister's campaign against corruption ended with her sweeping out the El Prefecto Sobalvarro (in whose office Alemán and I had met), several wardens, the head of internal security, and dozens of other personnel, causing an explosion of rejoicing among the inmates, so many of whom had been horribly abused by their hands. Things changed almost immediately in *el sistema*. The guards, fearful that they were next on the block, suddenly began kissing up to the prisoners they had victimized for years. Small pieces of meat and vegetables started to appear in the *chupeta*, the prison chow. And then things got really strange.

The change that affected me most directly was the appointment of Oscar Molina, the former spokesperson for the penitentiary, to the position of warden of La Modelo. Right away he seemed to make a conscious decision to clamp down on me harder, to make even the smallest things problematic for me. Molina said that the change in my regimen came about as a result of the interviews I had given to the Nica press, which had caused what he described as "big problems." He proceeded to torment me in little ways that would be hard to document or to prove and made sure that I couldn't complain too loudly. For example, the few times my parents came to the prison for a three-hour visit, someone at the prison would find a way to stall them until there was perhaps only half an hour left.

The most upsetting thing he did was to prevent me from seeing my attorney. This was a clear violation of rights under any circumstance, but with us in the middle of a deeply complex appeals process, it was entirely immoral, and had the effect of blunting my mobility and my defense effort. Although the Granada court had decreed specifically that my lawyer was to have unrestricted access to me, Molina found all kinds of ways to deny Fabbrith entrance, even on at least one occasion when he had brought a private doctor to examine me, a visit that had been carefully arranged and approved in advance.

Oscar Molina was the strangest of men. Thin like a skeleton, hollow eyed and bald, he looked like a vampire or maybe the grim reaper himself. Self-conscious and paranoid, Molina had no business running La Modelo. When the previous warden was removed from his job in Morales's sweep, the executive branch of the Sandinista government that oversaw the SPN took advantage of the opportunity and promoted a warden who was willing to operate on behalf of the party, turning the prison into an instrument of intimidation. On top of everything else, Molina had the bad luck to come into the job at a particularly sensitive time. With the Sinaloa crew in his jail and all the extra firepower and attention that came with it, Molina knew the spotlight was on him. And he had me on his hands—the other high-profile prisoner in the country, who, like the Mexicans, had been dominating the media.

On a whiteboard in his office, he had lines for the days that remained for his retirement. Every day he would X out a line. I saw this shrine when I was in his office. He would also randomly pop these pills without anything to wash them down. It was kind of spooky. Molina was constantly on edge, knowing the slightest slipup would cost him his job and his reputation. He enforced every last rule, and then went ahead and made up some new ones, some designed solely to turn up the heat on me. I could tell that I became a kind of obsession for Oscar Molina, as if I were the embodiment of all his problems. Many times, I would be lying on my bunk in the night, as scared of going to sleep as I was of staying awake, and I would look up at the door and see Molina's ghoulish face staring in at me. As I met his eye, he would stalk off in anger. It made me shudder to think that on top of all my other problems, the most direct and immediate control over my life had fallen into the hands of a completely unstable individual.

It seemed like *la violencia* got worse during that summer. The dangerously rough *galeria* below us seemed like something out of *Mad Max* and was constantly at a boiling point. Every one of the *reos* down there was heavily armed and what the guards would call *chiva*—in an "extremely volatile state." They would fling batteries at one another through the bars of their doors and piss in one another's food. Thick clouds of drug smoke filled their hallway all day, and I could hear them from above, chanting and banging in unison like a warrior tribe preparing for battle. We feared them, knowing that the slightest thing could trigger chaos. If something broke out, I knew I would either end up dead or would have to kill someone in self-defense. Guards brought one inmate from down there into our *galeria* for protection, a guy who had totally lost it. Babbling that the devil was walking the hallway deciding who to take, and this guy had prepared himself for battle. He had a sharpened broomstick with a shank fastened to one end and another shank hidden in his pants. He wore a plastic plate taped over his heart, magazines stuffed into his pants as kidney armor, and T-shirts wrapped around his forearms. To top if off, he managed to pull the electrical cables out of the wall and wired the metal door of the cell. He sacrificed showers to keep a fresh puddle of water under and out in front of the door. Anyone who came to open his cell would be electrocuted until the breaker blew. His notion was that he would "at least slow 'em" down. He sat like that in his cell, waiting for the trouble to start.

Later in the summer, we could hear shooting from the gun towers at night, although we never found out why. And a riot did break out, but not right below us as we feared. Twelve men from *galeria* 5 ended up in the hospital with stab wounds that night.

Crazy shit was happening all over. La Kimberly, the gay kid who had seduced the violently macho Alex on the *dos alta*, had moved on to another inmate, nicknamed Pulmon because he had been stabbed through the lung at one time. Pulmon, the *marido* in the couple, caught La Kimberly having sex with another inmate and broke up with him. La Kimberly responded by jamming a shank into Pulmon's leg. They got back together and went on just like old times—except for the limp.

A skinny kid named Pinky got cornered and stripped and finger raped—and the whole block knew about it. Elsewhere, a kid got stabbed through the heart on his first day in the prison. Another young *reo* burned himself and strung himself up with a rope but survived. We could all see this poor guy losing it, and it was only a matter of time until he ended his life. Later in the summer, I found him hanging dead in his cell. As the police carried out the body the other *reos* yelled, "¡Va libre! . . . ¡Oscar va libre!" *Oscar is being released.*

The end of summer brought its own miseries. I didn't think the mosquito problem could have gotten any worse, but the mosquitoes grew in number and ferocity beyond anything I had experienced before. They would find any tiny piece of exposed flesh—your face, your ears, your toes, your fingers—and eat you alive. The electrical power outages grew to twelve hours a day, adding constant darkness to the stink, the bugs, and the lethal heat.

Sickness and disease festered in every corner of the prison. Somehow, I managed to avoid the rotten infections of the toenails or puss-filled gums or whatever that would periodically sweep through La Modelo, but with the constant siege on the immune system a number of other bacteria got me. When a strange flu flattened most of the prisoners, I got it, too. But my own health problems grew steadily worse in those months. I was taking meds for my belly, for my lungs, for allergies that were making all the other conditions that much worse—and still, I felt weak and fatigued nearly every waking minute. My asthma was getting more intense, making me cough and wheeze all the time. Some days, the toxic smoke in the prison air would hit my exhausted lungs and my infected sinus and I thought I would collapse from the hacking and the agony. I would have attacks of intestinal flu that doubled me over in spasms of pain. I was convinced my insides were simply liquefying and pouring out of me.

I felt that I was dying a little bit every day, and in the face of practically no medical attention could not keep up with the accelerating breakdown of my poisoned body systems. I couldn't imagine lasting more than a year, no less thirty years. If I survived what passed for life in La Modelo, it wouldn't make a difference. The way things were going, I would just as surely die from untreated illness.

I refused to let my story end that way. I had no choice but to lean on faith—faith in God, whose presence I felt in the letters that came to me from around the world; faith in my parents, whose love was reason enough to keep going; faith in Tio Bob and in Fabbrith and in all the others who in different ways and in different places around Nicaragua and the world were turning over every last rock until they found the key to my release.

Near the end of August two hurricanes in two weeks swept over Nicaragua, as if God felt that he wanted to stir the pot just a little more. La Modelo got hit hard. Wind and rain pounded the prison, tearing away the plastic bags we had stuck over our windows. Water poured in, flowing down the hallways, filling the cells, soaking every last piece of clothing and every mattress. In the days that followed, you would swear that the building itself was crumbling around you.

Throughout that long summer, while I teetered on the edge of survival, my defense team was making progress. Just as crazy as it was inside La Modelo, equally crazy things were simmering far beyond the prison walls, and they were getting ready to boil over.

13.

Hospitalized

At first I had mentally compartmentalized my existence. At one level of consciousness, I lived the life of an inmate, focused totally on managing my situation there, keeping safe, surviving. When I needed to, I could flip a switch in my mind and become a legal and political advocate for myself, working with my mother and Dane on building an online community and leveraging the tools of the Web for support, working with Fabbrith on the appeal and other legal matters, and working with Tio Bob on strategy and tactics, finding a path through the maze.

Over those first seven or eight months, those two states of consciousness grew more and more intertwined. Moves made on the outside would directly affect my life on the inside. At the same time, things that happened to me in prison—people I met, things I heard, information I gathered and circulated—moved my case in new directions.

I knew that La Modelo was a hive of fabricators and informers, but we had discovered that there was a lot to be learned even from people who were spying on you or ratting you out. That summer I met a unique character in prison, a clean-cut, well-spoken man, grown soft around the middle in his late forties, named Chevez Pozo. Pozo carried himself like a mature and disciplined professional man, although he didn't seem as shocked or disgusted as you would expect by the conditions of the prison or the inhuman behavior of the prisoners around him.

Nicaragua is crawling with guys like Chevez Pozo, men who had done time in the military, the police, or, like Pozo, the shadowy state internal intelligence agency—La Seguridad del Estado. This man knew people, people like Judge Ivette Toruño, for instance, who came from the same town as him. In fact, Toruño had been the sentencing judge in Pozo's drug-trafficking case; he received the minimum allowable jail term. He could fill me in on many things, but that also meant that he was filling somebody in about me or could be deliberately feeding me disinformation. It turned out that Pozo was connected to another former *seguridad* agent who had gone on to become a judge: Peter Palma, the judge who oversaw my arraignment, who released Armando Llanes and Nelson Danglas, and who held me over for trial in Chipote and La Modelo and then got disbarred after he released me on house arrest.

Pozo came to me in prison with *un bisne*—Nica slang for a "business proposal"—from Judge Palma and a phone number. According to Pozo, Palma was advising us to get rid of my lead Nicaraguan attorney, Ramon Rojas, which we had essentially already done. Palma had put together another group of attorneys who he claimed could get me out. I knew immediately that Palma would expect some huge payment for this, but I had no way of knowing if it was even real. Nor did I know if I could trust Pozo, so I asked for a gesture of trust from him, some demonstration that he was the real deal. I insisted that he tell me who Palma was working with that might make my release possible, and I asked how much it was going to cost. The next day, Pozo came back to me with a price of $75,000 and the name Otto Navas, the corrupt son of a Supreme Court justice named Edgar Navas. This told us all we needed to know. We had already investigated Navas junior when he demanded $15,000 through Rojas to get me out shortly after my conviction. With minimal poking around it was revealed that he was a notorious judicial *bandido* who wielded light power in the Granada court system because of his father's post in the Supreme Court. I told him to go to hell and fired Rojas shortly after. But his extortion attempt was not a waste of time. When looking into the matter we uncovered that Otto Navas had a relationship that was too close for comfort with Estrada, the appeals judge who purportedly was loyal to Arnoldo Alemán. Palma's offer confirmed that Estrada was another person to worry about, even though Alemán was sure he could still control him.

Nonetheless, at my request, Fabbrith went ahead and met with Judge Palma for coffee, with Tio Bob running surveillance from a nearby table. Nobody on my team had any intention of moving forward with this scheme, but it was important to see what additional information we could get from Palma in our effort to try and map out the different groups of sharks circling around my case. Palma, despite his experience as a former intelligence officer, was nervous, still under fire from Mercedes and his recent corruption case, and was looking to cover his back. He claimed he had even received death threats from Doris's family. Palma did share our belief that the police had been the central operators in the campaign against me and were responsible for the press attacks and for spreading so many damaging rumors about me; but even though we had enemies in common with him, we knew he was no friend.

I never doubted that Chevez Pozo could do me as much harm as good, but I played the game with him, picking up intelligence that I would never have gotten otherwise. I knew he had contacts and access to real information. He came to my cell the day after Fabbrith's meeting with Palma and asked why I had a second person there running surveillance. After I realized that there was nothing I could say, I simply responded with a smile, "come on man, you know how this type of stuff goes." After all, Pozo had no problem asking me the question, which revealed that they, too, had someone running surveillance. We knew we couldn't trust each other, but we also knew that each of us needed something from the other. I didn't know it then, but Pozo would ultimately provide answers to many of the questions that had tormented me, day in and day out during the torturous months in prison.

Tio Bob had his hands full. He had relocated himself to Nicaragua and basically worked full time with my family for the better part of a year. Tio Bob constantly kept open the lines of communication with some and kept tabs on all the players in this saga, who by now had grown almost too numerous to count: the justices on the appeals panel and their various official and unofficial shot callers; the attorneys and prosecutors and

Julio Centeno in Managua; the Ministry of Government; the new director of SPN and all her underlings, including the warden, Oscar Molina; the
U.S. Embassy and consular staffs; contacts and informers in several local
government offices, national agencies, or departments; Arnoldo Alemán
and the middlemen between us and him; journalists and news producers,
and a new security team ready to move at the drop of a dime. And that was
just in Nicaragua. A complete cast was also onstage in Washington—State
Department officials, senators and congressmen, agency operatives past
and present, and so many more. Tio Bob had a few other things up his
sleeve, always keeping an eye toward the day when I might be released, but
he didn't talk about that.

One source of constant grief for Tio Bob and the rest of our team was
the Washington office of the law firm of Greenburg Traurig. Joe Reeder
had never even come down to Nicaragua, and his associates at GT hadn't
been in Nicaragua for months yet still felt they could influence the case
from the comfort of Washington and Dubai. We'd never forgotten that
shortly after my conviction, when Ángela Gross was still on the appeals
panel, Joe Reeder had met several times with the Nicaraguan ambassador, Arturo Cruz, and was convinced that he had Cruz's ear. Reeder had
written to us about a dinner he'd had with Cruz. The Nica ambassador
had taken the lawyer into his confidence, or at least that's what Reeder
believed. Cruz convinced Reeder that the best move we could make at
that moment was to figure out how to get Estrada off the appeals panel.
Maybe we could "convince" him to claim that an illness prevented him
from continuing with the case. Cruz had no faith in Estrada but knew of
"a terrific judge, with a great legal mind" who would undoubtedly make
the right call if he were on the panel. The judge he had in mind? Norman
Miranda, the one-time Sandinista who was now considered a chameleon
for his changing loyalties. When Joe Reeder told us about his exciting
"new development," we saw how truly out of the loop he was, but later,
when we put that knowledge together with our new understanding of
Cruz's primary mission in Washington, we realized we had to think differently about Ambassador Cruz. Suddenly his involvement in my case

on such a microlevel made more sense, and our suspicions about the connection between the missiles and my imprisonment grew much stronger.

Reeder was also on the phone with Ambassador Trivelli and the U.S. consul Marc Meznar in Nicaragua, making himself something of a nuisance at the U.S. Embassy, essentially barking up three wrong trees at once. The Washington lawyers simply had no idea of the complexity of the situation in Nicaragua or of all the back-channel maneuvering that Tio Bob and Fabbrith had going. After Tio came on board, we shared information with GT on a need-to-know basis. So as far as they knew, there wasn't much happening.

By September, the appeal had not moved one inch closer to a decisive vote. Never mind that the lack of action violated any number of Nicaraguan procedural codes, the simple truth was either that the case had become too radioactive or that Ortega was holding out for a missile deal. Anyone who came near the case lived in terror of making the wrong move, and circumstances were shifting so rapidly that very few of those involved could figure out what the right moves would be. Norman Miranda, the appeals judge who replaced Ángela Gross and who had recently flipped political parties to go back to the Sandinistas, had simply been sitting on the case file. With Judge Rodriquez's recommendation for acquittal and the Sandinista *bancada* pressing Miranda to confirm Toruño's guilty verdict, the case appeared to have him cornered.

As the political heat increased Miranda took several vacations over the course of that summer and fall, stalling my appeal. Sources of Tio Bob's managed to find out what was going on. In the face of all the evidence supporting my innocence that had become public and all the international attention, a straight confirmation of the guilty verdict from the Sandinista judge would be reckless, making it too obvious that I was nothing more than a political prisoner. But the fact was that it didn't matter what the appeals court ruled as long as the Sandinistas kept me in their possession. So they came up with a clever but underhanded way to hang on to me: It was leaked that Miranda was working on a vote for *annulment*. In other words, he could simply void Judge Toruño's verdict on some trumped-up grounds so that the case would have to be retried. The only problem was that annulment was not one of the legitimate options on the table.

Our appeal had asked only for the conviction to be reversed—a yes-or-no decision. Likewise, the papers filed by the prosecution requested that the conviction be upheld—again a simple yes-or-no decision. In this particular instance, Miranda could not vote for annulment, because it wasn't on the ballot, so to speak. If the information were accurate, it would confirm that Norman Miranda had thrown the rule of law out the window in order to fulfill the Sandinistas' wishes. This leak had not been confirmed at the time, but the very thought of it was devastating. If it were true, it would confirm that the Sandinistas were recruiting judges away from Arnoldo Alemán, and if two of the three voting justices were split, my fate would be entirely in the hands of the third, Alejandro Estrada. At the time, we had no reason to think that Estrada would cause more delays, because our friend Alemán told us he had things under control. But then we had originally thought he had influence over Miranda, and we'd been completely wrong.

In La Modelo, I was getting desperate and wasn't sure I could last much longer. My lungs were wheezing constantly. Even when I lay still, I could feel them gurgling and frothing. I cursed the insane warden Oscar Molina, who had ordered his guards to take away the nebulizer that had been prescribed for me. All kinds of new maladies were invading my body. My colon was severely inflamed, and I'm pretty sure other inflammation and swellings were causing problems—abdominal crowding was cutting off circulation in my legs. At the same time, electric pain shot through my groin. Maybe it was a hernia, but there would be times when I could barely walk. Molina prevented a private doctor from coming into examine me, but I was able to describe the symptoms to the doc over the phone. Fabbrith was able to smuggle in the antibiotics and other meds the doctor provided.

Part of what made Oscar Molina so bizarre and frightening was his unpredictability. The man who seemed to delight in my worsening medical condition, the obsessed jailer who would appear like a ghost at my cell door in the middle of the night, one day for no apparent reason granted my mother a visit to La Modelo, something that he had prevented for five solid months. My mother brought me food and vitamins, clean clothes and socks, and an enormous stack of letters from supporters, but, as much as I needed all that, nothing had as much healing power as her presence.

An uprising was brewing in La Modelo. Guards patrolled the rooftops with rifles while riot police lined the hallways. Everybody knew that war was coming between two rival *galerias*—hits had been ordered and vendettas has been sworn, some of them extending into our *galeria*. The accelerating cycle of violence and payback could only end in full-scale combat that would almost certainly spark a raid on *dos alta*.

On October 8, an interview was to take place inside the prison with people from the A&E network who were at work on a documentary about my case. I had planned to go on camera, until what I think of as a divinely inspired act changed everything. Early in the day, my abdominal swelling had gone down, and, feeling better, I decided to kick the soccer ball around in the hallway. In the course of the play, a random elbow—not a deliberate foul, but clean, accidental contact—caught me in the eye. Within minutes, my eye swelled completely shut and turned frighteningly ugly, displaying most of the colors of the rainbow.

The prison authorities panicked. They didn't want me going on camera looking like I had been beaten. Molina was supposed to make my life hard, but at the same time he couldn't let anything happen to me that would bring the press down on the prisons or the government. The guards on the block feared for their jobs, and I'm sure Molina did, too. I played the accident to my advantage. Knowing how much trouble I could save Molina, I declined to go on camera for the interview. I did the Nicas a huge favor, and they responded in kind. After eight months of ignoring the catalog of serious illness ravaging my body, they checked me into the hospital. I turned my back on La Modelo. In prison, they could keep me invisible, but once I was outside those walls and into a hospital, I would finally have some leverage.

It was just a black eye from a soccer game—happens all the time, all over the world—but that simple black eye helped save my life.

14.

Armando Llanes, Please Stand Up

L eaving the gates of La Modelo felt like being reborn. The moment we
passed through the final security checkpoint, my perspective changed.
Just outside the prison, I saw some of the more violent guards arriving for
work. Inside the walls, they were brutal oppressors who kept us living in
terror, but here, outside, I saw them as they were: just a few more of the
ever-so-common poor of Nicaragua. They looked almost as miserable as
us *reos*, pedaling their ancient, broken-down bicycles in the rain to their
lousy jobs.

The sense of luxury overwhelmed me compared with where I had
been. Although Oscar Molina still held the keys, this was a private police
hospital in a decent part of Managua. I had my first night of deep and
restful sleep in seven months, and I ate and ate and ate. Fresh steamed
vegetables and grilled chicken, fruit and blocks of cheese. I even had a
refrigerator in my room to keep the juices and yogurts that Tio Bob had
brought me. It wasn't just the reading lamp in my room that amazed me,
it was that there was a toilet seat, running water, a real mattress, even a
generator for when the power went out so I could actually turn on the light
and read the stacks of support letters.

The hospital guards treated me with respect as well, knocking and
entering the room quietly or letting me sleep when I needed to. The most
surprisingly wonderful thing about the hospital was the silence. You get
so used to the maddening noise of La Modelo that you don't notice it
until it's gone. No more yelling and screaming. No more banging of plates
and chairs and everything else against the bars. No more constant boom-
box drone. No more of the basketball clanging against the rusted, rickety

rim and backboard right outside my cell, a constant, unbearable noise that had become its own form of torture. The cleaner air also took me by surprise. I had been breathing the toxic fumes of La Modelo for so long that I had lost my sense of smell. I forgot what a pure breath felt like and nearly cried when the clean air filled my lungs. The comfort and relative wealth I acquired in the simple hospital room quickly brought on profound feelings of guilt and confusion when I thought of the subhuman conditions where so many men I had lived with still waited. I had spent the better part of a year living in utter poverty and suddenly was transitioning back into what felt like privilege. I carry that awareness around with me to this day.

Tio Bob and Fabbrith took full advantage of the unrestricted access that Molina allowed. We met in person, and they debriefed me at great length. This was the first time I really heard the details of what Tio was up to, and it took my breath away. He was working a thousand sophisticated angles and had thought of all the variables. He provided details about the disguise he'd prepared for me in the event that I was going to be released and had to get out of the country by land and about how to anticipate frustrating and dangerous obstacles, such as with the immigration department or other rogue factors that might block my departure.

This was when Bob told me that contacts of his had confirmed that Arturo Cruz's mandate in Washington was to conclude the negotiation for the SAM-7 missiles. We talked it through and began to see how this could have something to do with Cruz's getting himself involved with my case. Bob's theory was that the Nicas might see me as leverage—that they were holding on to me in order to pressure the United States into lowering their demands in the negotiations. The notion that a Cali kid like me, who had only come to Nicaragua to start a magazine, now played any role at all in an international arms deal struck both of us as almost comical.

Tio also updated me on a meeting he had with Miranda on the very day that I was transferred to the hospital. Miranda was coy with Bob, hinting that the judges had reached a consensus, but didn't let on what it might be. We had heard that Miranda was considering a vote for retrial, but Tio Bob wanted him to understand that, even without that illegal move, there was no way he would come out of this looking good. Bob knew just how to handle Miranda. He first explained that we planned to denounce the obscene delays and other violations of due process in front of an international human-rights tribunal and that we would make it clear that Miranda himself had been the one obstructing justice with his stalling.* Tio then added that the delays had jeopardized my health and that the move to the hospital, instead of making me safer, actually raised a whole new set of security problems. Then he closed by strategically telling Miranda that we had been approached by a group trying to extort us. Miranda got upset and immediately denied having anything to do with it. Bob's intention was to make Miranda realize that he was in a sensitive situation and needed to move with his ruling. If it came out that we were approached while the case file was in Miranda's hands, it could be interpreted that he was in on the scam. The meeting had begun with Miranda's acting cocky and self-important, relaxed enough to take calls from his romantic partner even as Tio Bob waited, but by the end Bob said that the judge was visibly shaken by the realization of the trouble ahead of him.

We also chatted about the ongoing conflicts with Joe Reeder and Greenberg Traurig. Joe had been making noise for weeks about taking action and had been talking to my mother and Dane about coming down to Managua with a whole delegation of lobbyists and such—the kind of people you'd assemble in Washington if you wanted a big show of power. But after learning things the hard way, we argued that such action would have no impact at all in Nicaragua except to convince everyone there that I really was the son of a privileged American who thought he could bring in an army of guys in fancy suits and limousines to rescue him. My family and even his own colleagues had told Reeder in many different ways what a bad idea it was, but egged on by my father, Jan, who was consumed by

---

* At the time of this writing I have submitted an emergency petition to the Inter-American Commission on Human Rights at the Organization of American States (OAS). Case number 743-09 was filed on June 15, 2009. See online exhibit [EX.46] for the executive summary of my petition.

his desperation to bring me back safely, he pushed ahead anyway. Just as I was moving from La Modelo to the hospital, Reeder sent a letter to Ambassador Cruz outlining his intention.

A totally random black eye had landed me in the hospital, but once I was there the doctors immediately saw how sick I was. A private doctor came in to do tests and started making a list of the results: kidney stone, giardia and other intestinal parasites, bladder infection, swollen colon, asthma, inflamed brochials, sinus infection, gastritis from starvation, insomnia, depression, and need for an X-ray of the bone above the eyebrow. The body I had taken such good care of and honed into condition throughout my life was beat down, poisoned, ruined.

Two days after I arrived at the hospital, the hallways filled suddenly with guards from La Modelo, many of them badly injured and bleeding from stab wounds. A massive riot had broken out in one of the cell blocks, a riot so violent that the guards had resorted to military reinforcements and concussion bombs to disperse the prisoners. Later, one of the guards told me that, although the papers had reported that one of the *galerias* had attempted some kind of mass escape, it was really just the warden, Molina, flexing his muscles, finding some lame excuse to teach everyone a brutal lesson. Twelve of the guards had been injured and rushed to the hospital, and now I could see little groups of guards I recognized huddling in the halls with looks of shock and fear on their faces. At the time it seemed so strange to be experiencing the aftermath of the riot as a detached observer in the hospital. I had no idea how soon I'd be back in the thick of it.

On October 14, just four days after I'd gotten there, the two doctors who ran the hospital came into my room and told me I was being sent back to La Modelo. They explained that the prison authorities had informed them that the hospital authorization was only for two to three days and that, even though they reported that they hadn't even completed their medical tests, it was out of their hands. Oscar Molina told a different story, claiming that the hospital had called him and told him my tests were done and I was ready to return to prison. It was all too familiar. Molina came up with different stories later, none of which made any sense. My guess at the time was that he just wanted me back where he could watch me. The man seemed to be getting stranger all the time. It turns out it was blowback from a move by someone convinced he was helping me—Reeder's letter.

As I steeled myself to reenter the prison that Sunday, it dawned on me that in four days at the hospital, no one had ever even examined my black eye.

The atmosphere of *dos alta* had grown more electric in the few days I was gone. In the aftermath of the riot, the guards had moved a bunch of new inmates to our *galeria*, to separate them from their enemies. That had only created new tension on our *galeria*, where many of these guys also had mortal enemies. When there is a new mix of inmates together, there is a primal yet purposeful stage of sizing one another up to establish social rank. Those first couple of days, *reos* were testing one another in little ways, flexing, offending, stealing, seeing what kind of trouble they might get started, looking for vulnerability. Despite the increased danger near my cell, I was seeing the penitentiary institution through a whole new set of eyes. Those few days off the block and outside the walls had opened a window of hope for me. For a moment I sensed that I had come to the beginning of the end of this ordeal, and that empowered me. Even after they threw me back in my cell, I could see above it in a way that had not been possible before. For reasons I can't fully explain, prison just didn't hurt as bad.

Over a cup of powdered coffee, Leo filled me in on the news of *dos alta*. He told me all the rumors about where I had gone, many of which reveal the history of conspiracy that plagued the minds of the inmates. Some thought I'd been taken to one of the other, more out-of-the-way prisons in Nicaragua. Others thought the government had taken me to some secret place to torture me, possibly even a secret cell right there in La Modelo. Some were sure the hospital story was a just a cover and that I had actually just paid a huge sum of money and gone free. And some of the prisoners actually believed I was in the hospital but only as a first step in my release. Nobody had known exactly what to make of my departure; my quick return must have been even more bizarre to them. It certainly was to me.

I heard from Leo that Chevez Pozo, the prisoner who had come to me with the proposition from Judge Peter Palma, had been asking a lot of questions about me. Pozo had been trying to find out what I had chatted about around the cell so he could get a sense of what I knew. Pozo was definitely keeping his eye on me for someone.

Pozo visited me in my cell the day of my return, and we began a strange little dance with each other. He told me he needed help with legal fees. I told him I could do better than that and promised him I would arrange to have my own attorney take on his case as soon as he was able. On that basis, he began sharing little tidbits of information: Mercedes had been paid $50,000 to make public statements damning me and poisoning the well of public opinion; a man who was running for mayor of San Juan del Sur had been the one who financed the buses that brought the mobs to Rivas for my hearing and trial, and Judge Toruño and the police had been aware of it. We knew a lot of this already, but that's how these little intelligence games work. I started off by telling him that I knew many things but was simply looking to confirm them with an additional source. This was so that he would feel less room to fabricate information. I might be asking him questions to which I knew the answer to see if he really had access to the truth. Pozo would have known this and had to give me something that I could confirm elsewhere so that I would trust him going forward. The best tactic for me was to act naïve on a lot of the topics to give him the impression that I didn't know what goes on behind the scenes. If he didn't know how much I knew, I could ask innocent questions and see what new information came to light. I could identify some of his sources, knowing certain information circulated only in specific groups.

Pozo and I bluffed each other and played each other for a couple of days and eventually got to the heart of the matter. He told me he could find out exactly what happened in Doris's store on the day she was murdered through his contacts in the police and the judiciary. He claimed that Armando Llanes was the main perpetrator of Doris's murder, and when the heat came down Llanes had confessed everything. And now Pozo was prepared to tell *me* about it, along with why it was pinned on me.

I can't count the hours I spent in the dark and dank of many prison cells imagining the scene of Doris's death and trying to fit together the pieces of the gigantic jigsaw puzzle the case had come to be. As excruciating as it would be to hear Pozo lay out his version of the murder in detail, I had been waiting many months for this moment. It felt like I had passed some test and earned access to this information after enduring endless months of prison and disease and terror.

Outwardly, I kept up my *reo* cool, but inside every nerve was buzzing. Every word that Pozo spoke felt like food to a starving man.

Some of what Pozo recounted as to the murder and its aftermath is impossible to verify without honest cooperation from law enforcement, but so much of it fits with the facts that we have at the time of this writing that I accept it as the most plausible account thus far.

Hearing it was devastating. This is the story that Chevez Pozo told me:

Doris closed up her shop and headed off to lunch, as she always did, but Armando Llanes stopped her on the street. They turned back toward the store and went inside. The two had begun to date but apparently had not slept together yet, which had begun to frustrate and agitate Armando. He was jealous and was there to scare her. Shortly after they returned to the store, Nelson Danglas and Rosita showed up, flying high on cocaine. Llanes himself had already drunk a couple of beers.

As Pozo told it, Armando had always caused trouble for the Llanes family. He had divorced parents and had grown up in Miami as a teenager with his sister and brother; he carried an American passport but got into some kind of trouble, allegedly gang related, and his family had brought him back to Nicaragua to live with his father and uncle. He had met Doris soon after his arrival, quickly developed an infatuation, and began pressuring her to drop everything and come live with him at his father's resort, the Monte Cristo Lodge, in the town of Rio San Juan.

Pozo said that inside the store the mood was at first nonviolent, but someone mentioned my name and the fact that she had been seen with me the weekend before. That set Llanes off. When Danglas and Rosita laughed at Armando's ranting, he grew even angrier and shouted at them to stay out of it. Doris thought Armando was kidding around, even when he put his hands on her throat, even when he threatened her.

"Te voy a matar." *I'm going to kill you.*

Suddenly, Doris realized that she was in real trouble and started to fight back with her fists and fingernails. Rosita grabbed her legs and egged Llanes on, teasing him that Doris was cheating on him, Pozo said. Armando Llanes tightened his grip around Doris's throat, and in a few moments she lost consciousness. Armando dropped her limp body onto the bed and then sat down to drink a beer. *He even opened another beer and drank it while he sat looking at Doris's body.* Nelson Danglas looked at the two of them and grew terribly nervous. Rosita lit up a joint.

Armando Llanes got up, put a pillow over Doris's face, and made sure she was dead, but he wasn't finished. At that point, he sent Rosita and Danglas into the other room. Alone with Doris, he raped her with his fingers, saying, "Is this what you wanted, bitch?" Llanes must have had a moment of reason then and panicked. He got the other two men back into the room and told them, "We really fucked up." *We.* Llanes gave his keys to Danglas and Rosita and told them to take whatever they wanted from the store and take his car. The impulsive decision was to make the scene look like a robbery gone bad.

Pozo's account was unbearable to listen to. It made me feel Doris's torment with all my senses. Pozo took the abstraction of Doris's death and made it visceral and real and heartbreaking. When I asked him how he had obtained so much detail, he reminded me that this was directly from a confession that Armando had given, which in turn was shared with the police and prosecutors used to come up with a version as close to reality as possible.

Pozo shared a great deal of information about the aftermath as well. A witness told the police that she saw Danglas and Rosita drive off in a white car. We already knew that the girl in the pizza shop across the street had reported seeing all three men enter the store, that Gabi had reported seeing one of Danglas's cousins wearing a blouse from Sol Fashion, and that the police went to Danglas's house and found the plastic bags he claimed that I had given to him. Nobody saw Llanes leave the store, but apparently, as the current boyfriend, he was one of the very first names that police had as a suspect from their interviews with Doris's friends and neighbors and from Rosita's and Danglas's confessions.

In a developing nation like Nicaragua, where the gap between the wealthy elite and the rest of the impoverished population is so great, the rich and powerful are virtually unarrestable. Armando Llanes and his family, considered at one time to be one of the ten wealthiest families in Nicaragua, fell into that category.* According to Pozo, the first police report sent by detective Jorge Uriarte to the Auxilio Judicial commissioner in Managua, Denis Tinoco, referred to witness statements pinning the crime on Llanes, Rosita, and Danglas. The murder was solved. It would have been no later than the day after the murder that Tinoco had the information.

Tinoco recognized the Llanes name and immediately picked up the phone and made a call. Tio Bob, knowing how things tend to go down, had always assumed that Tinoco offered cooperation for a price. Pozo also believed that Bob's assessment was true. In addition, Pozo claimed that Tinoco told a relative of Llanes's that they would also need to recruit help from Julio Centeno, the attorney general of Nicaragua. This was quickly achieved since Centeno had been an old friend of the Llanes fam-

---

* Armando's uncle, Ricardo Llanes Whitesell, is rumored to be an influential member of the Sandinista party. In addition, he is married to Johanna Hollmann de Llanes, who is the cousin of the San Juan del Sur mayor, Eduardo Hollmann, and directly related to the main owners of the newspaper *La Prensa*. She herself owns substantial shares in *La Prensa*.

ily and because, supposedly, an additional amount of $50,000 exchanged hands at Centeno's request.* From that point, it became Centeno's operation. Through Denis Tinoco, Centeno got a list of seven "potential" suspects, on which my name appeared, and then he got through to Isolda Ibarra, the Rivas prosecutor, and issued orders on how to proceed. Centeno was the mastermind.†

I asked why Llanes was one of the original four accused. If he had protection from the top, why would they allow his name to go public in the first place? Pozo shook his head as if I were a naïve gringo who could never see the matrix of connections and corruption in his country and said, "Brudda, it's the oldest trick in the book." Even though they had an agreement in place with a relative of Llanes's it takes time to get cash together, and this was Tinoco's and Centeno's insurance policy guaranteeing payment. Once everyone was happy, the charges against Llanes were dropped, and he was exonerated in the second hearing.

I may never know for sure who killed Doris or exactly why they decided to go after me for her murder when they could have just pinned it on the two Nicas, but my best guess is the most logical one: Initially, pinning it on Rosita and Danglas would be too risky if there were witnesses that saw a third participant. In addition, the police would run the risk of the press digging into the investigation for "the story." So they knew that charging another American would be an effective ingredient to shifting the focus of the press story away from Llanes and the dirty investigation. But I'm sure they saw dollar signs in me, too. Who better to put into the jackpot than a gringo, especially one with a good source of income and some public exposure? I imagine that neither Centeno nor anybody working with him thought it through very well, though. Centeno had probably heard that I had mouthed off to Reyes of the Rivas police and concluded that a "rich" gringo would figure a way out of trouble eventually but not before Llanes was long gone. Nobody could predict what a

---

* There was also a rumor that Julio Centeno was at one time an attorney of the Llanes family.
† This matched up with what we were told by a source in the Rivas prosecutor's office regarding Centeno's giving orders to Isolda Ibarra and Maria Esperanza Peña very early on.

sloppy job the cops would do fabricating "evidence" to frame me or how quickly the case would take over the public attention. Nobody knew that Mercedes would be such an effective organizer or that her childhood friend, Lesber Quintero, would ignite such a strong anti-American frenzy. It all got out of control too fast. Ortega knew about my arrest almost immediately, and people within the Sandinista party identified my conviction as an opportunity. It became political the moment orders were given to Toruño.

Pozo's account of the crime was lacking some details that had been established by police reports, but it provided a logical and conceivable framework into which many seemingly random bits of information fit perfectly. Much of it matched Rosita's confession, as long as you replace my name with Armando's and Armando's with Danglas's. In addition, Austin—JT's friend who had an undefined relationship with Doris— had confessed to Simon Strong that he was in love with her and actually proposed marriage to Doris on the Monday before the murder. The one condition that he put on it was that she had to stop talking to me. It was that night that Doris called me to tell me we couldn't see each other any longer. Austin later denied that he had asked for her hand in marriage, and I'm not sure he even knew about Llanes. For all I knew, Austin was the object of Llanes's real jealousy, not me. Whatever the case, one of the two of them had provoked her to make a decision about me, and she called me with a lump in her throat and edginess in her voice the night before she died. One could imagine that if she had decided to get married, she also called Llanes that same evening. Given what we had learned about Llanes's infatuation with Doris, maybe that could have sent him over the edge and provided the motive to come to scare her the following afternoon.*

---

* The cell-phone records of Doris Jiménez and Armando Llanes, although obtained by the police, were never publicly shared. Investigators from the U.S. Embassy and even Tío Bob tried to obtain the records, but the management of the company, Movistar, had the documents under strict protection. Suspiciously, several judges refused to subpoena the records. They could be requested and subpoenaed today by the police or the District Attorney of Nicaragua.

* * *

After hearing from Tio and my family about everything they had in the works and about Joe Reeder's potentially disastrous plan to descend on Nicaragua with his legal SWAT team, I had to agree that Greenburg Traurig was becoming more of a potential liability than an asset. I had already seen how quickly and easily the Nica government could increase the pressure on me inside the prison system if somebody got moody, and I simply couldn't afford anyone connected to me making a wrong move. Tio Bob heard that Reeder's letter to Cruz had been circulated around the Nica government and had pissed off enough people that Bob felt it necessary to get word to Cruz that the letter was, in fact, unauthorized by me and my team. Once Cruz got word that Reeder and my father Jan were just blowing steam and that Eric and his team were not aligned with them, he calmed down. This required a huge amount of damage control as it spread through the Nicaraguan government. In my cell, I drafted a letter terminating the relationship with Joe Reeder and his firm, which I had notarized by a former judge who was doing time in *dos alta*. The handwritten document was not transcribed but scanned and e-mailed to GT in Washington.

With the help of an attorney who was doing time on our *galeria*, I penciled another letter as well, this one to Oscar Molina. I accused Molina of denying me necessary medical care by removing me from the hospital. The letter showed that copies went the U.S. Embassy and to "international press," but that was a bluff. (It did get posted on my Web site.) But Molina didn't know that, and according to one of the guards in the prison, the letter spooked him a little. With the hospital directors and my own doctor on record advising that I remain in the hospital, this was a serious violation of rights, and if the U.S. press got hold of it, it could complicate things for the SPN. The gossip circulating among the guards was that Molina was in a real bind now. He had sent me to the hospital because the American television crew had seen my black eye, but I don't think his bosses who had given the order believed I really had other medical problems, much less very serious ones. His superiors at the Sandinista

Ministry of Government (MIG), Ana Morales, and her vice minister, Carlos Najar, wanted me in prison where they could prolong my suffering, but the results of my medical tests had thrown them a curve ball.

Fabbrith also drafted a letter in protest of the SPN conduct that was delivered to the Minstry of Government through the U.S. Embassy. In Nicaragua it is rare that a prisoner has a way to get a letter to a warden's superior in the government. I had put pressure on Molina from within the executive branch. It was a delicate matter. Our maneuver resulted in a meeting arranged for Fabbrith, me, and Molina to smooth things out. There was another man there who introduced himself only as a representative of the MIG. Everybody knew that Najar had been running things after Morales swept out the top level of bosses in the SPN, and this guy's presence was a clear reminder. Our exchange was a theatrical masterpiece. On the surface, we were polite and cordial, almost friendly, but that was all for show. I could feel Molina looking at me like I was some kind of personal demon sent to torture him, while I saw him as the personification of every evil force working to bury me. With all that simmering between us, we had our little chat and did the diplomatic dance I had grown so used to.

"I am sick," I began, "and would like to get the proper medical attention, if that would be possible, sir."

Molina flashed his grotesque death's-head grin. "Well, of course, young Eric. You just have to tell me these things, son. Why do you wait so long to tell me these things?"

I had one more line. "Sir, I just want you to know that I'd rather be in prison healthy than in the hospital sick."

Molina agreed on the spot to send me back to the hospital, although everyone in the room knew that plan had already been approved or else the meeting would have never taken place. I couldn't resist getting in a little shot, and, just before we stood up to leave, I turned to my attorney.

"Fabbrith, you can refrain from sending the letter of protest we drafted for the press. These men have done a good job so far, and there is no need to make this ugly."

As the guards approached to take me back to my cell, Fabbrith gave me a warm embrace and whispered quickly into my ear: "Number two is voting retrial."

The leak had been confirmed. Despite the fact that the option wasn't formally available to him, Norman Miranda had decided to cast his vote in the appeal for annulment, which would mean the case would have to be retried. He hadn't made any public announcement, but Fabbrith had credible enough sources to pass the information along to me. This was a body blow, just at the moment when I had scored my release back to the hospital.

On October 17, only three days after I had returned to La Modelo, I left again for the hospital. Big things had happened in those three days, and as I looked back, I actually thanked the Lord for some hidden blessings. It wasn't just that the first trip outside the walls had reset my attitude and allowed me to rewrite my experience of prison. I also realized that I had been out of the prison at the exact moment of the bloodiest, most dangerous riot that year. There had also been another episode in which guards had fired from the gun tower at some *reos* who had been trying to reach through the windows of *dos alta* to steal. The wall in my cell, just above my bunk, showed fresh bullet marks. Lastly, I would have missed out on the revelations of Chevez Pozo had I not come back. It's hard to imagine being grateful for being sent back to a prison where you never should have been in the first place, but as I left, I couldn't help feeling a new sense of strength and empowerment.

Oscar Molina seemed to be coming unhinged. He ran lead on my transport back to the hospital, during which he handcuffed my arm through the sleeve of my bulletproof vest so that I couldn't put it on.

"You don't need it," he said. "I'm your best flak jacket." Like the cops who had first driven me to prison after the trial, Molina and his bosses were speculating that the transfer back to the hospital would be the perfect opportunity for some kind of operation to break me out. He suspected that I knew an op was in place and didn't want to be accidentally injured. By exposing me, he thought he was protecting himself. We even

took a twenty-five-minute detour around the U.S. Embassy—a clear indication that they believed the United States was capable of stepping in
with military might. This subsequently revealed how relevant my imprisonment was in their minds as well. Every ten minutes, Molina reported
our whereabouts over his cell phone in a tone of voice that made me believe the person on the other end held a much higher rank than him.

The authorities must have known that the first few days in the hospital had felt almost like paradise to me and didn't intend to repeat that
mistake the second time around. The new rules were harsh. I wasn't allowed to see Tio Bob and Fabbrith, who were waiting at the hospital entrance. I was prohibited any future contact of any kind with Tio Bob. No
phone calls, no *sol* (prison lingo for free time outside in the sun), nothing.
Molina confined me to my room and ordered that a guard be in there
with me at all times but that we must not speak to each other. Then he
posted other armed officers around the area and had additional guards
floating around the hospital to look for anything suspicious.

On my second day back, Molina himself came to check on me, at 5:30 in
the morning. He woke me, excused the guard, pulled a chair up next to my
bed in the darkness, and began pouring his heart out. It was so strange and
unexpected to have my absolute nemesis open up to me. He told me about
all the pressures of his position and the difficult predicament he was now
in. He told me that he was very close to retirement and was trying not to get
fired by the new government that didn't tolerate mistakes. He really wasn't
in charge and made that clear. He told me explicitly that all of my activities
from that point forward, even a single phone call, required authorization
from the vice minister of government, confirming what we had assumed for
a long time, that the executive branch of the Nicaraguan government was
issuing any and all orders related to the handling of my detainment.

The case had gone somewhat cold as a news story, but it only took one
leak to *El Nuevo Diario* to ignite it again. In less than a day, a post appeared
on the paper's Web site, along with a picture of the door to my hospital
room, which someone must have gotten past the guards to take, unless one
of the guards snapped it himself. Now the whole country knew where I

was and what was wrong with me, and the press began stoking the fires again. The papers played to the readers' built-up resentment toward classic corruption tactics. Was this just another scam? Was this the usual trick of releasing someone to the hospital as a way of transitioning him out of jail and out of captivity? One headline read, "¿Enfermos o vacaciones en hospital?" (*Sick or on Vacation in Hospital?*). Lesber Quintero ran a piece saying that "reos enfermos es corrupción en vivo"—*sick prisoners is clearly corruption.* He wrote about human-rights commissions that believed that the preferential treatment of certain prisoners—such as me—revealed the deep corruption in the SPN. An online reader commented that "someone should try and poison Eric Volz in the hospital to put an end to this once and for all." Lesber even quoted his old friend Mercedes in the subhead to the article: "When he was with my daughter, he never got sick. Volz never even got the flu."

I was sick alright. By the end of the first week in the hospital, I was on more medications than I could count. My tuberculosis test had come back negative, but I was on two medications for bronchial inflammation. Although the doctor had determined that the smoke-filled air of La Modelo had caused the problem, there was no way she'd risk her career by writing that in her report. If a doctor ruled that the poor prison conditions had made me ill, she could be branded in the press as an ally of mine and subsequently an adversary of the Sandinistas.

My other prescriptions included clonazepam, an antiseizure medication they had foolishly prescribed to promote sleep. As soon as I found out what it was, I immediately stopped taking it. The allergy pills they prescribed had stopped working long ago. I had two inhalers, eye drops for pink eye, nasal antibiotic spray, gastritis medication, laxatives, antibiotics for a bladder infection, and a muscle relaxer that would completely knock me out. In my crazier moments in the hospital, I actually experimented with some of these medications, mixing them in solutions in water or juice and checking for telltale smells or tastes, in case I ever needed to drug one of the guards. It was a slightly deranged fantasy, but it kept my fevered mind occupied. My intestinal problems had eased somewhat, except for the kidney stone. The doctors wanted to treat it with a stick up my urethra that would have kept me hospitalized for months, but, while that had some appeal, I chose to treat it naturally, with lots and lots and lots of water.

Sadly, it was Tio Bob, not me, who was most victimized by this latest round of press attention. *El Nuevo Diaro* and *La Prensa* simultaneously reported on his former relationship with the CIA and the blowback of his final assignments. Ramon Rojas, bitter after getting fired by my family, had been the source of the leak. *La Prensa* described Tio as a fugitive from Italian justice. Having no idea what the fallout from the publicity might be, he simply got out of the country as fast as he could. His departure left a gaping hole in our defense effort. Tio was the captain of the ship, and if he wasn't there giving orders and instructions, some of the crew simply wouldn't know what to do next.

The leaking of Bob's CIA background ratcheted up the tension just a bit more. Molina and Najar and others took the possibility of an escape plan even more seriously. I knew it meant trouble for me. If Bob couldn't get back into Nicaragua, and if I were sent back to the penitentiary, they'd surely put me in a different *galeria*, one deeper inside the prison where escape would be more difficult and where the chances of my turning up dead would be greater.

But Tio did come back into the country a few weeks later, when the furor died down. To Bob, this was just part of the drill, but I was furious on his behalf. He was so skilled and so dedicated and had accomplished so much for me, and here he was dealing with his own personal past for something he made a point of acknowledging and explaining at the beginning of every relationship. One single sentence Rojas gave a journalist had landed one of the biggest blows to my defense effort since my arrest.

As I settled into a routine at the hospital, Oscar Molina established his own psychotic regimen. Even now that I had left the confines of his prison, he kept a personal eye on me, showing up unannounced at all hours of the day or night. I would look up and see his sunken eyes in his bony face, staring at me. I'd hear his voice outside my door, hissing orders at the guards, berating them for some reason or other or no reason at all. The guards who were chill with me would tell me that Molina was losing it, that he didn't trust anyone, especially them, and believed they had all fallen under my spell or something, which was why he kept surprising them with his unannounced visits.

One night, even though it wasn't allowed, someone brought me some fried chicken—a lot of it, so I could share with the guards on duty and they wouldn't report it. Molina happened to be there when it arrived, and he freaked when he saw the extra food. He turned my room inside out searching for who-knows-what and even confiscated a piece of chicken, probably to have it tested for poison or something. For the rest of the night, I could hear people hanging around outside my room, talking quietly to one another or chattering on their cell phones, constantly mentioning my name. Molina wanted me back in his prison, and they kept searching for justification—some way to show that I was planning an escape or making some other kind of trouble.

Molina seemed determined to keep me out of contact with anyone from my legal team. He disabled the public phone that I had been using to make calls for a couple of weeks until I managed to have the hospital directors get it fixed. He denied entrance to Lara Harris, the U.S. consular official who had replaced Dan Bazan, telling her that the vice minister hadn't approved her visits yet. When she finally got in to see me, Lara told me how Najar and the MIG had been giving her and other U.S. Embassy personnel the runaround. She said tensions had reached a high point between the two governments over my case, and she didn't hesitate to call me a political prisoner. Molina changed the guards assigned to my room, panicked that I was somehow manipulating them or turning them into assets of some kind. Eventually, he ordered that guards were no longer to stay in my room but only to be posted outside the door. This plan turned out to be even worse, with the guards opening the door and poking their heads in every half hour or so as if they wanted to be sure I never relaxed or slept very long. Molina even went so far as to confiscate a book

I was reading about the Nicaraguan civil war, written from a Contra perspective.

"You don't need to be brainwashing yourself with that Washington crap," he said, as he snatched it from my room. Maybe it seems like the least important thing, the loss of a book, but at the time, it really pissed me off. It reminded me of the very oppression I was reading about in the book and evoked my worst fears of Communist mind control. Did the FSLN really reach that deep into people's psyches? Had the country gotten to the point where even books were to be feared?

Molina's guards clashed with the hospital nurses, keeping them out of my room when they needed to do simple things like take my blood pressure or give me meds. The more the guards infuriated the nurses, the more sympathetic they would act toward me. Most of them made me feel at ease, but every now and then a nurse I had never seen before would show up to give me pills. I simply didn't trust anyone or anything anymore, and there was no way I'd ever swallow some strange pill from some strange nurse, although I developed a pretty good technique for faking it. The day one of the guards hassled the hospital director about bringing his cell phone into my room and demanded the phone, the doctor just laughed and then went off on the guard.

"Hell no! You are not touching my phone. When I am in your custody, you can take my phone, but until then, you *never* tell me what to do."

It took Fabbrith until the first of November to get Molina's permission for my team to drop off food, but the warden continued to deny all visits and phone calls.

Late one night I heard strange sounds from my door, the sounds of strained wood and metal being twisted and flexed, as if someone was leaning their weight against a locked door in an effort to open it. I knew that locking my door was not allowed and got up to check. I turned the knob slowly and opened the door, expecting to see an annoyed guard or two, but there was Oscar Molina, looking totally stunned to see me. Molina was busily tying one end of a length of rope to a couch outside my room. The other end was already tied to the knob on the outside of my door. Anger and embarrassment and desperation all flashed across the warden's face as he shot me a hard, nasty glare before yanking the rope and slamming the door shut.

It was funny to think that those initial four days of my first visit to the hospital had seemed so blissful. Those few replenishing days were so far removed from my current experience, which had begun to feel like the box at Chipote. Solitary confinement is cruel beyond imagining, and a slightly more comfortable setting wasn't making it any easier on the psyche. Molina and his men had me locked in that little place. They had stopped using the generator when the power went out, keeping me in darkness for half of every day and denying me the one companion I had—the television hanging on the wall. I was not allowed to open the blinds. I went one stretch of thirty-three days forbidden to leave the room except for two short walks for an ultrasound or to make my weekly ten-to-fifteen-minute call from the phone booth right outside the door.

It was like everyone was afraid to get too close to me. Nurses didn't like having to hassle with the guards and sometimes would not see me for days. I couldn't do simple exercise, afraid that someone would see me and report that I was healthy enough to work out. I could barely write in my journals for fear that some guard would bust in for one of their surprise inspections and either confiscate it or tighten down on me in some other way. I literally began pacing around my room like a caged tiger.

My physical condition actually worsened—amazing considering that I was in a hospital. I was having urinary problems on top of everything else and had started leaking semen into my urine. The doctors thought I might have an STD, but I couldn't let them test me for it, fearing that if somehow a positive result emerged and was leaked to the press, it would be taken as a sign that I was indeed some kind of unclean person, surely a rapist and surely guilty. We finally managed to have a private doctor do a test, which came back clean. I was in terrible pain from the kidney stone, and my whole body felt weak from the invasive testing that the hospital was doing. It occurred to me that if I ever got out of that hospital, it was possible that I'd leave sicker than I'd arrived.

In the first week of November, the second appeals justice, the spineless Norman Miranda, made his vote for annulment and retrial public. Miranda was protected by the president, who was delighted to have something to rub in the face of the United States and to use to show the Nicaraguan people his unwillingness to bow to U.S. pressure. Miranda's move scared the hell out of us. Now, Alejandro Estrada, the last judge, had the tie-breaking vote and was faced with even more pressures than had plagued Miranda.

A new sense of desperation set in. Only a couple of weeks before, I had believed that we had entered the final chapter, but now I felt like everything was falling apart. Oscar Molina had turned the promise of a replenishing hospitalization into torture. He had cut me off from my family and supporters even more severely than in La Modelo. The hope and excitement of Rodriguez's initial decision to reverse my conviction had all but evaporated.

The mounting pressure inside the appeals court was echoed all around us in the earth and atmosphere, as God unleashed the awesome forces of nature. In the week after Miranda handed down his vote, several earthquakes shook Nicaragua. It was the height of hurricane season as well, and the rainfall was so heavy that Nicaragua declared a state of emergency. Floods ravaged most of Central America, resulting in massive destruction and a tragically high death toll. Shut in my hospital room, cramped with pain, all I could think was that my world, *the* world, was coming to an end.

None of these cataclysms relieved the pressure on us. One morning a couple of weeks later, I woke up when something landed on my bed, hitting my legs. The door shut before I could see who had opened it. On the bed was the book that Molina had confiscated back in October, the one about the Contras. As I awoke and my head cleared, I realized that it was the November 21, the one-year anniversary of Doris's death, and that my mother was scheduled to visit that day. Maybe in Molina's twisted mind, his returning the book would somehow make Maggie think I was being well treated.

Two days later, the twenty-third, I marked the end of one full year in captivity. It would turn out to be a day full of new twists and developments, but for me it began as a day of spiritual reflection. My eyes were opening after a year in captivity, and I was able now to see some hint of purpose in this whole ordeal.

I saw with great clarity the flawed priorities of the life I had led. I had been reaching for money; telling myself that money begets power, that power begets mobility, that mobility makes positive social change possible. I had believed that ideas without resources would not get you very far. I had seen so many passionate initiatives fail for lack of competitive drive, even ambition. It made sense to me that if you want see results, you needed to infect the system like a virus and then effect change from the inside out. The plan looked good on paper, but it didn't take into account that there were moments when it had to be about me. I had to be the one on the mic and to have my name on the checks. I had to be promoted. I even started to buy myself expensive things. I had become *Don Eric*.

Now, removed from that material world, I could strive for something beyond myself. All that remained was a pursuit for true survival, which I could see now as a quest for a life in God's kingdom, through fulfillment of his purpose for me. My life was still about building bridges, but not just bridges between people and resources or between one culture and another but between the madness of the fallen world we inhabit and the inheritance of an eternal kingdom. What had been missing all along in my life was the quest for holiness.

As the light of awakening inside me grew stronger that morning, events outside the hospital were opening tiny cracks in the darkness. A friendly Nica named Julio, who worked in the U.S. consulate and had become a helpful ally, told us about an opportunity that had arisen with Lenin Cerna, the feared enforcer who headed the Sandinista internal intelligence apparatus. Lenin's wife had come to the consulate to request a visa to visit her ailing mother in the United States. Julio brought this to our attention because he knew it was a window for leverage. For a representative of the State Department to use its own bureaucracy to apply pressure like that was unprecedented, at least as far as we had experienced. It was a smart gamble, though, and an arrangement was agreed on with Lenin Cerna, the most immediate result of which was a meeting between my mother, stepfather, Tio Bob, and Vice Minister Najar of the Ministry of Government, who was directing all of Oscar Molina's actions.

The meeting revealed much. Tio Bob, Maggie, and Dane reported that Najar was the perfect model of a member of the Nica power elite. A high-ranking, very wealthy Sandinista, Najar was sharply dressed, well groomed, and carried himself with relaxed authority. More important, the vice minister is the embodiment of the "Russian shadow" in Nicaragua. His extensive role in the life of the FSLN landed him a seat in the highest ranks of the Sandinista power structure, and he was an even more powerful figure than his direct boss, Ana Morales. Najar was effectively only one step removed from Daniel Ortega himself. People of real power and influence in the Nica government generally shield themselves behind a complex hierarchy. Ortega tells his chief of staff to make life hell for Eric Volz. The chief sends word down to Najar, who breaks it down into specific directives. Maybe he tells Oscar Molina to stop me from making phone calls, so Molina, unsure how to proceed, breaks the only phone I could use. Vice Minister Najar may not have been the composer of my symphony of torment, but he was unquestionably conducting the orchestra. To have him come out in the open, as it were, to show himself and become personally involved with people representing me meant that the situation had become far too sensitive, too critical, to be left to less-experienced underlings.

Najar wasn't cowed in any way by Bob Lady, and that alone was impressive, not to mention the fingers missing from his left hand. He began the meeting by taking out his record of my prison history—a thick binder that seemed professionally prepared, with the documents carefully arranged and separated by neat colored index tabs. They had logs for prison visits with the times of entry and exit of the visitor. Many of the visits were falsified, confirming that they were conscious about covering their tracks. But Najar didn't really need the comprehensive documentation; he appeared to have every fact and detail of my life committed to memory. Najar confirmed what everybody assumed—that it had been Joe Reeder's letter to Arturo Cruz that had gotten me kicked out of the hospital and sent back to La Modelo the previous month. It was extremely important for my mother, Dane, and Tio to be able to confront the man orchestrating my misery, face-to-face. By the time the meeting ended, they had achieved their goal and extracted his approval for me to make phone calls and to receive visits from Maggie and Dane.

Oscar Molina inadvertently helped improve the relationship with Najar the next day. Sensing Tio Bob's growing stature and desperate to get Bob out of the picture, Molina went to Najar with a crazy, made-up story about how Bob had walked into the hospital and mouthed off to the guards about Molina's being a complete fool and a son of a bitch. Now that Tio had Najar's ear, however, he could speak to him directly and convinced him that nothing of the kind had happened. Tio even expressed concern for Molina, talking about the predicament the warden must have been in and the stress he was under. Najar caught on and fell out laughing, as if in unspoken agreement that Molina was on the edge of a meltdown.

"Okay, I got you," Najar said. "Just stay away from those guys." The fact Najar had called Tio over such a small detail was reaffirming, showing us that he, a top-level official of the executive branch, was getting involved in the little things.

Fortunately, after that meeting life did get better. I immediately started putting weight back on because I was eating better food. I was in contact with my family and my attorney. They even approved physical therapy for a foot injury I had sustained, and, even though the PT facility was just a short walk down the hall, it was like a different world to me. I could hear people laughing and joking—the sounds of freedom—and I soaked it up like a sponge. Pretty soon I even got the doctor to grant me access to the hospital gym. It hadn't been used in years, but I was able to cannibalize the different exercise bikes and piece a working machine together to get my body moving again.

Of course, I should have known from experience that just when things start looking up, something will bring it all crashing back to earth. On December 5, Fabbrith came to see me with news that the appeals court in Granada appeared to be hopelessly deadlocked. Rodriguez and Miranda had both ruled, but Estrada was flagging. He had been sitting on the sentence of the most-high-profile appeal of his career for over a month. Everyone knew he had already reviewed the case file, and everyone was watching him, waiting for a decision.

He was getting torn apart by the conflicting pressures coming down on him. He had the former president, Alemán, telling him to rule according to law, then he had the current president and the Sandinista operators Miranda and Gross pressuring him to annul the whole thing. But he still was holding out. Why? It seemed that he might have had an additional problem as well. Logic combined with what we already knew suggested that maybe his third problem was coming from a side scheme to try to get money. I can imagine Otto Navas, a district judge and the son of Supreme Court Justice Edgar Navas, and Judge Palma saying, "Just wait. Volz is desperate. I know he didn't go for it the first time, but we can still get money out of him." Maybe Navas offered temptations that tested Estrada's loyalty to Alemán. Otto Navas had strayed from Alemán's sphere of influence when the former president had denied him a Supreme Court appointment alongside his father. There was only so far he could stray, however. Alemán, though still serving his own sentence of confinement within the country, held all the cards. He controlled Estrada's career, and ultimately Navas's as well. He picked up the phone and called Otto Navas, telling him frankly, "quit fucking around." El Gordo still had control. Estrada had no place to turn.

The next day, Madeleine Albright visited Nicaragua. The former secretary of state met with Arnoldo Alemán and his wife, and she probably met with Daniel Ortega and his wife, Rosario Murillo, as well. We have reason to believe that she acted on our request to raise the issue of my case and appeal. Albright's visit coincided with a great deal of public political turmoil in Nicaragua. Newspaper articles were questioning the objectivity of the courts and even quoted the president of the Supreme Court acknowledging the influence of the Sandinista party in the court system, stating that "a judicial branch that is dominated by the political sector is not a judicial branch, it is a political branch. . . ." The realization that people within Nicaragua publicly denounced the political corruption of the courts in general even as they assured the United States and the rest of the world that my particular case was sticking to the letter of the law left a bitter taste in my mouth. By that time, even the staffers at the U.S. Embassy had begun referring to me as a "political prisoner."

Daniel Ortega also seemed to be running wild. He made outrageous public statements about how the United States was plotting to assassinate Hugo Chávez of Venezuela. At the same time, he began modeling himself after Chavez, even taking the step of strong-arming and confiscating significant American-owned holdings and investments. Ortega suddenly seemed out of step with his own people, making assertions that everyone saw as illogical and taking one giant stride after another on the path toward socialism. But he didn't give his people enough credit when it came to detecting the bullshit. The Nicaraguan people had been through all this once before, yet they could do little else but sit still and watch Ortega plunge their country back into the dark days of economic isolation, shortages, and deprivation. Opposition leaders were reporting death threats, and radio stations were being burned to the ground. To cap things off, Ortega appeared at the United Nations in early December, denouncing the United States "devil" with inflammatory rhetoric, and by all accounts sounding like he was stuck in the bygone days of the cold war. The man seemed to be playing with fire, adding fuel to the sense that everything and everyone around me was about to fall off the edge of reason.

One year earlier, I had sat in a cell in the Rivas police jail, waiting to be charged. Outside the jail, the fireworks of La Purisima festivities rocked the bars of the cells and shattered my nerves. I could hear the same explosions and throbbing music and partying in the streets now as I sat in the hospital, waiting and waiting, literally aching for freedom and growing deliriously frantic, nearly paralyzed with fear. To me, it sounded like war. On December 12, Fabbrith came and told me he believed a decision from Estrada would come any day. But the fact that Fabbrith's own house had been attacked with rocks led us to believe that Mercedes was at work again. She had been seen hanging around Miranda's office, and Fabbrith's broken windows suggested that she had heard through her own sources that the decision was not going to go her way.

The next day, Thursday, December 13, Sandinistas desperately flexed their muscles, ordered Arnoldo Alemán back into house arrest, and were openly threatening to return him to prison. The news about El Gordo dominated the media and gripped the nation. Alemán denounced the move as bald-faced blackmail and refused to be intimidated, announcing that he'd continue the fight from jail if he had to. As I felt my *padrino* and his influence slipping away, Alemán actually kept up the fight for me. Retreating into a private bathroom to escape the policemen guarding every corner of his house, the former president sat down on the toilet and phoned Judge Alejandro Estrada on his cell phone. Alemán took the gloves off and threatened Estrada, telling him in no uncertain terms that he would see to it that Estrada's career and reputation were ruined if the judge didn't immediately get off his ass and vote on the appeal.

For my part, I knew nothing of this at the time. Alone and trapped in my hospital room with half a dozen armed guards keeping watch outside my door, I stared dumbfounded at the endless televised replays of Arnoldo Alemán being marched back into his house by a police escort, through what looked like a battalion of cops. I watched as he went inside and the door slammed on what seemed like my last hope for freedom.

As the image on the screen dissolved into a commercial, my own door opened. I looked up to see Fabbrith standing there, with a smile unlike any I'd ever seen on his face. That smile told me everything I needed to know. We high-fived and embraced each other before any words were even spoken. He told me everything that had happened that day. The votes were in. Miranda for annulment and thus retrial. Rodriguez and Estrada for not guilty. We had won the judicial bout. All that remained was for the new sentence to be ratified, which by law had to happen within five days. Then my release order was to be signed immediately by the original trial judge, which meant Monday would be the day of my release, if the law was upheld.

That night I wrote in my journal, ". . . at this point, the only thing that could hold things up is Ivette Toruño avoiding signing the release order. And she most likely will." But, I told myself, ". . . a ratified appeal means the physical sentence document is final and signed. It can't be changed!" I had it right, on both counts.

My emotions ran wild for the next couple of days. I tried to stay calm, tried to prepare myself for the inevitable mayhem that would derail my release, but I couldn't stop my mind from racing. I relived every moment of the year gone by, every abuse and every triumph, every moment of pain and desolation, and every moment of strength and cleansing grace. The memories overwhelmed me—it was just too much, and all of it too intense for me to process and categorize. There was a great storm of memories and emotion raging inside me. On Sunday night, very possibly the last night before I would go free, I tried to remind myself that I had been through all this before. I had prepared myself for redemption and liberation, only to be thrust back into the oblivion of captivity. But still, the next day might be the beginning of a new and beautiful life for me. I rested, I read my Bible, and I prayed.

15.

Check and Mate

On Monday, the December 17, the Granada appeals court formally declared me not guilty. The sentence[EX.47] ordered my immediate release along with the return of the collateral required during my house arrest: my passport, a $10,000 bond, and the release of two mortgages. Norman Miranda's vote for annulment still stood on the books, but for the moment, a path was cleared for my release. Now it was just a matter of navigating the inevitable resistance of my adversaries.

I would have expected the Nica press to get wind of the decision right away, but by 1:00 that afternoon, there had been nothing on radio or television or in the newspapers. It was hard to figure why the media would keep quiet about this, and I felt the panic welling up inside me. Had someone slammed an iron first down on the release process? Had they found a way to get around the judicial order? What were the Sandinistas up to?

I couldn't let on that Fabbrith had shared his inside information on the vote tally with me the Thursday before, so I played dumb when the head nurse came in and told me that I was being "discharged" from the hospital and to "be ready." I figured this was disinformation from Molina to keep the hospital in the dark about the fact I had been declared innocent. I really didn't know what to think anymore actually. The nurses had been practically my only human contact for the two months that I had been confined to my hospital room. I was a wreck, but I could sense that there was something real about this. Something was happening.

As the day wore on, I found it harder and harder to even breathe. I retreated into scripture, trying to focus every scrap of consciousness on the words in front of me. The passage in the modern translation I read seemed written for only me, to be read precisely in that moment: *Like barbarians desecrating a shrine, they destroyed my reputation. . . . God, how long are you going to stand there doing nothing? . . . those who hate me for no reason. . . . Don't you see what they're doing? . . . Please get up, wake up! Tend to my case, my God, my Lord. My life is on the line. . . .* And, as though timed perfectly, just as I finished reading and closed my Bible, the door of my room opened and three friendly nurses burst in.

"Have you heard the news? They just said on the TV that you have been found innocent."

They cried, and I cried, and we all four embraced. If the Nica press was reporting the story, it was official, it was public, and it was spreading through wire services and phone lines, text messages and Internet cables and airwaves, and my captivity could really be about to end.

The hospital seemed to be buzzing. The hospital director came by and repeated the news about the verdict, and before long guards started poking their heads into my room, telling me of the verdict, letting me know that things were going to start happening, that I was going to be released, but nobody was sure when. Shortly after, I could hear someone arguing in a non-native Spanish accent outside my door. Two U.S. Embassy officials had come to get my signature in order to get me a passport. This could only mean that Ivette Toruño had declined to return my original passport and now one was needed on an emergency basis. We had even thought about this earlier, and I had pushed for the embassy to obtain my signature and keep it on file, but they had resisted, fearing it could leak and make it appear that they had advance knowledge of the appeals decision. If the SPN denied access to embassy personnel who needed my signature, the orders would have come from above, from the Ministry of Government, meaning from Ortega's executive branch. I knew what was up: The longer they could stall the release process, either through nonsense like denying a signature for a passport or through more sinister efforts to delay signing the orders, the more time the forces against me would have to organize themselves and block the verdict or my release. That effort, carried out through phone calls, backroom meetings, sponsored press campaigns, public confrontations, death threats, bribes, and so on, began as soon as the decision had been announced.

Once the story broke, the press went after it with everything it had. At 4:00 P.M., the multinational Spanish-language television network Univision ran a biased piece casting doubt on the appeals court verdict. The segment showed Julio Centeno, the attorney general, describing the new verdict of not guilty as a "babaridad," *a barbarity*. The local news was even worse. They were moving quickly to turn public opinion against me again, and everything they did seemed to have an impact.

Centeno and others put on their show, expressing outrage wherever they could find a live microphone. They promised the Nica people to present a reversal to the Supreme Court and argued that simply making the motion superceded any order to release me.* Mercedes was back, her face filling up the screen whenever I turned the set on. She had tragically lost her daughter, and I can only imagine what her loss must have felt like. But after she tried to turn her tragedy into a business opportunity, demanding settlements from innocent parties, I confess I had a hard time finding much sympathy for her. The melodrama she played out on the news sickened me. "Eric Volz has a license to kill!" she would wail. She would spread more lies about how we had paid off the judges, while she tried to display bravery by thrusting out her chin and declaring that she wasn't scared of me or anyone else. She called for an investigation into Judges Rodriguez and Estrada, who handed down the not guilty verdict, and, better yet, demanded they just be thrown in jail. The TV and radio call-in shows allowed anyone and everyone to spit their venom at me: How could that assassin go free? Why does the gringo get special treatment? "Don Dinero es el jefe!" (*Sir Money is*

---

* This was the first and only case in Nicaraguan history in which the prosecution (the attorney general) claimed that the mere act of submitting a reversal effectively overrides any release order and that the defendant is to remain in custody pending a decision on the motion. Furthermore, although it is completely unconstitutional and illegal, it has become an accepted practice in the Nicaraguan legal system for the prosecution to appeal a court verdict of not guilty in an attempt to change the verdict to guilty but not with the defendant behind bars. Fabbrith argued in the press that if this was lawful, then all defendants who have submitted appeals after being found guilty should be set free. What's good for the goose is good for the gander. Several Supreme Court magistrates are aware of this bending of the law but are not willing to point it out because hundreds of cases would have to be undone.

the boss.) In the saddest twist of irony, Nicas expressed outrage at the corruption and incompetence of their own courts. They were dead right, of course, but also dead wrong. The courts were a farce, but the appeals verdict that enraged the nation had been the one thing they'd gotten right in my case—and just barely. I was aware that the studios weren't giving airtime to those Nicas that supported me, but nevertheless it tore me apart that so many callers and commentators talked about how dangerous it would be now for any Nica woman to get too close to a gringo. It seemed possible that the legacy of my time in Nicaragua would be exactly the opposite of the vision I held when I had arrived. I had come with a simple idea of doing maybe just a little bit of good but ended up taking center stage in a production that only seemed to widen the divide and contribute to the hatred.

Marc Meznar, the U.S. consul, argued his way past Oscar Molina that first day—no small miracle—and got in to see me. He confirmed my worst fears, that Ivette Toruño, who had to sign my release order, immediately set about derailing the process. At first she simply refused to sign the order. Then Toruño brought other kinds of ridiculous dodges into play. She didn't show up for work, then she called in sick, then she started saying that she had returned the case file because the documents in it weren't properly stapled or that it wasn't legible or that the papers were not in the correct order. The case file would, in fact, "go missing" and would become the center of a kind of mass hysteria and my own personal agony for the rest of that week. As a result, the Granada court assigned an executor judge to track down Toruño, but he got nowhere. When Toruño didn't show up to work because of a "flat tire," Fabbrith immediately filed a writ of habeas corpus to force the judges to produce the file. Miranda, who signed the writ while the file was actually in his desk, and Toruño, representing the Sandinista agenda, had teamed up with the prosecution and were working together to keep the file hidden. It "magically reappeared" on Thursday morning after giving the prosecution time to prepare the paperwork to file their own reversal—in essence an appeal of the appeal.

Meznar also explained that all the prearranged agreements with the

Nica government went out the door. They weren't even returning his phone calls. He said, "Someone high up is worried and doesn't want you leaving the country." He feared for my safety. "The longer you are in here, the longer this takes, the more you get moved around, the more dangerous this gets for you," he told me. The Nicas had placed sharpshooters around the hospital, or so they said. Clearly, the police presence at the hospital had increased greatly. I could hear the radio chatter of the surveillance teams right outside the door to my room. Things were starting to feel extra sketchy.

By Tuesday, the U.S. press had descended on Nicaragua, seizing on the story that I was still a prisoner despite the release order. There was no doubt that the executive branch of the Nica government was desperately clinging to its "golden" prisoner, and only one explanation made any sense. I thought back to our conversations through the summer and fall about Arturo Cruz and his attempts to stack the appeals panel and what Tio Bob had learned about the extreme importance of the missile negotiation to both countries, and everything fell into place. Ortega knew that with the world watching, the United States could not ignore my situation, and that made me a valuable bargaining chip in his eyes. If my release was a priority for the United States, he could drive up the price for destroying the missiles by tightening his grip on me. Perhaps the attention made me valuable for the United States also. The U.S. State Department then got into the act, issuing public statements gently urging Ortega's regime to allow me to go free as soon as possible and promising to hold them responsible if anything was to happen to me. It is my honest belief that they wouldn't have lifted a finger had they not been flooded with thousands of letters and phone calls demanding that the U.S. government show some teeth. Even when they did engage, it infuriated me that they would never use strong enough language regarding my situation. Once the verdict had been overturned, it became an illegal detention.

I could also feel Oscar Molina tightening his grip. The hospital director avoided me but managed to pass the message that Molina wanted me back in La Modelo. He said I had been formally discharged from the hospital, but, instead of going free, I might find myself back in my prison cell. I felt like the Sandinistas wanted to get their last licks in, messing with me as much as they could before I got out, if I ever got out. Or maybe they simply wanted me back in a fortified facility and had no plans of releasing me. Molina canceled all my activities inside the hospital and again ordered that a guard be posted in my room at all times. Given the unrest outside and the fear that everyone else seemed to be feeling, I had no problem with that.

Trapped in my room with the television, I watched constantly as the battle raged over the airwaves. I desperately needed the TV news for information, but that also meant I was staring into the flickering face of my enemy. Broadcasters gave Mercedes an open forum, handing her a microphone and letting her call for the residents of Rivas and San Juan to "ensure justice." The channel I was watching cut Fabbrith off in the middle of an interview in which he was running down the list of mistakes made by the prosecution and convicting court. They had no problem letting Norman Miranda ramble on about how a new trial should take place, even as he strategically reminded people that although Llanes and Danglas probably should never have been released, they could not be retried. Nobody pointed out that neither of them had ever stood trial in the first place.

From the news I learned that the Granada courthouse was surrounded by guards and that riot police had been called in to reinforce the very hospital I was in. Everything I watched convinced me that my shot at freedom was disappearing, but inexplicably the guards kept poking their heads into my room all day, telling me to get ready because it looked like I'd be leaving any minute. My sanity started to crumble.

This is how surreal it got: A Nica government official named Omar Cabezas went on television to condemn the appeals verdict. He called it "*repugnante*"—*repugnant*—and repeated all the lies about me: I'd offered a million dollars to Mercedes, I'd paid off the appellate judges with cash, and so on. He claimed that "in order for Eric Volz to be able to move U.S. congressman, thousands of supporters, and Condoleezza Rice from the State Department, and the U.S. Embassy, he must be very powerful . . . and it proves that he is related to a senator very close to President Bush in the Republican party." Cabezas openly stated that he was in contact with the executive branch to make sure that I didn't leave the country and insisted that Judges Rodriguez and Estrada be investigated, prosecuted, and thrown in jail immediately. Omar Cabezas's title? Solicitor General *for Human Rights*.

Even my former attorney, Ramon Rojas, went on television to defend Mercedes's and the prosecution's right to take their case to the Supreme Court, but that wasn't the worst of it. When I saw Judge Ivette Toruño on the screen, declaring the case file "had been lost," I ran to the bathroom and threw up. Of all the terrible nights I had endured, that Tuesday may have been the worst. The adrenaline overload was poisoning me. Here, on the verge of freedom, I felt closer to death than I ever had.

When a nurse came in to record my astronomically high blood pressure on Wednesday morning, I could see how right I had been to worry the previous night. I know the woman was trying to calm me down when she told me she had overheard the higher-ups saying they didn't really plan to take me back to prison, but all it made me think was, *Now I've heard everything.*

The media circus opened that morning with Roberto Rodriguez defending his verdict in what he described as one of the largest cases the appeals court had ever handled. Rodriguez clearly believed he had a lot at stake and was defending not just this one decision but his own honor and freedom. When Marc Meznar visited later that day, he told me that Rodriguez had been receiving death threats to help me understand the judge's courage and conviction. Meznar told me that in the United States not only had the press gotten very much engaged in the story, generating a great number of new supporters, but also that Congress was inquiring

about me regularly and that U.S. Ambassador Trivelli had met personally with Morales and Najar, the people in charge of my detainment.

That same day, a subwarden from La Modelo came by to reassure me
about the tightened security measures, but I seized the opportunity to
show him that it wasn't sufficient. I handed him a newspaper that carried
a front-page photograph of the lobby of the hospital wing where we were
sitting at that moment. It wasn't quite "inside Eric Volz's room," as the
caption described it, but it was close enough. Whoever took the picture
had clearly breached the security perimeter. The newspaper lit a fire under the hospital directors, and within a half hour I could hear the sound
of windows slamming shut, doors being sealed up, workers being cleared
out of hallways, and chatter on every guard's radio about them staying on
high alert.

Centeno, Omar Cabezas, and one of the archbishops of the Catholic
Church in Nicaragua kept up their relentless attacks in the press, now
joined by representatives of women's rights groups. It had been bad enough
to hear the corrupt and ambitious politicos defaming me, but to hear
these female leaders talking about my case as "an insult to women and
justice" just made me wish a hole would open in the earth and swallow
me. Fortunately, my own secret weapon in the press war arrived that day:
My mom landed in Nicaragua.

The crush of reporters at the airport had been so out of control that
Tio Bob had just grabbed Maggie by the arm and run with her, both surrounded by security, to a waiting car. Sadly, that wasn't the story I heard.
One of the more hostile nurses came running in with the news that she
had just seen my mother attacked.

"Have you been watching TV?" she asked. "It was bad."

"What? What happened?"

"She got mobbed by a crowd. They dragged her away like a doll. Your
uncle was there."

That was the last straw. I thought to myself that these thugs could do
whatever they wanted to me but God help anyone who laid a hand on my

mother. I wanted to explode. In that moment, I was fully prepared to jump the first armed guard I saw, grab his gun, run, and just open fire on whoever happened to get in my way. I couldn't imagine any reason not to just throw it all to hell and go down in a blaze of gunfire right then and there.

Except none of what the nurse told me was true; it had just been an evil nurse trying to break my spirit. What had really shown on TV was my mom trying to outrun reporters to the car at the airport. To so many people, she had become the public face of my story, and reporters from inside and outside Nicaragua hung on her every word. She provided the emotional centerpiece of their stories, and she wasn't holding back. Not long after her plane touched down, the whole world could see her on television standing in front of the Granada courthouse, pleading for my freedom.

"Why won't anyone talk to me? No one will talk to me. The Supreme Court won't talk to me. WHERE IS MY SON? The Nicaraguan government has declared him innocent, but HE IS STILL NOT FREE!" She demanded that the authorities release me immediately and reminded anyone who would listen that with my conviction overturned, my continued detention was illegal no matter how you looked at it. If I had had any official diplomatic status, either as a member of the military or as a government employee, my imprisonment at that point could have been interpreted as an act of war.

Amazingly, as Maggie stood there in front of the courthouse, Isolda Ibarra, the lead prosecutor, walked up and demanded the camera's attention. She announced that the government was ready to submit its reversal,[EX.48] claiming that it would prevent me from being released. Fabbrith had already ridiculed that logic with his clever argument (see footnote on page 244). A bright reporter asked Ibarra how she had been able to prepare her appeal to the Supreme Court *without access to the case file, which was missing.* The prosecutor spun around and stormed off without saying another word. It wasn't until the next morning that Norman Miranda emerged from his office holding the case file in his hand for all the press and cameras to see.

"The case file has appeared," he announced with a show of mild outrage, as if he had been tricked. "It was on my desk. I have no idea how it got there. . . ."

Something had to give, and Tio Bob knew exactly where to apply pressure. On Thursday morning, he and my mother paid a visit to the U.S. Embassy in Managua, to meet with the DCM and the consul general. In the U.S. State Department, the DCM, or Deputy Chief of Mission, of an overseas embassy is the official directly under the ambassador. While ambassadors are the public face, it's often the career diplomat in the role of DCM who handles the day-to-day business of the embassy and knows how to get things done. As the saying goes, the DCM is likely to "know where the bodies are buried." In Nicaragua, Ortega was more likely to take a call from the DCM than from the ambassador himself.

Bob and Maggie had their presentation carefully scripted. Maggie took the lead, making an emotional plea for embassy support pressuring the Nica government to release me. As expected, she got a great deal of sympathy but not much commitment, which was Bob's cue to jump in.

"Excuse me, Maggie, but I have a question." He turned to the DCM. "Look, Eric Volz is an athlete. He can run. If he were to somehow be able to sprint the two blocks from the hospital to the gates of your embassy, would you take him in?"

The question was designed to get the U.S. officials to show their hand. The DCM shook his head and said that they would not be able to let me in but would have to turn me back over the Nicaraguan authorities. This was all Bob and my mom needed to hear. The U.S. government had made up its mind not to take action. They wouldn't interfere with the Nicaraguan legal system. His answer revealed the U.S. government's position. They were prepared to let me spend thirty years in prison, perhaps to die there.

"You see that, Maggie? They're not going to do anything for Eric. They aren't willing to help."

"Okay," Bob continued to the U.S. officials, "here's what's going to

happen. Maggie is going to go outside, to where the international news an-
chors are waiting for her, and she's going to tell them that she knows that
her son is being held as part of the SAM-7 missile negotiation between you
and President Ortega."

Check.

The DCM looked like he had been slammed back in his chair. His
face went white while Bob pressed his advantage.

"Also, if Eric is held over the Christmas holiday, we are going to file a
motion requesting that he be moved to house arrest. Former president
Alemán has already agreed to accept Eric as a guest in his home for the
duration of the house arrest."

Mate.

"Are you sure you want to do that?" the DCM asked, now flustered.
"Alemán is the most hated man in Nicaragua...."

"Is he? ... If anything, he is the most loved man in Nicaragua.... He
is the next president of Nicaragua. You've made him the most hated man
of the United States."

Bob knew that he had the U.S. government cornered. They had worked
for years to hack Alemán's reputation to bits, and now we were about to
turn him into an American hero overnight—the only man in Nicaragua
willing to protect me, to take me in and provide for my safety when no
one else would, and he would do so with the whole world watching.

Maggie and Bob left knowing that their message had hit home. They
had no doubt that the State Department would take action. They held
their breath, waiting to see what came next.

Two hours later, in the White House, U.S. Secretary of State Condoleezza Rice took a question about my case. Someone at State told me later
that it was the first time anyone could remember a Secretary of State making a public statement about a private U.S. citizen in Latin America. Rice
said only a few simple words at the tail end of an unrelated press conference, but in the indirect language of international relations, her words
carried great weight. "The court has spoken.... We expect him to be released." Now the highest level of the U.S. government had finally weighed

in. Even as Secretary Rice was speaking, at least twenty private phone calls were being placed by powerful U.S. politicians and State Department officials to their contacts within the Nicaraguan government, telling them in far more direct words that the game was over and that they needed to release me. An extra-special call was made directly to Ortega himself.

Roberto Rodriguez called Tio Bob with two critical pieces of information on Thursday afternoon. First, he had seen the appeal filed by the prosecution and thought it was shockingly weak, almost amateurish, given the profile of the case. The document was full of careless errors, even citing the wrong statutes in the penal code. Equally serious, but far less surprising, was Rodriguez's news of additional complications with the signing of the release order. When the original convicting judge could not be located within a certain amount of time to sign the release order, the appeals judges reserved the right to circumvent by signing the order themselves to make it official. Rodriguez had hit upon this remedy and had gotten Estrada to go along with the idea since only two of the three appeals justices were required to sign. But now Rodriguez was telling us that Estrada just wasn't signing.

Tio immediately got through to Alemán, and though the former president assured Bob that he'd get Estrada to sign, Bob had little faith.

"No," Tio said, "he's weak, he's backing out."

Alemán told Tio Bob to stay on the line while he dialed Estrada on a different phone. He wanted Bob to hear.

"What is this I hear that you're scared to sign," Alemán demanded as soon as Estrada picked up. "You are a goddamned criminal appeals magistrate! This is what you signed up for. . . . You have a moral obligation to sign for Volz's release. . . . The case is hurting our country. Do what is right."

That evening Oscar Molina tried to move me back to prison. I heard him outside my room, telling someone on his phone that my parents had "paid the bill" and that I was ready to leave the hospital. But a nurse leaked word of the move, and it quickly got to my mother, who practically flew to the hospital, as did just about every news truck in the country that wasn't already there. Maggie marched straight up to the gate and confronted one of the older guards.

She took his face in her hands and asked, "Is my son still inside?"

"Sí."

"Are they moving him to the prison?"

"No," the guard answered quietly. "He is inside, and he is fine."

"I am his mother. Can you promise me that he is okay?"

The guard was too overcome with emotion to say anything, but he nodded his head yes. By that time, the television trucks and newspaper reporters and photographers had jammed up every entrance and exit at the hospital. Oscar Molina would have to let me stay there a little while longer.

My team and I had come to believe that Friday was literally do-or-die time. On the most trivial level, we knew that we were on the eve of what was essentially a three-week holiday break. At the end of that day, December 21, the government would shut down until mid-January, a period during which the glare of attention would fade from me and my situation. On a more serious level, though, we had all but run out of legal moves. The U.S. government had assumed its stance and made its statement. If Ortega had chosen to keep me in custody after that, it would have been like flipping the diplomatic bird to the United States and the world: He no longer cared about maintaining a good relationship with the United States; about world opinion; or, for that matter, about the rule of law.

What could the United States have done at this point to turn up the heat on Nicaragua? Shut down the embassy and trigger a complete diplomatic meltdown? Impose economic sanctions? Send in the U.S. Marines? All because of one innocent American citizen in prison?

We understood that my value had changed for Nicaragua. For a long time, the regime there considered me an asset, a piece of leverage in its dealings with the United States. But now that the Nica court had found me innocent and the case had become world news, it short-circuited the Nicaraguan embassy in D.C. Our supporters managed to crash the embassy's server from such a high volume of e-mails. Ambassador Cruz literally couldn't operate and phoned Ortega to tell him enough was enough. He needed to release me.

Now I had become a liability. The regime didn't want to cave in and set me free, but neither could it hang on to me unless it wanted to ride out a hostage crisis. Forces much larger than I had become somehow personified in Eric Volz. Sending me back to prison would signify a major diplomatic break with the United States, and at that point there would be no incentive for the Nica government to care what happened to me.

I went to bed Thursday night as I did every night, with my only companion, my Bible.

16.

Deported

With so much happening and so much tension in the air, there was something eerie about the quiet on the morning of Friday, December 21. My day began with a visit in the hospital from my mother. Maggie and I had reached a point of simple despair; I couldn't even eat the chocolate cake she had brought me. We thought we had been able to maneuver the State Department to our advantage and that the U.S. government's posturing would have ensured my release, but nothing was happening. We had no idea what was going on anymore.

Maggie had mysteriously been granted a two-hour visit with me, much longer than had ever been allowed, and it dawned on us that the idea was to keep her occupied so she wouldn't be talking to the press, drumming up more outrage and support. When we got news that Molina was outside the hospital, waiting with a truck and guards, I asked my mom to get outside immediately so that the press would be alert and so that, if anything bad was in the works, it could be documented. She reluctantly agreed, and as we hugged each other for what could have been the last time in a very long while, I begged her: "Don't let them take me back to prison."

When my mom left the room, I began scanning the newspapers she had brought. There was nothing new. Rodriguez was letting the other judges have it, tearing them apart for their outrageous behavior regarding the case file and the release. The papers were full of conflicting predictions about what would happen to me next. Some said it would be a return to prison, others worried that I'd go free. Of course none of them had any real idea. None of them could know that Alejandro Estrada would finally put his signature on the release order that morning.

Rodriguez called Tio Bob to tell him the news, and at that moment the quiet of morning vanished. The next five hours were to be a dizzying, harrowing roller coaster that would take me from desperation to joy and back again many times over.

Bob hung up with Rodriguez and dialed Marc Meznar. Marc was to get to the Ministry of Government as quickly as possible so he could be there when the release papers arrived. Bob picked up my mother, and the two of them made their way to the office of Attorney General Julio Centeno. Bob knew that the release had already been signed, but he couldn't be too careful and wanted to make sure that he had covered all his bases by confronting Centeno. Everything needed to be on the table. Bob knew what he wanted to communicate to Centeno and had rehearsed countless times. As soon as they were ushered into the attorney general's office, where the inspector general also sat waiting, Bob took charge.

"Señor Centeno, I know you don't have much time. You are a busy man . . ." Bob began. "Maggie, do you mind if I speak for you?" Bob went on to lay out the facts of my case in what my mom described as an Oscar-worthy performance. Centeno sat speechless, mesmerized by Bob's presentation. Later, Bob just said, "I tore him a new asshole."

Bob took them through all the prosecution's "evidence" from the trial, which he systematically shredded, and went over all the improprieties and all the clear evidence of my innocence that had been ignored or disallowed. Then he got to his knock-out punch: "We have information that we have received—it's only *rumors*—that the Llanes family paid bribes to the judge; the *fiscal*, Isolda Ibarra; the victim's mother; and even fifty thousand dollars to you."

Julio Centeno erupted. "Absolutely not! I would never—"

"Exactly," Bob cut him off. "That's why we never said it in public. It's rumor, it's *bochinche*. Exactly the same as the one million dollars that you claim Eric tried to offer the victim's mother. And now you have said in public that there is suspicion that we paid off the appeals judges. Even though none of it's true, you have personally said these things in public without any evidence. What you are saying are rumors, too. But even if you believe they are true, punish the judges. Don't punish Eric Volz. They are *your* corrupt judges."

Bob went on, even describing the solicitor general of the country as being "all over the press like a woman in a market"—a clear swipe at Mercedes—for claiming publicly that we were handing out money in order to get the conviction reversed. In the middle of this, his cell phone started ringing. It was Marc Meznar, calling from the Ministry of Government.

"We have the letter," Meznar told him.

"Really, really, that's great, Marc," Bob was saying into the phone as he grabbed Maggie's arm and lifted her out of her chair. "I'll get the plane. I'll get the plane." He hung up and turned to face Maggie.

"Your son is free."

The two Nicaraguan officials jumped to their feet and congratulated my mother.

"Felicidades, Señora. Que dios le bendiga." *Congratulations. May God bless you.*

The inspector general grabbed Bob's hand and pumped it. "You did exactly what you had to do. Exactly. *Felicidades.*" He interrupted himself. "What is your name?"

Tío Bob spoke evenly, with just the slightest hint of triumph. "Roberto Lady."

Back at the hospital, the assistant director walked into my room and announced that I was being freed. I was suspicious right off the bat, sure that this was more disinformation to get me back into prison, and I told him so. This man had always been a gentle, reassuring voice of faith for me, but his tone quickly turned icy.

"Look, I've stuck my neck out for you. Don't get me involved in any of this shit, okay? I've got all kinds of fucked-up pressure on me because of your ass."

I shut my mouth and followed my instinct to go along with whatever was happening. All around me, I heard commotion—chairs being pushed back, doors opening, people shouting, the chatter from the police radios echoing around the hallways. Officers were barking orders, but I couldn't make out any specifics.

"Solo estamos esperando el jefe," they would say. *We're just waiting for the boss.* Or, "That's the order. Are you clear?"

I needed to gather some information for myself. I took the only roll of toilet paper in the bathroom and buried it in the garbage, then opened the door of my room to ask for some more. Outside my room, I saw a huge crowd—cops, prison guards, plainclothes officers, and military men. Something was definitely going down.

At 1:00 P.M., a huge number of the guards blew into my room. "Vamonos, Volz." Outside, we ducked through a hedge and hustled down a maintenance alley to an exit I didn't know existed. After so many agonizing months of waiting, everything was unfolding in a tremendous rush now. The guards loaded me into a waiting ambulance—in which they took all the seats, leaving me only the gurney to sit on, with my head nearly touching the ceiling. I had no choice but to sit with my back against the window, which was painted white except for ten inches at the top. We took off through the back gate, into an obscure Managua barrio. It felt strange to be driving along these unpaved backstreets, but I was relieved that the guards had thought this one through. They knew there would be press waiting, and they seemed to have outsmarted them. I figured a decoy ambulance must have left through the front gate. As soon as we turned onto a paved street, though, we came face-to-face with a huddle of cameramen.

"¡Hue' puta, fuck!" the driver shouted as he gunned the engine. As we peeled out, we could see the cameramen jump into their own cars and come flying after us. Thankfully, when we got to the highway, there was a military barricade, stopping all other traffic so we could pass. What happened next felt like it was right out of a Hollywood action movie, except that there was nothing at all entertaining about it. A dozen or more press cars suddenly materialized, coming at us from all directions. There were a bunch of small cars and pickups jammed with reporters and some television vans with dishes and aerials on top, and every one of them blew past the armed military guards as if they weren't there. The press cars jumped the median strip, plowing through flower beds and bouncing over curbs. Some of them took off down the other side of the street, racing headlong into oncoming traffic, in order to get closer. Guys were hanging out of car windows or holding on for dear life in the rear beds of the trucks. There was no way they were letting us get away.

Anyone could figure out our route, and if they couldn't, the whole chase was now being broadcast on television and radio. People I knew in all different parts of the world would tell me later that they had watched it live. Every intersection was a new adventure, with soldiers in camouflage and metro police trying to control traffic and onlookers. Even still, press cars would shoot out and block us so that people could jump out and snap a picture. Reporters would swarm over the ambulance and more than once had to be backed off at gunpoint by the guards. I was relieved and grateful to catch glimpses of our own security guys in the crowd, watching me pass, then reporting on their cell phones.

The crowds grew larger and rowdier as we made our way through the inner city. The cop driving the ambulance picked up speed and began taking more risks, driving on medians, swerving around slower cars, racing down the wrong side of the street if necessary. I prayed that we wouldn't hit any of the people who were pushing into the street for a better view, especially the children who were constantly darting out into traffic. We were barely in control. At one point, the driver had to swerve so suddenly to avoid one of the press cars that had pulled out in front us that the wheels on one side of the ambulance actually left the ground. We felt the ambulance teeter and slide, and we would have surely gone over, except that at that exact moment, our rear end slammed into the back of a semi waiting at a light. The impact threw us all over the inside of the ambulance but miraculously righted us, and we kept racing forward. We actually collided with two other cars before we got where we were going.

Maybe I had simply run out of fear or my emotions were just so deadened by the insanity of the past year, but I felt no real panic during this whole mad chase. I felt calm, even focused, directing all my attention through the narrow slit of clear glass at the top of the ambulance windows, scanning the hands of whomever I could see, watching for shooters or any other obvious threat. The fact was that the ambulance offered no real protection. We were totally exposed. I knew it but kept the fear compartmentalized so I could stay alert. Sitting on that rickety gurney in the back of the careening ambulance, I felt a sudden wave of God's love and protection wash over me. Whatever was going to happen, however it was going to turn out, so be it. Amen. I accepted it.

I was aware of the comfort this realization brought me and began absorbing the little snapshots of life that came in through my little patch of window: small children, barefoot and grinning, playing along the street; the lush green of the trees with their ripening fruit; the rusted old trucks coughing out sooty smoke as they changed gears. Most vividly, I remember being able to see into the rear window of a taxi, where a worried mother tried to fan the heat away from her tiny infant. I could see Doris doing that. She was so tender and comfortable with kids and always dreamed of children of her own. She would have been a wonderful mother. The sight of that young woman in the back of the taxi brought the situation back into perspective, reminding me once again where the real tragedy lay.

These were my thoughts as the airport came into sight. My heart began to beat faster, but only for a moment. The ambulance didn't even slow down but kept moving past the airport entrance. Farther on down that road was La Modelo. They were taking me back to prison. Just a few minutes later, we pulled through the penitentiary gates, and the ambulance stopped in front of the administrative building. Hope rose again; maybe we just had to stop here for some paperwork. I sat there for the longest sixty seconds of my life, listening to the driver take instructions on his cell phone from Molina. All I heard was the driver saying, "Si . . . si . . . mm . . . uh-huh . . . si," which only made the wait more agonizing. I could see the heavy internal security gate of the main prison directly in front of us. Either we would get out here and now and I would go free, or they'd push forward into the oblivion of *el sistema*.

The driver ended the conversation with a simple "correcto," snapped his phone shut, and put the ambulance in gear. I heard the tires crunching as we rolled forward over the gravel toward the security gate. The decision had been made, and as far as I was concerned, I was facing the end. I dropped my head and thought of the endless tears, the exposure, and the humiliation of the last year. I thought of the people who loved me and had been by my side for so long and the countless people who had come out of nowhere and everywhere to help and support me. I thought of the tireless fighting and plotting and strategizing, of the violence and the terror, and of the ceaseless prayers. And this is how it was all going to end. I looked at La Modelo and believed that I had come here to die.

At the gate, the guards all jumped out and ordered me not to move. I sat alone with my thoughts for another half a minute. Part of me had imagined this moment, just as I had imagined so many other possible closing scenes of this ordeal. I knew for sure that there was a reason I was here, and that knowledge centered me as I waited alone. I felt great honor and privilege to have been chosen to play such a role in God's works. As I remembered his promise to keep and protect me, I was infused with greater strength than I had ever felt.

I took in a deep breath and released it. Out loud, I said, "Okay. Just give me the strength, Lord."

A guard yanked open the back door and ordered me to get out. I picked up my little bag, got down out of the ambulance, and started walking toward the gate.

"Volz," the guard snapped. He nodded in the direction of the administrative building. "Por aquí," he said. *This way.*

Was I not going back into prison? A higher-ranked officer had taken charge and ordered all the guards to move away from me as they walked me back to the warden's office. I looked up and saw a prison photographer capturing the whole scene. *I'm staring into the face of my own doom, and these assholes are putting on a show.* Then I saw it all clearly; I really was going home. The guards, the cops, all of them knew it. This was their last chance to fuck with me, and, man, they were going to make the most of it.

There were too many people to count jammed into Molina's office. It was like a city subway car at rush hour, with everyone jockeying for position. Some wore uniforms but most wore suits. This was going to be the grand finale, and I guess everyone wanted to be there. I wondered how many of these guys had played a part in my suffering over the last year. Were some of them there to try to derail the process somehow? Were some of them on my side and wanted to see that nothing went wrong at the final hour? Was there anybody there just to make sure that Molina didn't find a way to screw it up? Or did they just want to be where the action was?

The guards hustled me in, and I saw Molina at his desk, surrounded by men who all seemed to ooze power. Even though I didn't recognize all of them, I felt in my bones that these were the men who counted.

"Eric," Molina said, "we have your release papers here. All that's needed is your signature." He slid them across the desk toward me.

Something in me made me hesitate. I had been abused for so long, in ways no one could have ever imagined, and I wasn't about to step into some sneaky trap at the last minute. Who knew what they might do with my signature? Who knew what the papers even were? I could see Molina growing impatient. He started pressuring me to stop messing around and sign the papers. There was a plane scheduled to leave very soon, and I needed to be on it.

It dawned on me right then that they were all waiting on me. I actually had control of the situation. It was the first time I felt any sense of control or even power in a very, very long time. I slid the paper back across the desk at Molina.

"I'm not signing," I said. "I'm not signing anything without my attorney or someone from the U.S. Embassy present."

There was a moment of stunned silence, and then the room erupted. After everything that had happened, I was now the one delaying my release. They all started screaming at me at once. Who the hell did I think I was? Was I some kind of arrogant little punk? Did I understand that I was going to spend the next thirty years in jail if I didn't sign? Molina told me that my plane was scheduled to leave, and if I wasn't on it, I'd be going straight back into prison.

But I stood my ground. They kept on yelling at me, at each other, or just venting their rage because that was the only thing they knew to do. Molina quickly realized the situation he was in and quieted everybody down.

"Atiende," he said. *Listen up.* "I know this kid. He's not going to sign. Get him a phone. Get his lawyer on the phone."

All of a sudden, everybody in the room was fishing a cell phone out of his pocket. A dozen or so appeared, but of course—*of course!*—this was Nicaragua, and not one of them had any phone credit. Not a single minute. This was the power elite of the Sandinista regime, the men who ran the police, the prisons, entire departments of the national government, and nobody had a working cell phone. I so wish I had been in a mood to laugh.

Finally, someone produced a phone with credit, and I started dialing. What I didn't know was that Tio Bob and Fabbrith had turned their own phones off because the damn things hadn't stopped ringing since dawn, and they had things to do. Luckily, as soon as I refused to sign the paper, one of the observers had stepped out of Molina's office to radio the official waiting for me at the airport, who was in turn able to get through to Bob, who was waiting there with Fabbrith and Marc Meznar. Fabbrith turned his phone on and answered on my first ring. I couldn't tell for sure whether Fabbrith thought I was insane or if he liked the idea of my messing with Molina a little bit, but he knew better than to add any new complications.

"¡Firma, Eric. Firma!" *Sign it now!*

I looked at Molina and told him I was ready to sign. The warden took out a pen and held it out to me, but I wasn't done with him. I was exhausted, but my mind was now clear. I knew better than to show my anger or to say anything stupid, but this was *my* time now. I knew by their presence and could tell just by looking at their faces that this drama of getting me out of the country had been orchestrated at the highest levels of the government, and they were all waiting on my signature. I had the floor for a change, and it felt good. I held up my hand as if to say *Stop* and reached into my vest and pulled out my pen. *My* pen. I wasn't even supposed to have a metal pen in prison, but this pen, this one pen, had been my lifeline, my link to the outside world. With that pen I had written my prison journals, taken notes on my hearings and trial and all our investigations. It was the single tool that allowed me to be Eric Volz—to *remain* Eric Volz—for more than a year in their hellholes.

I signed the order,[EX.49] and stood up. No good-byes, no handshakes. I just turned around and walked out the door. I was done.

I still had to get out of the country, though, and that wasn't going to be easy. The next thing I knew, I was in the back of small car, squeezed between two guys I'd never seen before, who introduced themselves as immigration agents. One of the agents pushed my head down between his legs, and we sped out of La Modelo toward the airport. The ambulance I had traveled in earlier in the day also left the prison as a decoy to throw the press off our trail.

In the car, one of the agents turned and spoke. "Okay, muchacho, you're free now, so tell us the truth. Did you whack her?"

"Man . . . you know you had the wrong guy all along," I said. "Why don't you worry about the fact there are still murderers out there." All I could think of was getting out of there. They were never going to stop hassling me. The guy pumped me for information, but I was done talking.

On another road, reporters ambushed the ambulance. The press chased it down and tried to block it, and in the effort to escape, the driver ended up spinning out in a patch of gravel. The reporters swarmed over the ambulance and quickly discovered that I wasn't inside. Word got out quickly, so that by the time we got to the airport, the crowds were waiting for us, even at the back entrance we used. With my head wedged between the fat legs of the Nica agent, I couldn't see anything, but I could hear the panic in the driver's voice as the mob came after the car. I could feel and hear him actually using the car to push people out of his way and imagined the outrage that would ensue if someone got injured now.

We got through the crowd and drove down the runway to the terminal. Here there was no decoy, no special arrangements, and they walked me straight into the main immigration hall, the central room where all passengers coming into the country go through the ritual of customs and passport inspections. Hundreds of people were milling about, eager tourists fresh off planes from up north, with their white winter skin, their flip-flops, and surfboard bags. A silence fell over the place as I walked in, surrounded by a detail of guards. It's unlikely that anyone traveling to Nicaragua that week didn't know who I was or that they had not at least heard something about my case. I wonder what must have gone through their heads when the first thing they saw upon landing was me in my bulletproof vest being marched through the airport by a squad of armed guards like some kind of war criminal.

The guards brought me into a small side office, where Tio Bob was waiting with Fabbrith and Marc Meznar. My mom, they explained, was upstairs in a VIP lounge, waiting for a commercial flight to Atlanta. The lounge had been guarded by soldiers with assault weapons, who were posted at the doors. To board the plane, she had to walk up a ramp lined on both sides by police carrying machine guns. I had a ticket for that flight, too, but that was just another ploy of ours. Reporters would have no problem finding out my flight information and would have bought tickets just to be able to follow me to the gate or onto the plane, and they would even be waiting for me in other airports. Bob had other plans for getting me home.

Bob tells me that when he first saw me that afternoon, he was alarmed by my labored breathing. He could hear me wheezing and thought I might have been having an asthma attack. Strangely, I have no memory of that. I remember only feeling anxious about what was happening but generally calm. Bob also says that the first thing I did was sit down, pull out my journal, and start frantically scribbling, apparently trying to write down everything that had gone on that day. I don't doubt that's true.

I think that keeping a chronicle, narrating the story even as it was happening to me, had become one of my most valuable coping mechanisms. It had become habit, a ritual that kept me sane. And it helped me write this book.

Earlier that morning, the moment Bob knew for sure that the justices had signed my release order, he phoned a pilot who was standing by with a private plane in Honduras. This was the kind of stuff that Bob Lady and his network did so perfectly. To begin with, this was no ordinary private plane but one of only a handful of planes in Latin America that are equipped with a deployable parachute attached to the frame. Bob was a little concerned; after all, we were painfully aware of the presence of small surface-to-air missiles in a government of questionable security. Tio Bob knew he couldn't let anyone know that the plan was to whisk me out of the country on a private plane, since the press would be watching the commercial flights like vultures, but he also knew he couldn't bring the plane into Nicaragua in advance of my release and keep it secret. The plan could only work if the pilot was able to swoop in, pick me up, and get back in the air as quickly as possible. The tower at the airport in Managua requires incoming private planes to file flight plans at least twenty-four hours in advance, which would also have represented a huge security risk. However, airports must allow an unscheduled landing when requested by a craft that is already airborne. Bob's pilot took off from a small town in Honduras with a filed flight plan to land in Tegucigalpa. He changed direction in midflight, crossed into Nicaraguan airspace, then radioed the tower in Managua, saying he needed to reroute and needed to land as soon as he could.

The plane taxied up to within walking distance of us, but the Nicas had a pickup waiting anyway. We gunned it over to the plane, where the pilot was waiting with the engines running and the luggage hatch open. Bob tossed him our bags as the rest of us leaped out of the truck, and it seemed like nothing could stop us now. Well, almost nothing. We were literally halfway into the plane when someone's cell phone rang. The Nica official who was with us was listening intently, nodding and saying, "Claro que si, mi jefe" into the phone. He hung up and announced that he was required to hold a formal deportation ceremony. It just so happened that he had brought a cameraman with him. So we stopped right there and put on a little show of exchanging passports and documents for the camera. The ground crew even stopped to snap photos with their own cell phones. As if the whole scene weren't absurd enough already, we couldn't ignore the fact that the official had dyed his gray hair jet-black for the occasion.

I jumped into the plane with Bob and Fabbrith, and, as the pilot rolled toward the runway, I phoned Dane and told him we were fifty feet away from leaving Nicaraguan soil. The pilot never stopped moving. He pulled straight onto the runway, and a moment later, we were in the air.

The plane climbed quickly, carrying me to freedom, but the Nicas just couldn't quite let go. Just after we left the ground, the tower radioed and instructed us to reprogram the flight path away from the standard and direct route out. The new plan they gave us veered many miles to the west, which made everyone nervous. Just to be safe, the pilot flew a course between his original plan and the new one, but nonetheless we spent the entire time in the air over Nicaragua scanning the ground below us for the telltale plume of white smoke from a missile launch. None came.

I stared out the window at the blue of the sky. We flew into clouds and then broke free above them, but it was hard for me to process the things I was seeing. I felt almost like I was flying into an hallucination. Part of me believed I was flying toward heaven.

At 3:19 in the afternoon, the pilot announced our departure from Nicaraguan airspace. The plane began its descent over the thick blanket of Honduran rain forest. Soon the slums and shanties of Tegucigalpa came into focus. It was the most beautiful sight I had ever seen.

17.

Totally Broke, Unfathomably Rich

Toward the end of the first week in January, barely two weeks after my release, I found myself sunk deep into an enormous plush couch in a penthouse suite of a swank hotel in New York City, courtesy of a national television network, surrounded by candy and fruit bowls, bottles of wine, and huge flat-screen TVs. At my disposal were the hotel gym, a personal trainer, room service, and a fat per diem to spend as I chose. And limousines.

I felt as if I had landed on another planet and was unable to process the idea that only a couple of weeks before I had been sitting in isolation and under armed guard in Nicaragua. Immediately after my release, I had begun a careful process of reentry while spending a few days in Honduras before coming home, taking tiny step after tiny step: dinner with Tio Bob and Fabbrith in a quiet restaurant, a gathering at the hilltop estate of a friend, a first solo outing—to a shopping mall, of all places. I walked in the woods, alone except for the company of a hunting dog, and was surprised by the vague fear I felt in the peace and purity of nature, intimidated by the simple grandeur of it all. After watching a mystical simultaneous sunset and moonrise during the winter solstice in Honduras, I sensed that my long night was over and knew that the sun would shine its light just a little longer into each coming day. On that night—my first as a free man—the world cycled into the winter season, marking a time of rest, recovery, and redemption. I tested myself in increments, trying to adjust again to people and to the world.

My story was far from over. I had no taste for the media blitz that was waiting for me in the United States, knowing that the media only sees the

269

personal tragedies and intimate struggles of individuals who have been through ordeals like mine as just more food for the hungry programming machine. But I also knew it was something I had to do. It was a whirlwind of interviews, not just with NBC and CNN and other American outlets and newspapers but also with the Spanish-language giants, like Univision and Telemundo. Many of these broadcasters had helped bring my plight to the public's attention, but the real responsibility I felt was not to them, it was to the many good people facing new kinds of danger in Nicaragua as a result of my victory.

Too many there were still facing persecution for coming to my aid. Speaking out on their behalf now fell to me. In the hours and hours we had all spent debriefing one another after my release, comparing notes, filling in holes in each of our stories, my defense team and I planned our media message carefully. We decided to focus the spotlight back on the corruption of the Sandinista leadership and to do what we could to protect the individuals who had stuck their necks out for me and who were still under attack in Nicaragua. I wanted to shine a spotlight on those who continued to allow killers to walk free. I wanted people to understand that Nicaragua's flag was in mourning for justice and to expose Ortega's violation of his own people's constitutional rights and dignity, maybe even to create an opening for the liberal opposition party in the future of Nicaraguan politics. There was a small window of opportunity, and I had to seize it.

I made the rounds in New York in taxis and black limos, moving from hotel to green room to boardroom to studio. Friends took me to restaurants and treated me kindly and gently, afraid to leave me alone. They told me stories, adding to those I had already heard from my family, about the kids who ran lemonade stands and car washes to raise money for my defense, about the people who ran marathons or held vigils or fasted, about the postings on Craigslist in every state, about the random "Free Eric Volz" signs on cars and vacant walls, about the grad student's thesis dedicated to me, and about bumper stickers everywhere. They told me about the climber who reached the top of Half Dome in Yosemite and found the message "Free Eric Volz" spelled out in rocks at the summit. I sat in the freezing, clanging chaos of New York, remembering the steaming chaos of Chipote and La Modelo, feeling the love of so many strangers washing over me.

And then I experienced it for myself. Sitting in a deli on Lexington Avenue, just a couple of blocks from Grand Central Station, the very heart of that great, rumbling city, an elegant and beautiful black woman stopped and stared at me through the glass. She came in and walked to our table.

"Are you Eric?"

"I am," I said, and the woman threw her arms around me and broke down, sobbing, telling me how much she had prayed for me and my family and how it was a miracle that I was standing in front of her. She did not— she could not—let me go. I thought to myself, This is it! This is the bridge I had once imagined. It might not look like I thought it would, and I hadn't built it with my own hands as I had once planned, but here it was, nonetheless. A bridge that brought strangers together, a bridge built on and strengthened by injustice and the triumph of good over evil.

Since that day, I have read a lot about and meditated often on the human connections that give meaning to our experiences. One passage from a close friend's letter that I read in my cell remains very present in my thoughts:

> If the true measure of our life is the depth of love that our friends and family have for us in their heart, then Eric, you are indeed a very rich man. Know that you are deeply loved by men and women of great character and personal integrity. 'Cause you see, in the end of our life, that is all that we can take with us.

Later that night, my friend reluctantly put me in a taxi alone to send me back to my hotel. As the driver pulled out from the curb, I settled into the seat and laid my head back to gaze out the window at the thrilling swirl of civilization around me.

"Where to?" the driver asked.

It took me a moment to respond.

"Just drive, please. Just keep driving."

Afterword

Nicaragua was now a more dangerous place to live than it had been before my release for a number of people. The windows of Fabbrith's house, for instance, were again smashed with stones, and one of his cousins was mysteriously stabbed in Fabbrith's driveway. We hired private security guards to protect the house, but even one of them was assaulted. Roberto Rodriguez received so many death threats and was subjected to so much slander in the Nica press that his wife phoned me in the United States and tearfully pleaded with me to speak out.

Daniel Ortega himself inflamed the public with statements about how "terrible and painful" it was that I had gone free. The president blasted his own justice system, referring to Roberto Rodriguez without ever naming him. The Sandinista *bancada* in the Supreme Court initiated an illegal investigation into Rodriguez's decision, forcing him to defend himself in the media and in a lengthy letter[EX.50] he had published. He was called to testify on his handling of my case. (The Supreme Court ultimately concluded that the appeals magistrates had acted "in accordance with the law" in finding me not guilty.) As for Judge Miranda, he was promoted to a position as a Nicaraguan representative at the United Nations in New York City.

What the public didn't know was that the courts actually had not been responsible for my departure from the country. Ortega himself had issued an executive order to the Ministry of Immigration. My passport holds the proof—a deportation stamp. With the sensitivity and publicity surrounding my case, no government official or bureaucrat, no matter how highly placed, would have taken it upon himself or herself to send me out of the country unless the order had come directly from the president. We published photos[EX.51] of that stamp and a document[EX.52] detailing the formalities of my release in an effort to protect Rodriguez. The revelation of Ortega's involvement became a public scandal dominating headline news for weeks in Nicaragua and was a blow to the president's public image. The Ministry of Government remained silent, and the heads of the Sandinista *bancada* of the Supreme Court who had initiated the investigation into Rodriguez—Rafael Solís and Alba Luz Ramos—did not show up to work for an entire week as they hid from the press. The list of people who were less prominent, but no less important to my defense, and who have suffered various indignities because of it is long. I will never forget them and offer my eternal gratitude and appreciation. I will defend them to the fullest of my capability always.

After the media tour, I traveled to Washington and got something of the same feeling from the politicos that I had gotten from the journalists and television personalities in New York. Many of the people who had been involved with my case greeted me with sincerity and made me feel the genuine pleasure they took in my safe return to the United States.

The State Department debriefed me. They asked lots of questions and wanted details. I had my list of questions, too. When appropriate, I described the role played by former president Arnoldo Alemán and provided detailed evidence of the unlawful methods and developing dictatorship of Daniel Ortega that I witnessed during my yearlong captivity. It's impossible to know what direct connection it had to my case, if any, but that next summer, the United States replaced Paul Trivelli as ambassador to Nicaragua. One of the first gestures made by the new ambassador, Robert Callahan, was to reach out to Alemán, who had by that time been released from house arrest back to "country arrest." Callahan made it clear to Alemán that the United States appreciated what he had done for me. Their meeting was historic in that it signaled a willingness in the United States to consider a new position on Alemán. (The Nicaraguan Supreme

Court went one step further and overturned Alemán's corruption conviction in early 2009.)

After my release, Camilo de Castro, the young producer of *Esta Semana*, kept his investigation going and ultimately broadcast the most significant piece of journalism about my case that Nicaragua had yet seen. Camillo's short documentary[EX.53] treated Doris's murder as an unsolved crime. It was no longer the Eric Volz case.

He began with an exhaustive analysis of Armando Llanes's and Nelson Danglas's porous alibis. Camilo broke down the alibis and revealed that further investigation was required. He concluded with a bold and direct statement that to me seemed to be the single most important thing I had heard anyone say about the case.

Looking straight into the camera, Castro said,

> I would like to close with the following: Three weeks ago I was in San Juan del Sur, and I spoke with some locals who know who the true killers are in this crime, but these people are terrified to talk about the case. They are very scared. One should ask, "Why are they so scared?" But I want to invite the people I spoke with to lose the fear and to come to us to tell their version of what happened. Because the worst thing that can happen is that another young woman with a promising future turns up dead in San Juan del Sur. A person who kills once can kill again. In addition, I would like to say to the authorities who are responsible for the safety of us Nicaraguans: I hope that they don't avoid continuing this investigation because it is not politically convenient. . . . This is a situation of life or death. . . . We cannot turn our backs on this case.

Camilo de Castro had gone on one of Nicaragua's most prominent news programs and announced that known eyewitnesses existed. This was thrilling and heartbreaking to me. For the first time, the Nica press was openly saying that there was work to be done on Doris's case and that the information, the truth, was there for those who chose to pursue it. At the same time, however, it supported what I had suspected all along. I believe that Doris's murder is not an unsolved case. The authorities had all the information they needed and had had it from almost the very beginning, yet they chose to disregard it in order to protect the real killers.*

Taking a fresh look at the circumstances of Doris's murder brought me back to November 21, 2006. My arrest had interrupted my grieving, but now I am able to process the loss of my dear friend. It is rare that a day goes by when the image of her face—her big eyes, dark and bright at the same time, and her warm smile—doesn't find its way into my consciousness. I see her standing on the side of a dirt road, waiting in surprise for me one day after we'd argued, her smile alone letting me know that everything was all right. I see her walking out the door, her arms full of food, heading out to provide for the neighbors or playing happily with little Valentina. I see her in her shop, chatting with the women of the town, basking in the pride of her creation, her accomplishment. I think about the comfort she provided, the feeling of home she created in those few short months we were together, and I feel the hole in the world where she used to be. I miss her terribly.

In the winter of 2008, a year after I escaped their prisons, Nicaragua held mayoral elections in all of its cities. Despite popular support for candidates from the opposition, the majority of seats went to candidates from the Sandinista party. These municipal elections were condemned by domestic observers and the international community as highly irregular. Evidence of fraud[EX.54] was formally presented to the Nicaraguan congress and even the Organization of American States. In the aftermath, the U.S. government announced the cancellation of its annual aid package to

---

* Shortly before publication of this book, Armando Agustín Llanes became known as "Private Llanes" when he enlisted in the U.S. Army. He completed his basic combat training at Fort Jackson, South Carolina, in the fall of 2009.

Nicaragua, citing that country's failure to satisfy certain basic require-ments of democracy. The same week, the Supreme Court of Nicaragua conveniently began their consideration of the prosecution's motion to re-verse the appeals verdict in my case—a year after the motion had been submitted.

The Nicaraguan Supreme Court has reviewed my case twice previ-ously. In both instances it determined that the case against me was weak at best. But this time seems to be different. Supreme Court magistrates have made statements in the press reflecting their intention to overturn the verdict of not guilty, reinstate my sentence, and issue a warrant for my arrest in Nicaragua and within Interpol, the international police organi-zation. If this were to happen, I would be a wanted man in the Republic of Nicaragua. I also would be prevented from traveling to any states "friendly" to Nicaragua, where I would run the risk of being detained and extradited.

I have exhausted all domestic remedies at my disposal in Nicaragua. My only remaining option has been to appeal to a supranational tribunal. In June of 2009, I filed an emergency petition[EX.55] in the Inter-American Commission on Human Rights, of the Organization of American States, seeking protection from and restitution for violations of my rights as pro-vided by the American Convention on Human Rights. The news of my petition provoked a wave of protests in Nicaragua. The president and vice president remained silent, but many of the highest-ranking Nica politicos aggressively defended themselves in the press. Doris's mother and some prominent women's-rights groups held a demonstration with banners and signs in front of the OAS building in Managua demanding that my peti-tion be rejected. I received such an extensive amount of death threats that a police special-investigations unit and a branch of the FBI have opened investigations.

The Inter-American Commission process is likely to last years. As of the time of this writing, the Nicaraguan Supreme Court has not handed down a final decision. Regardless of their finding, I know that I will never be completely free of this experience. I am relatively safe in the United States, which has no extradition agreement with Nicaragua, but I know that certain parts of Latin America, which I had adopted as my home, and where I had invested many years of my life, will never be safe for me again.

The SAM-7 missiles remain in Ortega's possession after failed negotiations with the United States.

The perspective in the book may have caused you to come to certain conclusions regarding various individuals. I have a legal obligation to remind you that subjects in this book are innocent until proven guilty.